Capital
Fictions

CAPITAL FICTIONS

The Literature of Latin America's Export Age

ERICKA BECKMAN

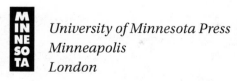

University of Minnesota Press
Minneapolis
London

Portions of chapters 2 and 4 were previously published as "Sujetos insol-
ventes: José Asunción Silva y la economía transatlántica del lujo," *Revista
Iberoamericana* 75, no. 228 (2009): 757-72.

Published by the University of Minnesota Press
111 Third Avenue South, Suite 290
Minneapolis, MN 55401-2520
http://www.upress.umn.edu

Printed in the United States of America on acid-free paper

The University of Minnesota is an equal-opportunity educator and employer.

Library of Congress Cataloging-in-Publication Data
Beckman, Ericka.
    Capital fictions : the literature of Latin America's export age /
Ericka Beckman.
    Includes bibliographical references and index.
    ISBN 978-0-8166-7919-5 (hc : acid-free paper)
    ISBN 978-0-8166-7920-1 (pb : acid-free paper)
    1. Latin American fiction – History and criticism. 2. Economics and
literature – Latin America. I. Title.
PQ7082.N7B355 2013
863.0093553 – dc23   2012016573

20 19 18 17 16 15 14 13   10 9 8 7 6 5 4 3 2 1

Contents

Introduction

CAPITAL FICTIONS

Disasters Foretold

Consider the following scenario: a Latin American dictator, in order to stay in power, sells the Caribbean Sea to the United States. The entire body of water is then carried away to irrigate the deserts of Arizona. To replace the lost sea breezes, the North Americans provide the Caribbean nation with a gigantic wind machine.

The scene comes from the novel *El otoño del patriarca* (*The Autumn of the Patriarch*) by the Colombian novelist Gabriel García Márquez (1975). This Nobel-prize–winning author has delighted readers the world over with his "colorful" depictions of life in Latin American republics. In keeping with García Márquez's well-known style, the most ridiculous things are presented as normal and natural; this is the essence of the estranging effect created by magical realism. This style is frequently chalked up to the backwardness of Latin America, a region where magic "still" exists, and enchantment waits around every corner. And yet, the power of the scene recounted above does not lie solely in its depiction of local color (e.g., the Latin American dictator so irrational as to sell the sea). Instead, it hails from the rationalized irrationality of modern capitalism itself, taken to its absolute extreme: Arizona needs water, and so a sea is purchased from a Latin American banana republic to irrigate it; once this massive ecological alteration is complete, a machine is used as a poor replacement for what has been lost. As a consequence, the inhabitants of the Central American nation are forced to get used to their new desert. The moment of the magically real comes with the transposition of the ultimate dream of capital—to overcome all physical and natural barriers—onto the plane of (fictional) reality. After the land of the "banana republic" is privatized and given over to commodity production, what does the still-poor country have left to sell? The sea itself, it may be imagined. After this, what might be next: the wind generated by the wind machine (for which electricity might be charged) or even the very air people breathe? The exercise of the imagination can go on until the resulting depredation creates conditions under which life itself becomes impossible.

What is striking to me about the scenario imagined by *The Autumn of the Patriarch* is not its propensity toward exaggeration, but rather its eerie proximity to the logic of capital in our own times. Here is another scenario, this time from real life. In 1999, the Bolivian government signed a $2.5 billion contract to privatize the city of Cochabamba's water supply. Under the proposed agreement, the consortium, which included the San Francisco–based Bechtel Corporation, was to own all of the city's water resources, *even the rain that fell from the sky*.[1] The proposition sounded ludicrous to Bolivian citizens, and the scheme was stopped only by massive protests. For indeed, how is it possible for private entities to own the rain that falls from the sky? Or, to take other real-world cases, how is it possible for corporations to patent life that existed before corporations, as in the case of human genomes, plants growing in the Amazon, or hybrid corn seeds? The logic behind such eventualities is, for many present-day economists, impeccable. As an example, a leaked 1991 memo authored by Larry Summers, then the chief economist of the World Bank, suggested that African and other "under-polluted" countries capitalize on their clean air quality.[2] Summers later claimed that the memo was not meant to be taken seriously; whether or not a satire, it perfectly renders the thought processes employed by the World Bank and IMF, for which it is perfectly logical and normal that countries sell off public assets at bargain prices to foreign investors and capitalize on cheap labor and unspoiled resources.[3]

But what passes as impeccable economic logic today is rooted in a *fiction,* raised to previously unimaginable heights: that natural resources, together with human creativity and labor, "exist" only so that they might become alienable commodities. In the form lived today, under the hypercommoditized logic of neoliberalism, these fictions allow us to believe that the end of human existence is the market, not that the market exists to serve human needs. As a result, exaggerated scenarios such as that imagined by García Márquez in *Autumn of the Patriarch* become the real of our lives.[4]

Read today, García Márquez's image of the magically real powers of capital to claim ownership of and to transport the Caribbean Sea to water the arid zone of the United States seems prophetic. But if it is prophetic, it is so because it looks back to the ruins of a previous moment in which capital and its attendant fictions took hold over Latin American societies in an unprecedented fashion. Between roughly 1870 and 1930, Latin American nations were brought swiftly—if unevenly—into the fold of global market relations, mainly as exporters of "raw" or "primary" commodities, and as importers of European and North American manufactures.[5] At the height of European imperial and industrial expansion, the mainly independent nations of Latin America joined an emerging world order rooted in the primacy of the commodity form.[6]

It is to this ur-past of late nineteenth-century capitalist modernization, and the fictions that sustained and contested its transformations, that this book turns. I am most concerned with the intellectual production of Latin America's lettered elite, a class that during the second half of the nineteenth century reached consensus regarding the desirability of "progress" and "civilization" by way of economic liberalization. What elites had to believe so that integration into the world order of capital could be seen as not only desirable, but inevitable, is one of the key questions asked by this book. The question is all the more relevant because of the frequently dismal outcomes of capitalist modernization in Latin America, which then as today have been marked by grave inequalities on the level of individual societies, as well as by poverty and subordination with respect to the major centers of capital. For if the Export Age marked the consolidation of commodity-driven republics, it also marked the consolidation of a pattern of structural financial instability, marked by phenomena such as hyperinflation, commodity booms and busts, and astronomical foreign debt. A second major question asked by this study, then, is how elites (frequently politicians but also novelists, poets, and journalists) came to terms with the frequent disasters resulting from market integration and liberalization.

This book proceeds as an inquiry into how late nineteenth-century elites thought about and responded to the world(s) emerging from early economic liberalization and modernization. I call these responses "capital fictions," or fictions of and about capital during Latin America's period of high economic liberalism. I use this term repeatedly throughout the book to designate two overlapping discursive arenas: first, the fictions generated by capital (e.g., that the creation of a republic dedicated to producing coffee for the world market is a natural and normal facet of social life); and second, the specific expressions of those fictions within an assembled corpus of images and texts. This corpus, focused on the cultural production of the region's lettered creole (white) elite, draws from a wide range of sources. These include novels about stock market speculation in 1890s Argentina and rubber extraction in the early twentieth-century rubber boom. My source texts also include economic essays predicting, in the 1870s, that Bolivia, Guatemala, Colombia, and any number of nations were on the cusp of becoming rich beyond their wildest imaginations, a mode of discourse I call "export reverie." My corpus also includes little-studied objects of Latin American commercial culture such as banknotes and advertisements, alongside high artistic discourses like poetry.

Along the way, the book examines the rhetorical styles embedded within appeals to market utopias, constituted by images of "magical" coffee beans and "mythical" bananas. I also study the narrative solutions developed to account for the increasingly volatile nature of Latin American economies, as national fortunes rose and fell wildly with speculative bubbles and currency crises, leaving trails of destruction in their wake. Then as now the crises kept getting bigger, and as a result became harder and harder to explain.

Here it is relevant to mention, however briefly, that the great era of export-driven modernization studied in this book ended only with the great crash of 1929. As depression and war sent global capital into a long slumber, Latin American nations initiated another moment of history, frequently called "The Age of Development," during which the entrenched export model was partially reversed with state-led development and protectionist policies designed to stimulate industrialization. While the contours of this era remain well outside the boundaries of the present study, it is a temporal marker that divides the ur-past of economic liberalization (the Export Age) with the return of certain aspects of this past under programs of *neo*-liberalism. Beginning in the 1980s and intensifying in the 1990s and 2000s, countries across the region opened their markets to foreign capital (often under pressure from the IMF and World Bank), privatized state services, and in many cases reinstated an extractive, export-driven model of growth. It is with this recent history in mind that this book, like García Márquez's scenario, looks back to a previous moment in the hopes of catching a fleeting glimpse of our present.

Commodity Maps: Fictions of Global Exchange

One of the key concepts guiding this work is that of the "fiction," a term that designates the centrality of ideology and imagination in governing economic life. I draw here from Karl Polanyi, who argues, following Marx, that modern capitalism can function only once certain fictions come to be accepted as real; namely, that we begin to assume that labor, land and nature exist so that they might become commodities. But, he writes, "[l]abor is only another name for a human activity which goes with life itself, which in its turn is not produced for sale but for entirely different reasons, nor can that activity be detached from the rest of life . . . ; land is only another name for nature, which is not produced by man; actual money, finally, is merely a token of purchasing power, which, as a rule, is not produced at all, but comes into being through the mechanism of banking and state finance" ([1944] 2001, 75–76). These fictions, in turn, provide the ground for actual transformations of material life and as such are absolutely fundamental to how the whole system works: "Nevertheless, it is with the help of this fiction that the actual markets for land, labor and money are organized; these are actually bought and sold on the market" (76).

The specific ways in which such fictions can be grasped and expressed on the remote peripheries of world capitalism is one of this book's central concerns. As an initial example of how these fictions might be expressed on the peripheries of the system discussed by Polanyi, we might begin with the fiction of Latin America itself, a name that accords unity and uniformity to an impossibly heterogeneous grouping of societies, but that nevertheless self-actualizes as a real position within the global division of labor. This position is represented in the map reproduced on the following page. The map, included at the beginning of Victor Bulmer-Thomas's classic study *The Economic History of Latin America* (2003), represents the region's main sources of export wealth circa 1930, after thirty-some years of intense market integration.

The map reproduces the landmass extending south of the Rio Grande to the tip of the Southern Cone, indicating the borders of the countries within it. No further geopolitical indications are given: no names of cities or towns, rivers or mountains appear. Instead, the spaces between borders are filled with crudely yet cheerfully drawn representations of commodities. As ciphers standing in for commodities, the drawings depict oil rigs, individual sheep, bunches of bananas, bars of iron, copper, and silver and pots of coffee. We also see whales spouting water off the coast of the Atlantic, and pearl necklaces emanating aureola-like rays over Venezuela. As a result of the fact that the commodities depicted on the map refer to what political economists have called "primary" or "raw" commodities, the form they take is in fact quite modern and possible only within the historical coordinates of nineteenth-century world capitalism.[7]

What is striking about the map, then, is the extent to which Latin America—a coinage of the late nineteenth century—can be represented as a storehouse of a particular order of commodities. In the famous first sentence of volume 1 of *Capital,* Marx writes that under the capitalist mode of production, the wealth of societies appears as "an immense collection of commodities" (1976, 125). The map takes the metaphor of the collection literally, to show its expression on a spatialized, geopolitical plane: Latin America

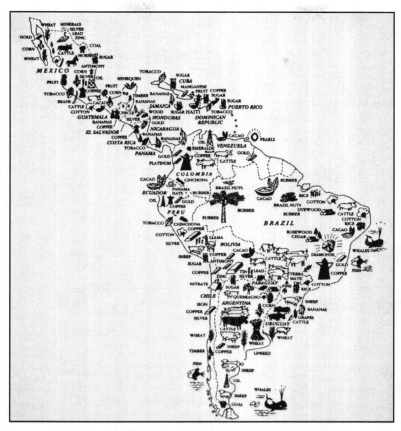

Latin America as collection of commodities, circa 1930. From Bulmer-Thomas (2003). Reprinted courtesy of Cambridge University Press.

comes into being for capital as a combination of commensurable and exchangeable commodities.

For Marx, the *appearance* of the world as a collection of commodities is misleading; in similar fashion, the idea that certain commodities "make" Latin America is also misleading, for two main reasons. First, because the map literally leaves out the larger system in which these commodities are produced and exchanged;

and second, because the map's lack of industrial markers leads us to believe that the commodity system is not only spatially, but also temporally removed from the order of modernity. But the appearance of coffee pots and cotton plants makes sense only when we consider that they are produced within a wider, indeed global system of exchange. And just as there is nothing natural about a society specializing in the production of coffee for the world market, there is nothing primitive or premodern about it either. The production of these commodities occurs simultaneously, if invisibly, alongside the production of the locomotives, textiles, and threshing machines for which they are exchanged. These other commodities are implied in the map, but *we can't see them;* nor can we see the markets for which the Latin American products are destined. Instead, these larger coordinates are present only in a ghost-like fashion, like phantom limbs whose stirrings can be felt but not seen.

This is where the concept of the commodity *fiction* I have been discussing gives rise to a related but separate concept: the commodity fetish. I use this term in a Marxian sense to identify the appearances and illusions that alter our perceptions of reality and as a consequence also alter the actual conditions under which production and exchange take place. Again, the map is illustrative: once Latin America is isolated from the larger system in which commodity specialization becomes possible, the resulting distortion actually does make the little coffee pots and giant rubber trees seem like animate, autonomous objects.

One of the key questions asked by this book is how the mysteries of the commodity can be represented and understood in a region whose role in the world economy was simultaneously generated by a larger system and circumscribed to a limited role within it. How might commodities and money *appear* in places whose economies are simultaneously driven by the global commodity order and, because nonindustrialized, seemingly anterior to it? Which kinds of fictions and fetishes arise, and how can they be expressed? As an initial approximation to how I answer these questions in the chapters that follow, we can turn back to the map as a guide. Chapter 1, for example, reads as an inquiry into *export* commodity fetishism, examining the rhetorical styles developed by Latin American intellectuals to showcase nations' commodifiable natural resources and crops. Chapter 2, in turn, examines the discursive modes deployed to represent the prestigious *imported* goods (invisible on the map) for which export commodities were exchanged. Chapters 3 and 4 examine the invisible and yet uncontrollable stirrings of *money,* by which the materiality of the commodity seems to disappear altogether into the winds of transnational exchange. Finally chapter 5 turns to examine the human exploitation invisibilized by the "collection" of raw export commodities as arranged by the map, specifically, the violence standing behind the outsized rubber tree drawn to fill the space of the Amazonian rainforest.

In each of these cases, the fictions and illusions generated by the larger market system find specific expressions in the range of images and texts studied in this book, a corpus I have organized under the rubric of capital fictions. Each chapter focuses on a different aspect of economic life—among them, export production, import consumption, financial speculation—to examine how different textual forms encoded and symbolized the transformations heralded by the global commodity order.

"Tobacco and sugar," the twentieth-century Cuban anthropologist Fernando Ortiz famously contends, "are the most important characters in Cuban history" ([1940] 1978, 12). Here and elsewhere in the region's cultural production, the humble export commodity—so simple and yet strangely animated—is personified and accorded a starring role in fables of culture and identity. In like manner, the export commodity will also play a starring role in this book's inquiry into the symbolic and imaginative practices embedded within economic life. As it traipses and trips across the world, the export commodity sheds its body to become exchange value in the *salto mortale* discussed by Marx, to come back dressed as a top hat, piano, or locomotive, or, in the case of the region's repetitive crises, to evaporate altogether into thin air. The imaginative apparatuses enlisted to explain these and other mysteries of value constitute the core of this book's critical endeavor.

Latin America in the World- System

Already in 1848, Marx and Engels noted the global pretensions of capitalism: "[t]he need of a constantly expanding market for its products chases the bourgeoisie over the entire surface of the globe. It must nestle everywhere, settle everywhere, establish connections everywhere" (1978, 476). At the same time, however, the geographical and social terrains through which capital circulates are never uniform but intensely variegated and uneven. That is, while capitalism exhibits a marked tendency toward the universalization of commodity and money forms, capitalist expansion produces radically different results in different historical contexts. All too often, however, liberal and Marxist teleologies alike have tended to erase this contingency by assuming a single and uninterrupted trajectory of capitalism across the globe. In this telos, northern European historical experiences mark the correct and normal path toward capitalist modernity, while those of peripheries and semiperipheries mark the belated, incomplete, and/or anomalous path toward that norm. But as theorists of "underdevelopment," "dependency," world-systems analysis, and uneven geographical development have argued in varied contexts, centers, peripheries, and semiperipheries are themselves creations of a single system and could not exist outside of a mutually constitutive relation.[8] Within this tradition, my own analysis assumes that the radically different social systems produced by global capitalism do not result simply from the "incomplete" absorption of bourgeois mechanisms, but instead are the concrete outcome of different strategies of accumulation used at different moments in different settings. My intention is to move beyond linear-stagist and diffusionist readings of capitalism to explore how this system has been able to accommodate—and profit from—wildly different social formations and landscapes. Hence while industrial production, wage labor, and bourgeois legal institutions are key components of capitalism (without which it could not exist as we know it), it does not logically follow that these features will be reproduced faithfully in other social contexts or even less that this failure to reproduce European social formations should be viewed as a failure to achieve modernity.[9]

I should stress that I am not making the claim that key features of European bourgeois societies—formal equality, wage labor, bourgeois institutions—were predominant in late nineteenth-century Latin America, nor that their absence was meaningless. Instead, I am insisting that even as certain key features through which capitalist society reproduces itself were absent, national societies were themselves radically altered by the intensification of commodity and money relations occurring during the Export Age. On the dependent periphery, some aspects of modern commercial society fade from view (such as industrialized specialization and rationalization), and yet others acquire special importance. This observation leads directly to a recalibration of what we might expect from peripheral cultural production, long considered in similarly linear-stagist terms as only imperfectly or belatedly repeating European norms. As Richard Rosa (n.d.) has explored in his study of the role of credit in nineteenth-century literature, Latin American modernities lacked the industrial aspect many have come to assume is a hallmark of bourgeois societies, and yet they were deeply shaped by the unruly behavior of transnational finance. Pace cultural theorists such as Fredric Jameson, the predominance of finance capital marks the onset of "late" capitalism and postmodernity. But as Rosa shows, finance has been an important aspect of Latin American modernities since the Independence period, when nascent nations accorded their first loans with British bankers. With this, Rosa provides a new entry point into the study of cultural production of the "long" nineteenth century, showing how recognized literary works by authors such as Andrés Bello, Jorge Isaacs, and Jorge Luis Borges interact with and mirror transnational credit relations.[10]

In taking the Export Age as a point of departure, I am inspired by previous studies of the ideologies and wish images that undergirded great periods of modernization in other parts of the world. Raymond Williams (1973) on England's Industrial Revolution and Walter Benjamin (1978) on Haussmann's Paris have shaped my thinking in this regard, along with a more recent corpus of scholarship on periods such as Britain's eighteenth-century "financial revolution," or the United States post–Civil War "Gilded Age."[11] My own use of the term "Export Age" is meant to conjure these other periods of intense modernization, and in so doing to establish the era as a valid point of departure for the study of the cultural articulations of modern capitalism.

The idea that Latin America lies somehow outside of or anterior to modern capitalist social formations is itself a "capital fiction," or fiction of the first order. Although Latin America has frequently played the sleepy backwater to the dynamic centers of industrial Europe, the time has come, I think, to reposition this region's cultural production at the vanguard, and not the rear guard, of the history of global capital. For if it is true that today capitalism is revealing its logic as one of instability, mobility, and extreme inequality, what better place to examine this logic than in Latin America, a region whose modern history is founded on precisely these characteristics? Hence one of the main intentions of this book is to remove Latin American cultures from what Dipesh Chakrabarty has named the "waiting room of history" to examine their possible contributions to the experience of global modernity (2008, 8). With attention to historical detail, this book isolates some of these peripheral sites of capital and examines the manifold fictions, fantasies, and illusions that accompanied tumultuous and uneven processes of economic modernization. All the while, I continue to draw from a Marxist tradition of critique, whose insights into the fictional foundations of bourgeois political economy remain unsurpassed in critical potential: commodities that appear to dance, money that appears to multiply and then evaporate, financial abstractions whose hold on reality seems unchallenged by their immateriality.

Writing the Export Age: Literature and Political Economy

My chosen object for excavating the capital fictions of the Export Age is late nineteenth- and early twentieth-century Latin American intellectual production, with a special emphasis on literary texts. Beyond contingencies of training and personal interest, there are two main reasons for this emphasis. In the first instance, it corresponds with a close, but largely overlooked, relationship between the discursive fields of political economy in nineteenth-century Latin America. As others have shown, the ubiquitous figure of Latin American nation-building was the *letrado,* or "man of letters," an elite social and political actor (most often male) who was equally at home whether writing novels or writing constitutions and drafting diplomatic accords.[12] To take just the case of Colombia, until well into the twentieth century, it was difficult to name a national president who had *not* at some point in his life penned a book of poems. Within this tradition of letters, different aesthetic forms such as poetry, the romantic novel, and the historical essay became important legitimizing discourses for Latin America's tiny European-identified and mostly white elite. For this elite, designated as "creole" in Spanish America, writing acquired special prestige as a civilizing discourse in what until the twentieth century remained predominantly illiterate societies. In past decades, scholars have paid special attention to the role of different forms of writing as key apparatuses in the forging of political power, especially as it pertained to the biopolitical governance of the nation-state.[13] The wave of cultural-studies-inspired critique that revitalized nineteenth-century Latin American literary studies in the 1980s and 1990s has provided excellent insights into what Doris Sommer (1991) has called the "foundational fictions" of literature and state. *Capital Fictions* (in which the echoes of Sommer's well-known coinage can be heard) maintains this focus on the politicized charge of nineteenth-century literature, but does so with an eye to the *economic* dimensions of writing. This shift in focus is justified by the fact that the political independence of new nations was accompanied from the start by a condition of *non*-independence in the sphere of global market relations. From the mid-nineteenth-century onward, *letrados* did double duty as presidents and novelists, and as diplomats and historians; they were also customs agents, Treasury ministers, and architects of liberal trade policies. Moreover, as I show throughout this book, texts of the period were filled with references to the incessant flow of money and commodities through the body politic. In novels and poetry, as well as in a virtually unknown corpus of financial treatises and advertisements, the present study uncovers the role of the *letrado* as a principal architect of the liberal reforms that swept across the continent from the 1870s onward, just as it identifies a range of literary texts and genres as key sites in the construction of economic imaginaries.

A second reason for focusing on cultural production as a guide to the capital fictions of Latin American modernities hails from the imaginative and representational apparatuses embedded within *both* literature and political economy. In this sense, my use of the term "capital fictions" refers not only to the ideological fallacies that allow capitalist economy to function as it does. Instead, when we turn to the study of specific texts and genres of the Export Age, the term acquires additional meaning in reference to works of the imagination whose value resides not so much in their truth or falsity, but rather in their capacity to seize on the *fictitious* dimensions of capitalist economy itself. As many have already shown, the very notion of the material economy relies on strategies of representation to make itself intelligible. Behind its claims to scientific objectivity, the discipline of economics likewise relies on a series of tropes, metaphors, and storytelling devices.[14] With an eye to identifying the specific elements that animated early capitalist imaginaries in Export Age Latin America, the first chapter of this book demonstrates the extent to which early liberal reformers enlisted the precepts of bourgeois political economy to imagine the immense benefits of market liberalization before they had become a lived reality. In this manner, political economy took on a highly speculative and utopian dimension by imagining scenarios, subjects, and lifeways that did not yet exist. This capacity to imagine worlds that do not yet exist, it should be noted, closely mirrors the work we associate with modern literary texts. And just as political economy approximates the function of literary fiction, so too does literary fiction resemble the formal qualities of economic instruments such as money. As literary critics such as Marc Shell (1978, 1993, 1995), Walter Benn Michaels (1987), and Patrick Brantlinger (1996) have shown in other contexts, literature and money bear close similarities as forms of representation that mediate between the tangible and intangible, the real and fictitious.[15] Inspired by critics such as these, my analysis seeks to uncover specific points of contact between economic and literary fictions in Export Age Latin America.

From a disciplinary perspective, then, this book not only aims to add something to literary and cultural history by way of political economy, but indeed it also hopes to open new ways of thinking about political economy through the imaginative contours of literature. Here it is important to mention that just as literary studies have overlooked the specific dimensions of economic life in modernizing Latin America, most economic histories of the period have sidestepped the representational means through which liberal polities could be imagined at all.[16] And while it is perhaps true that *all* literary projects mediate between the real and the imagined, there is still much to be said about the uniqueness of the fictions born of Latin America's first major experiment with capitalist modernization. The mirroring structures of belief undergirding literary and monetary fictions, for example, necessarily acquire special meaning in a region long accustomed to violent cycles of boom and bust wherein commodities and money "danced" (a key figure of the era), only to disappear into thin air with an oncoming crash. From within this context, paying attention to the circulation of money and commodities and to the exchange of meaning and metaphor in written texts promises to provide unique insights into how capitalism was imagined and lived.

One of the contributions of this book is, hopefully, to provide a new periodization and analytical frame for late nineteenth- and early twentieth-century Latin American literary production. This gesture becomes particularly relevant in light of the specific period studied, during which a specialized form of literary discourse wrapped itself in the cloak of spiritual disinterest with respect to the encroachment of market relations in daily life. Not coincidentally, it was precisely during the Export Age, as Latin American countries were becoming more and more integrated into global circuits of capital, that literature began to define itself as not only separate from, but indeed hostile toward, the world of commodities and money. As scholars such as Julio Ramos ([1989] 2001),

Aníbal González (1993) and Susana Rotker (2000) have shown, the last decades of the nineteenth century witnessed a straining of the historical relationship between writing and state institutions outlined above, as writing was increasingly incorporated into specialized print markets. One of the paradoxical outcomes of this shift away from state institutions and toward market-driven specialization was the birth of an aesthetic discourse that defined itself in resistance to the economic sphere. This development, associated with the genesis of the cultural current known as Spanish American *modernismo,* sacralized art as a disinterested counterpart to the economic interests at the core of bourgeois liberalism. This vision of art, in turn, was inscribed as a founding principle of Latin American literary studies in the early twentieth century, through critics such as Pedro Henríquez Ureña, Alfonso Reyes, and Ricardo Rojas. As I argue throughout this book, however, the more literary production proclaimed its independence from the economic sphere, the more it revealed itself to be embedded within that very sphere. This is true on the level of individual writers' roles as economic agents, which went beyond professional writing to include the activities of merchants, speculators, and debtors, among others. This embeddedness is also revealed on the level of representation, as texts and genres sought to make sense of an array of emerging economic practices: among them, the forceful clearing of indigenous lands to make room for coffee cultivation, the pleasures of luxury consumption, and the excruciating experience of personal and national bankruptcy.

Stories of Boom and Bust

The story told by this book is divided into two parts, "Boom" and "Bust," terms that refer to the unstable logic of capitalist expansion in Latin America. In this manner, the trajectory of the book is designed to mimic that of the Export Age itself, moving from the emergence of liberal utopias of global market integration and national prosperity, to grim realizations that this dream was not being realized. The first part traces the emergence of fantasies of national prosperity through free trade, export specialization, and prestige-based import consumption. The second part, in turn, shows how cultural production attempted to account for the salient outcomes of early capitalist development: among them, volatile commodity markets, frequent currency debacles, huge race- and class-based disparities, and "eternal" debt to foreign lenders.

More than demarcate linear stages overcome with time, the categories of boom and bust are meant to evoke Latin American engagements with global capital as permanently volatile and uneven, a quality we can see with special clarity from the vantage of the Export Age. For heuristic purposes, I have found it useful to isolate different moments in this cycle to tell a story about the rise and fall of creole illusions about the free market in the late nineteenth and early twentieth centuries. The chapters themselves are organized within this temporal scheme of rise and fall to focus on particular aspects of economic life that became salient as the Export Age wore on. The book thus begins with a consideration of early dreams of production, found in liberal newspapers and commercial pamphlets, to move to fantasies of prestige-based consumption lodged in poetry, advertisements, and journalistic chronicles; the second part of the book examines how widespread financial crises transformed *money* into a key site of fiction making, especially by way of the novel. Finally, the last chapter of the book returns to the realm of production, this time to study how elites attempted to account for the exploitative practices that accompanied export-led modernization.

The consolidation of Latin America's first liberal experiment was accompanied by a generalized acceptance of the classical economic doctrine of Ricardian advantage. This doctrine held that countries should specialize in those commodities they could produce most efficiently for the world market, with the promise that this arrangement would bring prosperity to all parties involved. Chaper 1 introduces the concept of export specialization as imagined by nineteenth-century liberal reformers and studies its corollary in a discursive mode I call "export reverie," by which liberal visionaries imagined the intense benefits to be wrought through incorporation into global commodity networks, conjuring national wealth before it had materialized in production. To examine the contradictions emerging from this future-oriented, speculative rhetoric, I turn to a little-known pamphlet by the Cuban writer José Martí, *Guatemala* (1878), written to promote foreign investment in this country. In this text, I argue, Martí conjures beautiful visions of rich agrarian landscapes, self-sustaining growth, and mutual cooperation between plantation owners, European investors, and indigenous workers. Yet these fantasies—which reached their democratic and inclusive heights with Martí—would always be undermined by the material logic of export-led modernization, which tended to privilege the creation of privately owned surplus value over the needs of citizens. At stake in this chapter is a rereading of Martí (often figured in heroic opposition to market society), but also an understanding of the hopes and illusions on which early liberal projects were based.

Chapter 2 moves from the export side of economies to the import side, and from liberal-democratic fantasies of production to exclusionary fantasies of consumption. My point of departure is Spanish American *modernismo,* a cultural current long noted for its celebration of European luxury goods and works of art, as well as for its suppression of American subjects, objects, and geographies. Focusing on a discursive mode I call the modernist import catalogue, I show how embellished lists and inventories of imported commodities helped to forge a language with which to appreciate and "love" luxurious foreign commodities. My examination of the modernist import catalogue passes through the Nicaraguan poet Rubén Darío's landmark book *Azul* (1888); virtually unknown advertisements by the renowned Colombian poet José Asunción Silva (who earned his living as an import merchant in turn-of-the century Bogotá); and a journalistic appraisal of a Havana department store by the Cuban poet Julián del Casal.

If the realms of production and consumption are the most visible and apprehensible in capitalist economies, the realm of circulation marks the unbreachable gap between value and representations of value. Chapter 3 turns to this sphere to examine a literary genre that emerged in the wake of the great financial crash of 1890 in Argentina: the stock market novel. In the decade following the crash, around a dozen novels centered on the stock market attempted to make sense of the sudden creation and disappearance of value during the cycle of financial boom and bust. Centering my analysis on the most famous of these novels, Julián Martel's *La bolsa* (The stock exchange [1891]), I show how the novel—under the twin guise of artistic disinterest and civic outrage—stepped in to provide ideological therapy for the nation in times of financial crisis. With the crash, the "fictitious capital" of the stock market evaporated. In the ensuing panic, the novel stepped forth to issue *new* fictions, arguing, for example, that if the destructive elements of capital (associated with Jews and women) could be domesticated, things would be set on their right course again. This, however, was utter fantasy; for in Argentina and elsewhere, the restoration of belief in the financial system only serves to recreate the conditions for crisis to occur once more.

If the stock market novels attempt to stabilize belief so that economic actors might gather the courage to weather the storms of capital once more, this restoration of belief became all but impossible under conditions of unrelenting crisis and bankruptcy. By the end of the century, several Latin American nations, in spite of following liberal recipes for success, were bankrupt and, even worse, bereft of credit. Chapter 4 moves to study decadent aesthetics as a response to financial ruin. To do so, I return to the Colombian import merchant and writer José Asunción Silva to study his post-humously published novel *De sobremesa* (*After-Dinner Conversation*), which was completed between the author's own bankruptcy and subsequent suicide in 1896. While it is usually approached as a novel about art, I argue that it also offers an allegory of national economic failure by way of a masculine subject whose psyche bears a striking resemblance to crisis-prone national economies at the end of the nineteenth century.

In chapter 5 I trace how, beginning in the 1920s, literary texts inscribed themselves within the demise and decay of the export-led model of growth. Many critics have read this turn to autochthony or regionalism as corresponding to literature's rejection of European(ized) city life in search of a more "simple" or "authentic" rural reality. But during the Export Age, the jungles, forests, and plains depicted in regionalist novels were by no means outside modern capitalist social relations, but rather at the very center of commodity export regimes. Rather than representing the negation of urban space, then, the rural-extractive sector represents its hidden complementary counterpart. I focus on the Colombian novelist José Eustasio Rivera's *La vorágine* (*The Vortex* [1924]), a novel set during the Amazonian rubber boom, and its depiction of the destructive logic of frontier capitalism. Read against the other texts studied in this book, *La vorágine* glimpses the traumatic "real" of Latin American export economies, providing a striking image of the human and ecological consequences of natural resource extraction.

The conclusion examines the afterlife of nineteenth-century fictions of capital in Gabriel García Márquez's *Cien años de soledad* (*One Hundred Years of Solitude* [1967]), the most famous novel of the "Boom" generation of the 1960s. While many have read García Márquez's aesthetic as corresponding with mythical and hence nonmodern elements of Latin American history, my reading argues that it in fact allows for an understanding of *capital* as the foundational myth of export-driven modernities.

The analysis I advance in the outlined chapters is made possible by the combination and mutual critique of two main methodological paradigms: on the one hand, a Foucauldian and new historicist–inspired approach to discourse still operative in Latin American literary and cultural studies; and on the other, a much older tradition of Marxist dialectics. Foucauldian discourse analysis, associated with the rise of feminist and queer studies in the discipline, has expanded the parameters of Latin American literary studies to explore formations surrounding sexuality, race, criminality, medicine, and illness.[17] This approach has also radically expanded the sheer number of texts, genres, and objects available for scholarly inquiry.[18] Yet, for the most part, at least in the latest wave of Latin American literary and cultural studies, this approach has not focused on capital as a force shaping the region's modernities. By the 1980s, Marxist approaches to culture became increasingly identified with a mechanical economic determinism and reductionism. Additionally, Latin Americanist interpretations of Marxism (from dependency school economics to literary studies) have faced the problem of operating within a European-centered telos that has frequently interpreted local divergences from bourgeois modernities as signs of backwardness or incompletion rather than historically significant in their own right.

And yet, in spite of these limitations, a reinvigorated form of materialist critique is sorely needed if we are to adequately understand the vast inequalities that continue to shape and constrain our capacity to imagine a different world. For in the two decades following the end of the Cold War, when Marxism fell out of favor in academic circles, the importance of capital as a vector of social power has not diminished. If anything, given the force of ongoing crisis and the upward redistribution of the world's wealth, the salience of class in shaping social relations from the everyday to the geopolitical has only intensified. Marxist critique still has much to teach us about the unpredictable and variegated cultural formations created within the global order of capital. Here I am thinking especially of the beautifully nuanced and complex analysis of literary texts provided by Latin American Marxist critics such as Roberto Schwarz and Angel Rama, and Left feminist critics such as Jean Franco, whose continued relevance lies in their relentless attention to social contradiction within a wider framework of capitalist relations.[19] And though it is true that much Marxist literary analysis in Latin America and elsewhere has focused on class to the frequent exclusion of gender, race, and sexuality (just as more recent studies of the latter categories have frequently excluded class), this study maintains that we need not necessarily choose between these points of inquiry.

The geographical focus of the study aims to be continental rather than national; this choice is justified given the similar economic model that arose across the region during the Export Age. This choice is also justified by the fact that my object of study—capital—is by definition mobile and can be grasped only by taking a wide geographical frame. From within this broad context, however, I have paid attention to national specificities, explaining their particularities when necessary and contrasting different articulations of the commodity order. Readers will note that I use the term "Latin America" to demarcate the region in question (specifying only when the cultural discourse in question is exclusive to one subregion, as in the case of Spanish American *modernismo*). Given the fact that the greater part of my study focuses on Spanish-speaking countries, this nomenclature needs some justification. While "Spanish" or even "Hispanic" America would perhaps be a more accurate term, my point of departure is an economic model that became dominant throughout the region as a whole. My use of the marker "Latin America"—a term that rose to prominence precisely during the Export Age—aims to conjure this broad sweep of history, without losing sight of the particularities and variations within it.

Cycles

Before turning to the capital fictions of the previous century, a final word on historicity. As I mentioned at the beginning of this introduction, the capital fictions excavated in this book continue to animate our present. I have attempted to respect the dead by not folding their disasters and cataclysms into our current and ongoing ones. And yet it is impossible, I think, not to notice some continuities and repetitions between the pathways of capital in the past *fin de siglo* and the one we are living today. By the 1990s, Latin American countries were once again drawn into global markets on unprecedented levels under a new round of liberal reforms: the wide-scale privatization of state institutions, the opening of markets to foreign investors, and the return to an extractive, natural-resource–based model (justified through a neo-Ricardian discourse of advantage), were all hallmarks of this neoliberal shift. In the post-1989 world, the "free" circulation of capital became ubiquitous again. Throughout the 1990s, neoliberal economists were once again promising that foreign investment and natural resource specialization would create untold wealth: to look no further than the title of an advertising campaign financed by the

Peruvian government and published by *Forbes* magazine, free markets were again "Leading the Way" toward prosperity and equality for Latin American countries ("Peru: Leading the way," n.d). At the same time, the vast concentration of wealth sparked by the privatization of state-owned companies has created the region's first billionaires (such as Carlos Slim in Mexico) and sparked a resurgence of export-elite opulence that recalls that of over a century ago. In São Paulo, Brazil, a luxury emporium with a neocolonial façade was built between a river and a hillside slum to purvey Chanel purses and Ferraris to the city's ultra-rich, whose shopping experience is protected by a small army of guards and a helipad for quick entries and exits (Benson, 2005). Even more significantly, *crisis* came back; after decades of relative economic stability between the 1940s and 1970s, the 1980s and 1990s were marked by currency debacles, dollarization, and IMF-imposed "shock therapy." The hopes associated with neoliberal restructuring, under strain since the 1990s, came to a symbolic end when a booming Argentina—*finally* on its way to first-world status and lasting prosperity—defaulted on its loans in 2001. In Colombia and Mexico the narcotics trade serves as but the latest articulation of a long history of export commodity booms, creating unprecedented amounts of wealth and with it unprecedented levels of violence. Without assuming a neat overlay between moments of accumulation a century apart, this book turns back to the Export Age with the intention of creating resonances between the capital fictions of the past and those that continue to flourish in our midst.

I. BOOM

Chapter 1

PRODUCTION

Imagining
the Export Republic

In 1872 an article entitled "Las riquezas de Bolivia" ("The wealth of Bolivia") appeared in the New York–based, Cuban-owned newspaper *La América Ilustrada*.[1] The anonymous article confidently identifies Bolivia as "one of the richest countries of this rich land of América": "The fertility of its soil is incomparable, its products are varied and infinite, and its entrails hold an abundant store of man's most valuable minerals."[2] The country's indigenous majority, described as "peaceful and industrious," promises to provide the necessary labor to create lasting national wealth. So ideal are the conditions for wealth creation in Bolivia, the article goes on to note, that it all seems part of a larger plan. "It seems, in reality, that chance has wanted to unite in Bolivia all the elements of wealth necessary for an intelligent and resolved race to plant in her the foundations of a great [nation]" (34).

From the perspective of the twenty-first century, the assessment of Bolivia as "one of the richest countries of this rich land of America" surely deserves our attention: for according to all economic indicators, Bolivia is not the richest, but one of the *poorest* countries of a region that is itself poor. But in the 1870s, on the cusp of Latin America's most intense and far-reaching experiment with economic liberalism yet, Bolivia's success seemed all but assured.

The title of this forgotten text itself recalls a much more famous work, Adam Smith's *Wealth of Nations* (1776), the foundational text of bourgeois liberal economic thought. This and other foundational texts of political economy had circulated widely in Latin America since the Independence period, and as noted in the Introduction, the best-known writers of the nineteenth century were avid readers and exponents of the science of wealth. And as I show in this chapter, from the mid-nineteenth century onward, political economy emerged as an intense site of fantasy and imagination for liberal thinkers. For by following the immutable "laws" of political economy, fledgling nations might produce wealth and prosperity well beyond their wildest dreams.

The intense optimism buoying "Las riquezas de Bolivía" and scores of other texts like it was stoked by the spectacular growth of European markets from the 1850s onward, and their unquench-able thirst for tropical agricultural products like sugar and coffee, as well as for raw materials for industrial production, ranging from nitrates and tin to rubber and timber.[3] More fundamentally, lib-eral hopes were sustained by faith in the possibility of export com-modity production to create long-lasting wealth and prosperity for their nations. Two basic elements of production—land and natu-ral resources—were in abundant, exuberant, and seemingly end-less supply across Latin America, forming a vast reserve of possible wealth for new nations. "All that was needed," writes the economic historian Victor Bulmer-Thomas in a gloss on nineteenth-century liberal thought, "were capital and skilled labor to unlock the nat-ural resources in Latin America's vast unexploited interior and unrestricted access to the wealthy markets of Western Europe" (2003, 5).

"Las riquezas de Bolivia" recognizes this division of labor, in which export commodity production figures as the starting point for a vision of future wealth: the extraction of "man's most valuable minerals," an abstract name for those metals for which a demand had been established in foreign markets, would lead to the con-struction of railways. Railways, in turn, would allow for more commodity production to occur, "swiftly" allowing the nation to become "rich and prosperous" (1872, 34).

As a representative of scores of similar texts from the period, "Las riquezas de Bolivia" is an example of what this chapter iden-tifies as a poetics of capital in Latin America, one I call "export reverie."[4] This mode emerges as the waking dream of nineteenth-century liberal visionaries, providing beautiful visions of national and regional wealth before it had actually materialized. Characterized by optimism, ebullience, and effervescence, this discourse flourished especially at the dawn of the Export Age in the 1870s and 1880s, when it seemed as though the realization of America's vast stores of natural wealth was not only possible but imminent, awaiting only the touch of human labor and creativity for its realization.[5]

Liberal elites viewed their own labor and creativity as men of letters (*letrados*) as necessary to getting this process underway; to this end, the mode of discourse I call export reverie became a key vehicle for expressing the hopes and dreams of export-led modernization. While not formalized as a genre, the ebullient and optimistic tones of export reverie reverberated across the continent in newspaper essays, commercial manuals, exposition catalogues, inaugural speeches, and advertisements. As a discourse, export reverie is recognizable through a double gesture: first, the identification of the untapped agricultural or mineral resources, followed by an ecstatic prediction of the wealth and happiness that export commodity wealth would bring.

For liberal visionaries, this transformation had been a long time coming. For decades after Independence in the early nineteenth century, new republics had been racked by political discord and civil war, tendencies blamed for stifling the development of commerce. But after decades of stops and starts, the 1870s allowed creole elites to catch a glimpse of a world uniting under the sign of commerce. Newspapers—one of the key supports of this global vision—printed allegories of the "banquet of nations," along with engravings of railways, worker bees, and chimneyed factories, all wish-images of the mobility and productivity promised by the free market. Financial instruments such as banknotes and bond certificates showed idyllic scenes of transatlantic commerce, signified by images of locomotives standing next to bags of coffee, signifying a harmonious circuit of exchange (Raventos 1984, 22; Clark 1971, 43).

With images such as these, the market and its instruments became intense sites of utopian longing, united under the sign of "progress": as the historian Silvia Álvarez Curbelo notes, this term

Icons of productivity: late nineteenth-century advertisement for the Chaves chocolate factory, depicting cacao plants, beehive, and locomotives. From Raventos (1984).

carries interpretive power not as a homogeneous set of economic policies, but instead as a "shared grouping of signifiers" (2001, 156).

In his critique of the triumphalist discourses surrounding world markets in the 1990s, Paul Smith argues that the very term "globalization" announces a project that has not yet materialized. Far from a fait accompli, globalization emerges as ideology *before* it becomes material reality, or as "a signifier that has yet to quite realize its own referent" (1997, 49). Contemporary globalization functions, then, as a grouping of "millennial dreams," in which "the process of annunciating its dream has extensive effects in the formation not just of the material circumstances under which the world labors, but also of the ideological and cultural conditions under which it lives and which have to be made apposite for the desired condition" (1997, 18).

Near the end of the nineteenth century, Latin American liberal thinkers conjured their own set of "millennial dreams," announcing the project of market integration before it was lived as a reality. I analyze these millennial dreams under the rubric of "export reverie," a discourse that melded political economy, civic rhetoric,

The export reverie visualized: late nineteenth-century note issued by the American Bank of Guatemala showing a scene of coffee production *(left)* and the arrival of a locomotive *(right)*. In keeping with this distribution, the national seal of Guatemala appears at left, while that of the United States is on the right. From Clark (1971).

and aesthetics to present dream visions of a more perfect future in the hands of the market. Following Paul Smith's analysis, an oneiric vision unfolds and in so doing, drastically alters the ideological and cultural conditions under which social life can be imagined. And just as our own historical epoch (neoliberal globalization) has witnessed a drastic change not only under which the world labors, but under which the world itself is imagined, the millennial reveries of nineteenth-century Latin American liberals set out to do nothing less than remake the social fabric of their nations.[6]

Liberal enthusiasts took their mission very seriously: as the historian Paul Gootenberg notes, in the second half of the nineteenth century, "Latin America emerged as the purest and most tenacious pole of liberal orthodoxy of the modern world economy" (1988, 64). Integration into the global commodity lottery under nineteenth-century paradigms of liberalism involved a gigantic leap of faith into the unknown. Late nineteenth-century Latin American elites, in order to proceed with their reforms, had to believe in the necessity of free exchange and private property in the creation of modern, prosperous republics. In order for the vast reorganization of space, human activity, and lifeways necessary for

liberal reform to occur, elites also had to believe in the ductility of
the country's landscapes and population. Belief was all the more
important because the creation of a republic specialized in export
agriculture was no small task: it required the felling of forests to
make room for plantations, the building of railways and ports to
connect to mines, and the massive relocation of populations to create labor forces. And as I show in this chapter, the enormity of the
challenge at hand necessitated the creation of rhetorical strategies
to imagine the outcomes of export-led modernization.

In the view advanced by this chapter, late nineteenth-century
liberalism did not involve simply adherence to a set of political
beliefs or economic policies. Instead, liberalism created a political
imaginary that itself served as a conduit for expansive and radically
transformative desire. For real economic transformation to occur,
it had to be preceded as if in dream. Alternately, we might say that
the "spirit" of capitalist transformation ran across the region before
its material body appeared. To return to the article "Las riquezas
de Bolivia," lettered elites had to conjure wealth as an idea before it
might materialize on the ground.

This chapter has two chief aims. The first is to revive, by way
of export reverie, the sense of possibility and hope at work in early
liberal imaginaries, wherein invigorated commodity *production*
for the world market promised untold wealth for Latin American
nations. Second, this examination has the goal of exploring the
imagination as a starting point for political economy. The prediction that Bolivia will "swiftly" become one of the richest nations
of "this rich land of America" attests to the immense expectations
expressed by liberal discourse in late nineteenth-century Latin
America, as nations poised themselves on the cusp of a grand
transformation. Specialized commodity production for the global
market promised to create widespread prosperity, self-sustaining
"progress" and modernity, and, at least in its most utopian democratic incarnations, it also pledged to incorporate excluded masses
(particularly indigenous peoples) as citizens of the nation-state.
But as I show in this chapter, these liberal fantasies continued to
run up against contradictions, experienced on levels both external

and internal to the Latin American nation-state. First, with respect to the global market, specialization in "raw" materials (a name with huge symbolic potency) implies a ready space in the global market, but under conditions of inequality and dependency. Second, with respect to the internal composition of Latin American societies, the civic impulse of early liberal fantasies would always be contradicted by the very logic of capital accumulation, which promises prosperity and mobility for all, while privileging the creation of *private* wealth. The first part of the chapter outlines the rhetorical means through which early liberals conjured the benefits of specialized production for the world market before these benefits had been realized on the ground. The second part turns to examine a little-known pamphlet by the Cuban writer and patriot José Martí, entitled *Guatemala* (1878), as providing special insights into the promises and contradictions contained within early liberal imaginaries.

Political Economy and the Fiction of Specialization

During the last quarter of the nineteenth century, the consolidation of liberal regimes in Latin America resulted in the creation of export-driven economies, organized around the production of a handful of commodities for the global market. Yet the transformation of a country like Guatemala or Colombia into a specialized producer of coffee, or Bolivia into a producer of tungsten and tin is logical only if we accept another of the grand fictions on which classical political economy rests: the theory of international trade advantage. This doctrine, first outlined by the British political economist David Ricardo in his 1817 *Principles of Political Economy* and rearticulated over the course of the nineteenth century, held that nations should specialize in those commodities it might produce most efficiently for the global market.[7] The promise was that such specialization would foment unprecedented prosperity for all parties involved: the world's resources would be allocated efficiently and productively, and technological advance would spread equally across different parts of the world. The question of the division of labor within a given society had been fundamental to early political economy, most notably in Adam Smith's *Wealth of Nations* (1776). Ricardo extends Smith's analysis of specialization to consider the optimal *global* division of labor, by which different nations or colonies would specialize in the production of different commodities. His famous example of international trade advantage looked to England and Portugal to decide whether either country should attempt to produce what the other already produced: textiles and wine, respectively. The answer Ricardo provides is an emphatic "no." Assuming that each country was able to produce each commodity, Britain should not try to produce wine, because it would lose out on potential profits to be gained through textile manufacture. On the other hand, Portugal should direct its energies toward wine, which it could produce more cheaply than England, and with the profits buy textiles from the island nation. Just as earlier political economists did not ask how capitalists came to own the means of producing textiles or wine in the first place, Ricardo's theory of advantage does not ask how nations came to possess their advantages. Instead, factors of production are taken as self-evident, as are the historical processes through which the demand for textiles or wine might be generated in order to constitute an advantage in the first place.[8] At the same time, the question of differing costs of labor between one place and another is taken as a given and absorbed into the calculus of advantage and disadvantage; the inequalities that create advantage in the first place, that is, are erased from view. At least in its application, Ricardo's theory also removes geopolitical relations from the picture. For while the political economist set out to prove that English and Portuguese advantages resulted from the rational play of market forces, the Methuen treaty of 1703 had already stipulated that British textiles would enter Portugal, and Portuguese wine would enter Britain without taxation. Here as elsewhere, history is abstracted from the science of wealth and transformed into economic law.

While Ricardo's famous example was restricted to the industrial center and agrarian margin of Europe, the theory of advantage with which his name is associated would have its most dramatic and lasting effect in laying the ideological foundations for a truly global division of labor. In this division of labor, nonindustrialized nations and colonies would produce agricultural and mineral products in exchange for European commodities (including wine, textiles, locomotives, threshing machines, and so on). An even more extreme version of trade advantage emerged to deal with countries whose chief advantage was deemed to be "nature" itself. As Fernando Coronil writes, "The international division of labor is not solely a social division of labor but also a global division of nature," in which the periphery is consigned to contribute cheap labor and raw materials (1997, 29).[9]

Since the Spanish Conquest in the sixteenth century, the "New World" had been codified in European imaginaries as the space of nature par excellence, lacking in culture and history. Under colonial mercantilism—an economic system in which wealth was measured in specie—Spain treated its American colonies as a reserve of precious metals like silver and gold. Under nineteenth-century capitalism, the countries of Latin America would continue to contribute products of nature, but this time according to the logic of advantage built into the global commodity lottery. This advantage was constituted through the tropical products that northern societies could not produce for themselves (e.g., coffee, sugar). It also included raw materials unavailable or long since depleted in Europe (metals, petroleum, timber, arable soil). On the other side of the equation, European industry offered American nations manufactured goods they did not produce (steel, locomotives, threshing machines), as well as those that European societies could produce more cheaply with industrial production (e.g., textiles, shoes).

Early liberal thinkers in Latin America characterized this emerging division of labor between nations as the natural expression of the laws of political economy. Elements of a narrative surrounding export commodity specialization had already emerged as early as 1850, on the cusp of a previous wave of post-Independence liberal reform.[10] As an example, we can turn to the era's most indefatigable liberal crusader, the Argentine writer and future president D. F. Sarmiento. In his political essay *Argirópolis* (written to propose a confederation of states to be formed by Argentina, Paraguay, and Uruguay, a proposal never brought to fruition), Sarmiento gives an excursus on classical political economy from the perspective of Latin American nations. "[N]uestro interés está en vender la mayor suma de productos posible y comprar la mayor suma de productos posible y comprar la mayor cantidad de artefactos europeos. No es rico el que tiene plata, sino el que produce y sabe gozar del fruto de su trabajo" ("[O]ur interest is in selling the greatest quantity of products possible and in buying the greatest possible quantity of European goods. He who has money [*plata*] isn't rich, but instead he who produces and knows how to enjoy the fruits of his labor"; [1850] 1968, 97). Now surely this was a lesson with which creole national leaders, who fought for the demise of Spanish colonial mercantilism in the first decades of the nineteenth century, were quite familiar. Indeed, Independence leaders had been readers not only of republican political theorists like Rousseau, but also political economists like Smith, Hume, and Montesquieu. But for Sarmiento, writing in 1850, this lesson had not adequately been learned and clearly needed repeating to his readers. This was especially true in Sarmiento's native Argentina, ruled by the caudillo Juan Manuel de Rosas. Sarmiento's most famous work *Facundo: Civilización y barbarie* (1845) reads as an impassioned diatribe against the barbarism of the isolationist and iron-armed dictator. The terms "barbarism" and "civilization" were themselves invoked to differentiate modes of production on a global scale, with European commercial societies representing the pinnacle of civilization, and the rest of the world still mired in barbarism. In *Argirópolis,* written five years after *Facundo,* Sarmiento rendered the link between civilization and free commerce even more explicit: "Esta es una ley universal. Del libre intercambio de productos entre una ciudad y los demás mercados del mundo, depende su engrandecimiento y su prosperidad" ("This is a universal law. A city's expansion and prosperity depends on the free trade of products with the rest of the world's markets"; [1850] 1968, 68).

As a mark of the liberal ethos I am studying in this chapter, Sarmiento displays utter confidence in the "universal law" established by political economy: fundamentally, that lasting prosperity can be created only through the free exchange of useful commodities among nations. But what might Latin American nations, long cut off from centers of industry and technology, produce for the "civilized" world? Here a second law of classical political economy acquires enormous importance. For it is self-evident to Sarmiento that Latin American nations should specialize in the production of a specific order of goods for European markets: raw materials. "Nosotros no seremos fabricantes sino con el lapso de los siglos y con la aglomeración de millones de habitantes; nuestro medio sencillo de riqueza está en la exportación de las materias primas que la fabricación europea necesita" ("We will not become manufacturers until centuries pass and millions of inhabitants are gathered; our simple means of [producing] wealth lies in exporting the raw materials [*materias primas*] that European industry needs"; 97).

Sarmiento posits that because European societies had *already* become manufacturing nations, Latin American societies were not in a position to compete in this arena. Therefore, entry into global circuits of exchange would be granted through the production of "raw" commodities and consumption of "la mayor cantidad de artefactos europeos [posible]" ("the largest quantity of European goods [possible]"; 97). This is not to say that Sarmiento and others of his generation did not aspire to introducing industry in the region; quite the contrary, this eventuality remained the explicit goal of modernization programs well into the twentieth century. What I want to stress is the temporal dynamic in Sarmiento's statement: *for now,* Argentina must accept its limitations in the realm of production.

In keeping with the fundamental tenets of trade advantage, Sarmiento assumes that this arrangement will be beneficial to both Europe and Latin America, even as his own understanding of this doctrine assumes a fundamental asymmetry between the two parties. For "primary" commodities, produced by "simple" means, are by definition worth less than the manufactures they are traded for. Sarmiento does not ask why this should be so, but rather assumes that certain production techniques produce more valuable commodities, and that in the global arena, these techniques are available only to countries that already have them. There is a tautological character to this statement: industrialization is the product of industrialization. Only with the passage of "centuries" might this change.

Sarmiento's insistence that Latin American nations must export their simple products in return for European manufactures would become a litany so frequently heard so as to become an article of liberal faith. The liberal reformer Florentino González, for example, writes that New Granadins [Colombians]

> cannot compete in manufacturing with Europeans and [North] Americans. Any directive aimed to increase manufacturing, despising the resources of agriculture, has no place in a Government inclined toward the well-being of the nation of which it is in charge. Europe, with an intelligent population, possessing steam technology, already skillful in the art of manufacturing, achieves the mission of transforming raw materials within the industrial world. We must accomplish our mission, and we cannot have doubts about it, when we look at the prodigality of natural resources with which Providence has endowed our land. (Qtd. in C. Rojas. [2002, 106])

The secular religion of political economy hands Colombia a "mission" it must fulfill within the civilized global order. Additionally, González reveals a crucial element on which the legitimacy of nineteenth-century discourses of commodity specialization rests: the ability to manufacture products serves as a measure of a nation's *intelligence;* conversely, its absence reveals a lack of intelligence, thereby justifying Colombia's role as purveyor of raw materials to Europe. Concomitantly, in concert with the teleological movement of nineteenth-century "progress," manufacturing nations belong to a higher stage of historical development than nonmanufacturing ones. Spatial distance, as Johannes Fabian has argued, is measured as a temporal distance between Europe and its (neo)colonial peripheries, here in direct correlation with a society's main mode of production (2002).[11] Hence the theory of value inscribed into the global division of labor does not measure merely the quantity of labor that goes into the making of a commodity, but rather the *quality* of that labor (educated versus noneducated), as well as the stage in the production process it occupies ("raw" versus "finished," "natural" versus "manufactured"). It matters little to this ideological schema that a product like unrefined sugar is in its own right a manufacture (passing through labor-intensive and technologically sophisticated processes of cutting, juice extraction, boiling), or that industrial societies in Europe and North America remained strongly tied to more "primitive" methods of production like agriculture and mining. Instead, terms like "raw" and "primary" materials acquire ideological significance within spatially—and racially—inflected hierarchies of value.

There was little doubt among early liberal thinkers, then, that specialization in "natural," "raw," "primary" or "tropical" commodities was less preferable than the production of manufactures. Nor was there doubt that Latin American production techniques— defined from the outset as primitive—required less intelligent labor than those required for production in European countries. And yet, to recall the Colombian liberal Florentino González's words: "We must accomplish our mission, and we cannot have doubts about it." As if already cognizant of the potential pitfalls residing within the recommended economic model, the author insists that all doubts be banished nonetheless. At least at this moment, to reject Latin American countries' "mission" within the global division of labor was tantamount to a rejection of civilization itself.

Political Economy: A Not-So-Dismal Science

For nineteenth-century liberal thinkers, political economy offered a set of universal laws governing production and exchange, at the same time as the extension of these laws to the functioning of the world market placed Latin America in a position of subordination vis-à-vis industrial centers. Asymmetry, that is, was assumed as part of the cost of doing business with the "civilized" world. It is thus all the more remarkable that political economy became an active site of *fantasy* and *imagination* for these same liberal thinkers. For while openly cognizant that Latin America's declared trade advantage in natural resources was itself a disadvantage within the global system of trade, liberals displayed utter confidence that, in the long run, the region's nations could overcome temporal and material barriers to become wealthy beyond their greatest expectations. This is the leap of faith that underpins the mode of discourse I have introduced as export reverie, a mode of discourse able to express the dream of the nation's wealth through specialized commodity production for the world market. As we see in Sarmiento's early text, written in 1850, once this leap of faith is taken, a beautiful future begins to emerge.

In *Argirópolis* Sarmiento predicts that by following the precepts of free trade, Entre Ríos (a river-bound region of today's Argentina) might become the *"richest country on earth"* ([1850] 1968, 86–87, emphasis added). This is no small claim, especially for an author who spent much of his career outlining the historical, cultural, and racial obstacles to economic "progress" in Latin America. Importantly, the expository tone of Sarmiento's excursus on political economy ("this is a universal law") acts as a support for a dream vision. Argentina's current emphasis on ranching, dismissed as "barbaric" and isolationist in earlier texts like *Facundo*, will be replaced by the production of exportable grains (88); at the same time, European immigrants will arrive to the region's vast and underpopulated expanses to forge a superior labor force. These imagined workers, acting in concert with imported technology and manufactures, will revolutionize the productive forces in the country so much as to "increase forces by hundred-fold to produce in one day the work of a century" (98). If, according to Sarmiento, the science of political economy dictates that it will take centuries for Latin American nations to catch up with European ones, the same science seems to predict that a zealous commitment to its principles might reduce those centuries to mere days. The author himself recognizes that the future he predicts might seem outlandish, the stuff of mere *dreams*. He proudly assumes the charge: "Ah! Dreams, indeed, but dreams that ennoble man; for nations, it is enough to have them as the object of their aspiration to see them realized" (85).

Dreams for Sarmiento are not the negation of material reality, but instead the necessary starting point for its transformation. The country has not yet begun its production process in earnest, but its very enunciation *as a dream* is poised to set a much-desired process in motion. Dream-work, and in a more fundamental manner, language itself, foretells a grand material transformation before it has actually gotten underway. A key node within the discursive mode I have named "export reverie" is what I call "liberal fortune-telling," in which the nation's fortune—in the word's double meaning as both future and wealth—is conjured in language and image before it materializes as a tangible reality. While the immutable and universal laws of political economy provide the immediate intellectual framework for fortune-telling, its rhetorical work depends on leaps of the imagination. Fortune-telling opens onto a glorious future in which anything is possible: productive forces shorten centuries into days, and increased commodity exchange creates stable, prosperous polities in a single stroke. Two sides to political economy emerge: on the one hand, it is a science with objective and observable laws governing the production of material wealth; on the other, it serves as an active site of imaginative and even magical thinking.[12]

If in Europe political economy had in the 1850s been named the "dismal science," a term coined by the Victorian critic Thomas Carlyle, this discipline began to carry quite the opposite charge in Latin America. For if in the Great Britain of Carlyle or Dickens, political economy represented the spread of calculation and interest to all spheres of human life, in Latin America this science represented sheer promise to fortune-tellers like Sarmiento. Because its precepts and suppositions had not yet become dominant, political economy was the site of utopian thinking and great optimism.

With regard to the futuristic temporality of liberal fortune-telling, we might note that speculation is a precondition for all human interventions into material reality. Here we might remember Marx's famous dictum that all production begins in the human mind; what separates the "worst of architects from the best of bees," he writes, is the human ability to foresee the consequences of purposefusubmmmmml activity (1976, 284). Yet the speculative enterprise at the heart of liberal fortune-telling takes on special contours in Latin America, a region that since the Conquest had been imagined by Europeans as a "blank slate" awaiting inscription by culture and civilization. As Angel Rama writes in *The Lettered City*, this perception of blankness allowed Spanish colonizers to imagine entire cities on paper before they were actually built (1996, 2). Carlos Alonso, in turn, has argued that whereas the colonial conquest inaugurated the Americas into European imaginaries as sites of novelty and marvelousness, nineteenth-century nation-building projects mobilized the narrative of futurity to gesture toward the promise of full-fledged, European-style modernity. In line with a wider discourse on progress, Latin American nations "came to be identified comprehensively and unequivocally with the future" (1998, 15). As part of the rhetorical construct Alonso identifies as "the burden of modernity," the ideal of national consolidation was placed tantalizingly within reach, only to be forever postponed. The "narrative of futurity" Alonso identifies is particularly useful in understanding the liberal fortune-telling, since it is the as-yet-unrealized sources of wealth that the rhetorical construct seeks to act on and exploit. The concept of futurity animates the very category "raw" materials, as objects whose true value will be realized at a future date. This sense of futurity is also sustained by the nineteenth-century narrative of progress, through which raw-material-exporting nations will eventually acquire more "sophisticated" production techniques, thereby allowing them to become wealthy and modern at some later date.

Even more critically, perhaps, tropes of novelty and blankness inflect the decidedly radical character of the transformations imagined. For if, on one the hand, "nature" functioned as a chief obstacle to modernization (marking the *absence* of human endeavor), its perceived virginity simultaneously enabled fantastic visions of the future. As an example, we can turn to Manuel Pardo, as he marvels at the seemingly infinite stores of wealth lying beneath the Peruvian soil, awaiting the magical touch of human intervention:

> The natural elements our country has to insure prosperity and [good] fortune are such that the application of the most basic principle of social economy [*economía social*]—even if only by work of the imagination—is frightening in its consequences. . . . [One] fears becoming a visionary or utopian when comparing the colossal scale of these consequences with the stingy dimensions of our impoverished present. ([1860] 1988, 65)

Again, the principles of political economy are employed as a springboard for a vision of the future. Because these principles have not yet been implemented, they can be articulated only through the imagination. The resulting image of possible wealth, while garnered through the rational application of principles, is so powerful as to defy this very rationality. Relishing his role as liberal fortune-teller, Pardo asks his readers to compare the fantastic vision of the future with the "impoverished" reality of the present. Following the development of dormant resources, Peru will receive technological improvements like railways and locomotives, enabling the country to create even more wealth. The arrival of these improvements, Pardo writes, will create unprecedented opportunities for a radical reorganization of social reality: "If in other countries the locomotive facilitates production and commerce, in ours its mission is higher: *to create that which does not yet exist*" ([1860] 1988, 44–45, emphasis added). Once again, the metaphor of the mission is applied to the (secular) liberal project. Paul Gootenberg, speaking of this text, has defined Pardo's project as one of utopian industrialism (1993, 82). As in Sarmiento, specialization in agricultural products and raw materials for the world market is not an end in itself, but a station on the way to full-fledged industrial development. What is most compelling about Pardo's rhetorical style is its headlong plunge into the future and absolute lack of doubt. His prose carries with it the energy of a steam train, an energy whose force paradoxically depends on the fact that real railways had not yet been built. In this way, Pardo offers a succinct and compelling definition of the liberal project in late nineteenth-century Latin

America: "to create that which does not yet exist," first in the mind, and then in reality.

The confident zeal with which liberal fortune-tellers predict the end result of free market integration overcomes any possible doubts about the desirability of the project itself. As a rhetorical maneuver, liberal fortune-telling is powerful precisely because that which is promised has not yet been realized, but also because of the sheer energy with which the wish image poises itself to banish doubt in its eventual materialization. As in Paul Smith's discussion of fantasies of globalization from the 1990s, this rhetorical work constitutes an important, perhaps necessary part of material transformation, establishing the ideological dispositions necessary for the transformation to begin in earnest (1997). Thus while we might be apt to charge Sarmiento, Pardo, and others with mere "dreaming"—a fear expressed in these authors' own statements—this dreamwork indeed constitutes a fundamental point of departure for a radical reorganization of material and social relations. Hence the point of this discussion is not simply to point to the divergence between material reality and imagination as setting up the failure for fantasy to materialize; this argument would be too easy to make in Latin America, where liberal dreams of national prosperity have more often than not been disappointed. Rather, it is necessary to examine how liberal fantasies *succeeded* in creating the conditions of possibility under which social and natural landscapes might be altered. After all, the wide-scale alteration of the social fabric to fit the new demands of the global commodity lottery was no small task: it required the felling of forests to make way for plantations and railways, the construction or elimination of settlements, and the assemblage of new labor forces to extract metals and agricultural products from the earth. Literally and figuratively, mountains had to be moved to get the process of modernization underway. And while the eventual outcomes of export-led modernization diverged greatly from liberal aspirations (in ways that liberal dreamers could never have predicted), the very articulation of those aspirations laid the ideological groundwork for material transformation to occur.

By the 1870s, the export reverie, with its glorious predictions, had morphed into a recognizable and indeed ubiquitous form. As an example, we can turn to the numerous texts published in the commercial newspaper *La América Ilustrada*. As its name suggests, this newspaper relied on the mass reproduction of engraved images, ranging from pictorial representations of guano production in Peru to coffee production in Ceylon; in another issue, a man in his workshop, surrounded by tools, is named "man of the century." These images, however compelling, do not begin to match the effusiveness of the journalistic essays appearing in its pages. In "Las riquezas de Bolivia," used to open this chapter, an anonymous author outlines this country's ample reserves of land, labor, and untapped metals. As home to the "man's most valuable minerals" (1872, 34), Bolivia contains exciting reserves of wealth. The article assumes that these metals will be exported in exchange for railways, which in turn will create a chain reaction toward full-fledged prosperity. In "La República Dominicana" ("The Dominican Republic"), another anonymous article appearing in *La América Ilustrada,* language emerges as a crucial component of the production process when the author states that prosperity is assured, because "the word 'railway' is already being pronounced" (275). The country does not as yet have railways; but its very enunciation in speech and in writing is enough to set a much-desired process in motion. Rhetorically, this process begins with the identification of "raw" nature as a site of productive transformation and culminates in the wish-image of the railway, a metonym for industrial development at the end of the nineteenth century. This imaginative dimension is present even as the export reverie hails its own expository quality. In "El Porvenir de Colombia" ("The future of Colombia"), signed by Justo Arosema, the author hopes to convince the reader (and possible investors) with "the truth and frankness" of his account of national resources; at the same time, export reverie as a discursive mode depends on the mobilization of "hope and fervor" surrounding the possibility of generating wealth. Today, it is impossible to assert that Colombia is "a rich and prosperous nation," because years of bloody civil war have "significantly retarded industrial development." And yet, he assures us that this very poverty, while not exactly a source of pride, marks "a point of departure toward a great future, to which [the country's] great conditions call it" (1873, 92). In this rhetorical construction, Arosema foresees the transformation of material lack into surplus, rehearsing the very process through which Colombia's soil and labor might create lasting and self-sustaining wealth.

Beyond these examples, the form I have been analyzing as export reverie circulated in forms ranging from journalistic articles and commercial pamphlets to political speeches, advertisements, and exposition catalogues. This mode also circulated widely in speeches to inaugurate chambers of commerce, catalogues for national exhibitions, and in commercial manuals on coffee production. Even the Nicaraguan writer Rubén Darío—often distinguished as the first Spanish American writer to abandon civic impulses in favor of a discourse of "art for art's sake" studied in the next chapter—employed this form in his newspaper *El Mundo Nuevo,* in a series of essays highlighting different countries' state of development and capacity for production *(Prosas políticas).* And as I explore below, the renowned Cuban author José Martí frequently employed euphoric visions of different Latin American nations' exportable wealth.[13]

Export reverie served as a potent site of transformative agency within early liberal imaginaries in Latin America, pointing confidently toward a future that had not yet fulfilled its gigantic promise. But this rhetoric, while immensely productive in discursive terms, carried within itself numerous absences and contradictions. The open-endedness of the dreams gave them rhetorical power at the same time as this very characteristic elided the precise conditions under which commodity production for the global market would take place. Which agents would engage in production and under which conditions? Through which mechanisms would the resulting wealth be distributed? Once dormant resources were awakened to become export commodities, which kind of social organization would result?

The Limits of the Early Liberal Imagination: José Martí's *Guatemala*

The absences and contradictions of early liberal imaginaries become particularly prominent in a little-known text by the Cuban writer and Independence leader José Martí, titled *Guatemala* (1878), a pamphlet-essay written to celebrate the arrival of liberal reform to this country. José Martí experienced this moment firsthand while living and working as a schoolteacher in Guatemala, one of the countries to which he fled after having been exiled from his native Cuba. For the young Martí, just twenty-four years old and awed by the liberal revolutions being lived across Latin America in the 1870s, looked out and saw nothing less than the beginning of a new era:

> Now ruins are finished and foundations commence! Towns lose their convent-like appearance, their apathetic flavor, their sickly shade, and gain, to the sound of centrifuges amidst luxuriant vine leaves and aromatic coffee bush, the colors of youth and the revelations of life. Liberty opened these doors. ([1878] 1975c, 7:125)[14]

It is not only the ideological dimensions of Martí's prose that I want to highlight (faith in abstract values of universal liberty and progress), but rather its linguistic economy. As a hallmark of Martí's literary talent, his prose performs the transformation it seeks to represent, crafting images to contrast an epoch of sickly stagnation (metaphorized, in a liberal-secularist vein, through religious images) with one of life-giving productivity. Similarly, the rhythm of the prose seeks to capture the rhythms of material progress: the first, exclamatory sentence announces a new beginning, while the second performs a transition from a period of dying and loss to one of movement and gain. The expansive, euphoric impulse identified earlier as a key component of Martí's liberal discourse is in full force. The image of the centrifuge contributes to this reading, as both a sign of industrial modernity and as a metaphor for outward movement. As a machine used for separating liquids from solids, the centrifuge operates according to a principle of movement away from the point of origin. It seems that this metaphorical meaning is more important, since the centrifuge was not a fixture in nineteenth-century coffee plantations; instead, it was a prevalent device in the sugar plantations of Martí's native Cuba. The term *pampano* (vine leaf), in turn, conjures the spindly growth of grapes—a crop not grown in Guatemala—whose movement extends metonymically to the fragrant coffee bush. For the moment, no human agents are represented, though their presence is strongly felt through their intelligent cultivation of the land. Similarly, the legal cornerstone of liberal polities—private property—is for the moment absent. Instead, we are given a highly aestheticized representation of coffee bushes and buzzing machines, culminating in an image of potently expansive "liberty."

Two aspects of *Guatemala* deserve distinction with regard to the earlier examples of liberal fantasies of production considered above: first, the text is in essence an extended promotion for Guatemalan export commodities, an aspect that highlights the emergence of advertising as a practical application of liberal political economy in the 1870s. Second, and often working at cross-purposes with the promotional message of the text, *Guatemala* reads as a political treatise dedicated to defining the ideal contours of the export republic. Martí is well known as one of Latin America's most radically democratic thinkers, a position that most often assumes his opposition to emerging forms of capitalism in the Americas. *Guatemala,* however, written by Martí when he was just twenty-four years old, displays a faith that "free" markets and commodity specialization will foment equality, democracy, and stability. But this optimism, too, has its limits. For read against the grain of its endorsement of liberalism, *Guatemala* succeeds in identifying sites of conflict and contradiction residing within the early liberal imaginary. As I show below, the free market emerges as the ground for a utopian vision of the Latin American republic *and* the greatest obstacle to its realization.

The celebratory, indeed effusive register employed in Martí's pamphlet *Guatemala* operates as a direct response to the Liberal Revolution of 1871, in which an ascendant class of coffee planters established control of the state. One of the crucial results of this revolution was the promotion of agricultural exports, especially coffee. In the passage above, abstract references to liberty and grapes—drawing from a classical vocabulary much loved by Martí—coincide with a direct reference to "aromatic coffee groves" that began to proliferate across the highlands of Guatemala. The liberal revolution celebrated in this text succeeded in changing the natural landscape of the country, its labor regime, and its rhythms of daily life, as the country took a definitive turn toward export-driven modernization.

It is necessary to point out here that Martí is best remembered today *not* as a defender of free commerce, but rather as a staunch critic of capitalist forms of exploitation, a position he articulated especially forcefully during his decade-long stay in the United States in the 1880s and early 1890s. *Guatemala,* however, speaks from a very different position, one filled with wonder and awe at the productive forces being unleashed by liberal economic reform in Latin America. Written in the early part of Martí's career, the text corresponds to a youthful optimism that, as Latin American countries became increasingly absorbed into global circuits of capital, would be challenged by the realities of class subjugation and imperial domination. For surely, from the vantage of the present, we can see clearly that Martí's predictions were wrong: Guatemala would never become rich through export agriculture; instead, it emerged as one of the poorest and most violently unequal countries of the Western Hemisphere. To note this divergence between the future Martí envisioned and the reality that transpired is not to accuse him of blindness or naïveté. Instead, my intention is to examine the specific outline of a utopian vision that, as time wore on, would become impossible to sustain, even as fantasy. In this sense, I am not so interested in contrasting a "liberal, young" Martí with his more "mature," "radical" incarnation, as I am in uncovering the tensions and contradictions residing within early liberal projects themselves. For *Guatemala* is itself strongly dialectical, attempting to reconcile contrary forces of stability and expansion, polis and market, patriotism and material self-interest.

Like many of Martí's works, *Guatemala* melds a range of different genres and rhetorical registers. In part, it is a travelogue, simulating a journey through modern Guatemala, moving between cities such as Antigua and Guatemala City, between the Caribbean and Pacific coasts, and through the fertile highlands:

> Retalhuleu is the name of a department that abounds in wood, and succulent cacao, and the exquisite American coffee bean.
>
> This and sugar cane are produced in Mazatenango, faithful tributary of commercial Quezaltenango.
>
> In Quezaltenango, in addition to the agricultural riches already mentioned, wool livestock abound. Unexploited, this industry is a sure source of wealth. Carders, export merchants and weavers will have much to do there. ([1878] 1975c, 7:132)[15]

Guatemala articulates a dream of a productive and virtuous polis under liberal reform; at the same time, as shown by the passage above, it positions itself to bring the dream into reality by publicizing the country's different sources of wealth. Martí first published his pamphlet in Mexico, and in the introduction he explains that he wants foreign readers to know about the immense resources the country has to offer. Here the celebratory of Martí's text opens onto an emerging discourse of publicity and advertising, pointing out "unexploited" opportunities and "sure" sources of wealth to the reader.

This turn toward advertising is an extension of the rhetorical mode of liberal fortune-telling studied above, insofar as it attempts to make writing economically *productive*. This is liberal dreaming in its most practical application: as promotion. Martí not only imagines a country well on its way to wealth and prosperity; in addition, he tells his reader exactly how he or she might take part in the grand transformation. Other parts of the text detail abundant land reserves in Guatemala and then ask "Who wouldn't buy?" (133). It is as simple as "going there, planting, and becoming rich" (134).

Poetry and advertising, musings on political economy and practical commercial advice commingle throughout *Guatemala,* as indeed they do in a series of commercially inclined journalistic texts Martí published between roughly 1875 and 1884.[16] The comfortable way in which genres and rhetorical styles mix and merge is indicative of what Julio Ramos has termed the "hybrid" character of Martí's writing (2001, 87). This hybridity works toward a specific end in *Guatemala,* insofar as it reflects early Martí's faith in the harmonious and organic movements of the market itself. The text's effusive, playful, and easy style attests to Martí's belief in this early moment of his writing career that the free market will live up to its many promises: prosperity for all, the spontaneous and harmonious distribution of wealth within and between polities, constant moral and material improvement. Martí's optimism is also grounded in the market's promise to spread more egalitarian and democratic social relations. It is this promise that underwrites Martí's loving description of Guatemala's sources of exportable commodity wealth to his readers. In line with liberal utopianism, there is absolutely no conflict posed between the material interests of individuals and those of the nation as a whole. Nor is there any conflict posed between the interests of the reader addressed by the pamphlet (whom Martí directs to "sure" sources of wealth), and the interests of the Guatemalan nation. On levels internal and external to the nation-state, individuals' actions in the market sphere are viewed as fomenting the common good.

Yet Martí's faith in the free market as an entity able to foment the common good in *Guatemala* is traversed by a series of contradictions, as the text itself reveals that the emerging export republic will be neither stable nor equitable. Thus while seemingly uniform in its effusive embrace of liberalism as it was being implemented in the 1870s, *Guatemala* expresses a number of tensions and ambiguities with respect to that very project. Read closely, and against the grain of its own effusive optimism, this pamphlet allows us to identify a "dialectics of modernity" (Rama 1974) sensitive to the uneven and unequal logic of capitalist expansion on the export-driven periphery. Two mains sets of contradictions concern me here. First, while Martí relies on georgic and pastoral tropes to imagine Guatemala as a virtuous and stable agrarian republic rooted to the soil through the cultivation of numerous crops, the text itself recognizes that the true motor of export-driven prosperity is a single export commodity: coffee. The tension between the ideal of variation and the reality of monocrop specialization is compounded by a second set of contradictions, this time pertaining to the social organization of the export republic. If on the one hand Martí insists that all Guatemalans will share equally in the wealth generated by export commodities, his simultaneous emphasis on *private* property and wealth creates a possible contradiction with respect to the principle of equitable distribution the text espouses.

Agrarian Romance

To a large extent, the capacity of Martí to imagine a republic that is at once modern and virtuous, expansive and stable, has to do with the fact that Guatemala's entry into the global market occurs primarily through agriculture, an activity with deep symbolic, aesthetic, and moral meaning for Martí. Agriculture is a basic activity needed for human survival, one that antecedes the arrival of liberalism by millennia. As such, agriculture retains strong ties to the precapitalist or noncapitalist past. Moreover, as a classically republican sign of virtue and virility, agriculture retains moral force as an antidote to the instability of modern market relations.[17] Martí makes this clear when he writes in another text: "Children should be taught to read with this phrase: Agriculture is the only constant, sure, and entirely pure source of wealth" (1975e, 8: 298).[18]

Gayatri Spivak is the most recent critic to identify José Martí as representative of an agrarian utopianism whose grain of resistance might be revived in a present characterized by the relentlessly dispossessing forces of capital (2005, 92). This gesture is consistent with classic criticism on Martí—ranging from that of Cintio Vitier to Roberto Fernández Retamar—which has focused on the most radically anticolonial and anticapitalist elements of his enormous oeuvre. *Guatemala* (written during the same period as the texts Spivak cites as evidence of his anticolonial ruralism) adds a more contradictory strain to this line of argumentation: for while the exultation of the rural points to a classically inflected, egalitarian, and use-driven social economy, it *also* incorporates the destabilizing, unequal, and exchange-driven elements of bourgeois liberalism. And while Martí's diagnoses of the world order would change (see the last section of this chapter), his more ambivalent moments deserve our attention, not only to give us a more accurate picture of Martí's politics but also to identify a powerful strain of contradiction within nascent liberal imaginaries themselves.

As an example of how Martí simultaneously gestures toward a classical and proto-bourgeois worldview, we can turn to one of *Guatemala*'s many depictions of agricultural beauty and abundance:

> I come from a land of tall volcanoes, fertile hills, and wide rivers, where gold extends in a vast placer along the mountains of Izabal, where coffee—the best form of gold—grows aromatic and abundant in the expanse of the Costa Cuca. There the blonde ears of corn grow apace of golden wheat; colossal bunches hang from the high plantain bushes. ([1878] 1975c, 7:118)

Initial images of virgin nature (tall volcanoes and wide rivers) morph into ones of agrarian abundance. Like other export reveries of the 1870s, *Guatemala* draws from the georgic tradition in post-Independence Latin America, a classically derived literary mode inaugurated with Andrés Bello's "Silva a la agricultura de la zona tórrida" (Ode to tropical agriculture, 1826) that extols the virtues of farming and rusticity. As Mary Louise Pratt has pointed out, Bello's ode focuses exclusively on American agrarian products, studiously leaving out the mineral wealth sought by Europeans since the arrival of Columbus (1992, 178). Martí's text continues in a similarly rustic vein, and yet his vision of agrarian abundance becomes ambiguous when he singles out coffee as Guatemala's "best form of gold." Here gold an as abstract referent for value—which may be moral or aesthetic—combines with a vision of gold as *money,* the form of value arising in commodity exchange. Paradoxically, coffee is at once part of a harmonious agrarian landscape *and* a singular element within it. This supplemental position is itself consistent with coffee's special commodity status in late nineteenth-century Guatemala. For like indigenous crops like maize—a millennial foodstuff of Central America—and transplants like wheat and plantains, coffee is a product of human interaction with nature. Coffee is not a food crop, however, but a stimulant; moreover, from the mid-nineteenth-century onward, coffee was not grown for consumption in the country, but for export to Europe and the United States. In Guatemala, a class of coffee planters had consolidated the liberal state; and as Martí's pamphlet shows, coffee was the main reason foreigners were arriving, in search of concessions to build plantations.

On one hand, then, Martí's text corresponds with a classical principle of agrarian variety and nonspecialization. On the other, it identifies coffee as a singular agent, with a logic and trajectory all its own. Coffee appears on nearly every page of *Guatemala;* more importantly, the crop gains its very own style of representation, as a metaphoric and literal stimulant to the country's economic growth. Figured as the "rich, generous gift [*don*] of America" ([1878] 1975c, 7:137), and as "sublime juice" ([*jugo excelso*], 135), coffee grows like a "dream," "fantasy," and "sensual caprice" (133). These figurations of coffee as a site of imagination and fantasy give way to moments of utter abandon in the text:

> Ah, yes! The sumptuous bean that ignites the blood, awakens passion, keeps sleep away, restlessly leaps in the veins, generates flames and aromas in the brain; it makes Urapan famous, it supports Colima and distinguishes Java; the *hashish* of América, which allows one to dream but doesn't dull the senses; the victor over tea; hot nectar, perfumed coffee bush, it grows like an illusion does with lovers, like the movement of a cloud pushed by the wind in the hills and plains of hospitable Guatemala. (133)[19]

In this panegyric to coffee, Martí's voice imitates the disquieting and stimulating effects of the caffeinated beverage. Plucked from the varied agrarian landscapes pictured elsewhere in the text, the coffee bean literally and figuratively takes flight, acquiring identity as a highly mobile and transformative object. Leaving behind the rhetorical registers of commercial catalogue, political essay, and georgic mode, Martí's voice comes under the spell of coffee as a magical and transformative substance, associated with heightened smell, sight, and even sexual desire. So powerful is the pull of coffee on the author's imagination that it becomes a referent for poetic language itself.[20] This aesthetic impulse is guided neither by nature nor by harmony, but instead by a principle of fantasy.[21]

Martí's lyrical representation of coffee in *Guatemala* bears much in common with what Timothy Morton has called the "poetics of spice" in eighteenth-century British literature (2000). Morton shows how since the origins of early commercial capitalism (often called "the spice trade"), "spice" has operated as an enduring trope for instability and excess, mediating boundaries between East and West, luxury and necessity, self and Other. In the texts Morton examines, "[s]pice is employed as a figure about figurative language itself, and as a token of the distant, the exotic, the erotic, and the poetically inspired" (60). It is for this reason that "spice," as a conduit for libidinal desire, became a model for the fetish object in early commercial culture. Martí's representation of coffee functions as a poetics of spice insofar as it mobilizes flow, imagination, and enjoyment across spatial divides.

Martí's descriptions of coffee in *Guatemala* might also be approached as an example of an emerging discourse of export commodity fetishism in late nineteenth-century Latin America, wherein the commodity "appears" in specific ways on the peripheries of global exchange. In Marx's classic discussion, the fetish names the illusion through which people in capitalist societies come to believe that commodities are autonomous agents, arriving as if on their own to market. *Products* of labor, that is, appear to us as sovereign entities ruling over the hands and minds that produced them. As an illustration, Marx conjures the image of a wooden table: on its own, the table is "an ordinary, sensuous thing":

> But as soon as it emerges as a commodity, it changes into a thing which transcends sensuousness. It not only stands with its feet on the ground, but, in relation to all other commodities, it stands on its head, and evolves out of its wooden brain grotesque ideas, far more wonderful than if it were to begin dancing of its own free will. (1976, 163)

Marx is primarily concerned in this discussion with the process through which labor is forced to recognize itself in alienated form, in that which it has produced. Herein lies the "grotesque" nature of the commodity fetish. From another angle, Marx's naming of the commodity fetish introduces a spatial and temporal dimension into the commodity relation, one that becomes especially important when we turn to the distant outposts of capitalist exchange. In Marx's analysis, the commodity fetish assumes the existence of a sophisticated division of labor, in which the "hidden abode of production" (1976, 279) is radically separated from spheres of circulation and consumption within a system so vast that no one agent can grasp its whole. For this reason, the commodity fetish is an illusion and not a simple fallacy: for within the system of exchange, it really *does* seem as though the commodity arrives on its own to market. This illusion becomes even more compelling when we turn to the global reach of the commodity system, in which commodities traverse not only huge expanses of space and time, but also vastly different social formations. In the case I have been discussing, coffee produced by mainly coerced indigenous labor in the agro-exporting periphery (discussed in greater detail below) travels to societies characterized by free wage labor and heavy industry.[22]

It is in part the very unevenness of the global system of exchange, I would argue, that lends itself especially well to representations of the commodity as a source of magic on the periphery. In *Guatemala,* coffee bushes are represented as beautiful bearers of fruit; but magic and fantasy arise once coffee beans are plucked from the bushes that extend like "placers" over the varied countryside, and put into circulation as commodities. It is in this moment of exchange that Martí's own language, in concert with the coffee beans shipped abroad, takes flight with images of passion, stimulation, and fantasy.

The fantasy associated with coffee is a double-edged sword, as the rhetorical excess it generates carries with it the seed of danger. To recall Morton's deconstructionist analysis of spice, coffee calls forth stimulation, excitement, and open-endedness, but in doing so it also calls forth the possibility of slippage and unpredictability. And drawing from a Marxian analysis of fetishism, isn't it possible that the autonomous energy ascribed to coffee might come to dominate the agrarian landscape that Martí clearly wishes to remain varied? For what would happen if coffee cultivation started to *replace* rather than supplement or complement the production of food for consumption by people in Guatemala? Given the imaginative and fantastic properties Martí explicitly associates with coffee as an export crop—not to mention the wealth it promises—why would anyone *not* want to plant it?

At the same moment as Martí was writing *Guatemala,* unprecedented amounts of land and labor were being turned over to coffee production in response to international demand. Within the material logic of the commodity lottery, the varied sources of wealth put forth by Martí's text were in reality being whittled down to coffee; from this standpoint, what Martí identified as the nation's "best" source of gold was becoming its *only* source of gold. For by the 1870s, coffee was beginning to dominate the country's economy. This steady transition to a monocrop export regime carried with it a series of consequences that Martí's text, *written before this transition was complete,* is unable to foresee. If on one hand, coffee provided a thrilling source of national income, increased specialization in this crop also fomented greater sensitivity to market demand. And if coffee allowed Guatemala access to modern circuits of production and exchange, the underside of this access was increased dependence on those very circuits for economic survival. The outer-directed drive of coffee, celebrated in Martí's pamphlet, was hence additionally a source of great vulnerability. And near the end of the nineteenth century, coffee markets themselves became notoriously volatile. As more and more regions raced to fill demand—Guatemala, Brazil, Colombia, Venezuela, Ceylon, Indonesia—the price of coffee fluctuated wildly on the global market. Agriculture, that is, imagined in idyllic terms by Martí, was becoming a site of active financial speculation. Subject to overproduction and speculative bubbles, coffee production was at once a lucrative and dangerous business. In Guatemala, the coffee economy would expand until 1897, when increased output from Brazil, the · world's largest producer, caused the national market to collapse. Precisely because the Guatemalan economy had been reorganized around coffee, recovery from such crises became exceedingly difficult. In the early twentieth century, North American demand for bananas created an additional source of commodity wealth for the country, which, far from heralding the kind of diversity Martí had envisioned, marked a further entrenchment of monocrop agriculture and dependency.

Yeomans, Capitalists, and Indians

In the 1870s, Martí's enthusiasm for coffee as lead export crop went hand in hand with his enthusiasm for the equitable distribution of land and wealth in the republic. In order to understand his high hopes for the coffee republic, we might contrast its potential with the sugar republic from which Martí hailed, Cuba. Whereas sugar represented the brutality of slavery, monocrop dependence, and large-scale plantations, the advent of coffee promised a very different social order: one rooted in free labor and the possibility of small-scale production.[23] In *Guatemala,* this democratic potential is expressed through dictums such as these: "Es rica una nación que cuenta muchos pequeños propietarios. No es rico el pueblo donde hay algunos hombres ricos, sino aquel donde cada uno tiene un poco de riqueza. En economía política y en buen gobierno, distribuir es hacer venturosos" ("The nation that has many small landholders is rich. The country in which there are a few rich men is not rich, but rather the country in which every person has some wealth. In political economy and in good government, distribution makes a fortunate people"; [1878] 1975c, 7:134). In strongly utopian terms, individual freedom is not simply compatible with but indeed demands equality in the republic. Similarly, the individual interests encouraged by liberalism foment the common good.

Borrowing again from a well-established set of agrarian tropes, *Guatemala* imagines a republic of farmer-citizens: "Let us push away books and papers and let us go, like Cincinnatus, like Washington, like my teacher of Greek, to plant wheat, to look after cattle, to cultivate cherries" (137). Here Martí expresses an ideal of the small-holding yeoman, who like Cincinnatus, the famed citizen of the Roman republic, and George Washington (responsible for the naming of the city Cincinnati after the Roman citizen), defends the republic in times of war and in times of peace retreats to his farm. We will note that coffee is both absent and present in the passage, as the mention of cherries brings us to George Washington's fabled staging of virtue and by way of metonymic association, to the cherries of the coffee bush.

Martí's image of the yeoman stands at odds, however, with the fact that production is specialized around coffee and that the landowner operates according to the rhythms instated by the export market. It also stands at odds with the rapidity with which the text vaunts the flexibility and speed with which property can be bought and sold under the new system. Another contradiction involves the fact that Martí's imagined yeomans, supposedly rooted to the soil by virtue, are simultaneously foreign investors motivated by profit. Since its inception in the 1850s, coffee production in Guatemala had been dominated by European *colonos,* or settlers. Martí recognizes and indeed celebrates this reality in his text by imagining German, French, and Belgian planters lining up to receive land concessions from the liberal state ([1978] 1975c, 7:124). The predominance of European settlers involves a second leap of faith on Martí's part: not only will private material interests complement the common good, but the interests of *foreign* investors will complement those of the American polis. Yet, under the same market system Martí assumes in his text, there is nothing to assure that equitable distribution and cooperation will prevail over individual accumulation and competition. This presents a grave danger to the notions of civic duty staunchly defended by Martí. For it is not necessary that foreigners be loyal to Guatemala to reproduce their capital. It is even less necessary for the European or *ladino* planter to limit his holdings to a single piece of land, so as to leave parcels to others.

But most contradictory of all in Martí's agrarian utopia is the role it envisions for indigenous people. In its most radically egalitarian manifestations, Martí's utopia seeks to reverse centuries of colonial oppression, a message for which he is justly well known.

As a metaphor for this liberation, Martí declares his intention to destroy the *cacaxte* and *huacal,* Nahual-derived words for the wooden boxes indigenous people carried on their backs to move heavy loads: "I will take away the Indian's *cacaxte,* the ominous *haucal,* and put in their hands the plough, and consciousness in their sleeping breast" ([1878] 1975c, 7:117). No longer treated as beasts of burden—a dehumanizing trope with a long history in Latin America—indigenous peoples will take part in the nation's liberal transformation as autonomous producers. While the *huacal* and *cacaxte* are figured as tools of colonial oppression, the plough itself functions as a symbol of both productivity and enlightenment.

Martí's own text, however, recognizes the less-than-idyllic circumstances under which the modernization of indigenous lifeways will take place. For the awakening of indigenous consciousness to the benefits of modernization will, in the last instance, rely on force. As Greg Grandin remarks, "Guatemala's entrance into the nineteenth-century international coffee market remains one of the most brutal in the hemisphere" (2000, 111); "[e]ven the most generous liberals, who acknowledged the intrinsic worth of Indians, understood Guatemala's economic development in racial terms" (128). In a story with parallels in many parts of Latin America in the 1870s, the liberal Guatemalan state created private property from previously protected church and indigenous lands; more force was used to create a new labor regime for the resulting coffee plantations that began to extend over the countryside. Hence even though Martí's text imagines modernization in Guatemala through lexicons of freedom and equality, it is forced to reckon with the perceived necessity of forced dispossession. Recognizing that land and labor are not infinite resources, he reasons that force is justifiable when it upholds the common good, in this case, the republic's imperative to create wealth through export agriculture:

> And already there is a shortage of land for those who wish to possess it. . . .The indigenous race, made accustomed to uninspiring idleness and to selfish possession by an inexcusable and barbarous education, doesn't plant or let planting take place; the Government, energetic and patriotic, obliges it to sow, or to allow

others to do so. And what they, the lazy ones, don't use, he, the eager supporter of the homeland, breaks into pieces and distributes. Because only in the name of good is force just. For this only, I always thought. ([1878] 1975c, 7:134)

While Martí vaunts the tradition of the independent and self-sufficient yeoman, his text is much more critical of the subsistence economies of indigenous peoples, which restrict production to what he terms *egoísta posesión* (selfish possession). Indians, that is, produce for themselves and not for the nation as a whole. Again, the fact that the crop best suited to the new regime of production, coffee, is grown primarily for export, is occluded. So too is the fact that the property and surpluses generated through dispossession will not belong to all Guatemalans, but to the owners of coffee plantations.

In 1877, a year before the publication of *Guatemala,* the Barrios government had implemented a labor draft law, known as the *mandamiento,* designed to secure indigenous labor for coffee plantations.[24] Under this policy, which remained in place until the 1920s, Indians were forced to work for a number of days a year on a plantation; this practice was gradually replaced with a system of debt peonage. J. C. Cambranes notes that measures such as these were deemed "painful but necessary" by Guatemala's elite (1985, 183), a position Martí echoes. As partial compensation for dispossession, Indians will be educated in preparation for their full incorporation as citizens. After noting that the use of force against Indians is "just" when carried out in the name of the common good (a common good, it should be noted, whose contours are determined by a minority population), Martí returns to the message that property should be distributed justly. However, because Indians have been rendered lazy by their "barbarous" education—another effect of colonial oppression for Martí—they will have to wait to claim their share of the wealth. At different points in the text, Martí (who traveled to Guatemala as a schoolteacher) advocates the establishment of normal schools to create what he calls a "new apostolate" ([1878] 1975c, 7:158) or class of indigenous leaders. In merely suggesting that indigenous people should participate in the political life of Guatemala, Martí makes a radical proposition. Indeed, his

utopian brand of liberalism was so radical that he was expelled
from Guatemala shortly after writing his pamphlet for criticizing
President Barrios's administration. But the fact remains that Martí
can imagine the incorporation of Indians as citizens only *after* they
have been forcibly removed from their lands and forced to work;
in spite of *Guatemala*'s constant defense of equitable distribution,
the text imagines a social order in which equality has already been
rendered impossible.[25]

Wine from Bananas

Martí's adherence to liberal economic ideals was neither constant nor uniform. Even a text like *Guatemala,* full of faith in the
promises of liberalism, is not blind in its embrace but rather con-
ditioned on liberalism's ability to deliver certain benefits in the
future. Already in 1883, this belief seems shaken. Writing as editor
of the commercial journal *La América,* he complained that coffee
was being produced "in excess" in the region—a seeming impossibility in *Guatemala*—and urged diversification (1975a, 7:190).
In the near-decade he spent in New York City following his expul-
sion from Guatemala (and, after this, from Venezuela), Martí wrote
searchingly and critically of the failure of Latin American liberal
governments to foment either democratic political participation or
equitable distribution. And as he turned his attention increasingly
to the question of Cuban independence from Spain, Martí warned
presciently of the imperial aspirations of the United States in Latin
America. In his famous essay "Nuestra América" (Our America,
1891), Martí made an urgent plea for unity in the face of "the giant
with the seven-league boots" (Martí 2001, 295) poised to dominate
the region politically and economically. Cuba's sugar wealth, under
Spanish control, had become particularly appealing to U.S. interests. And Martí now recognizes, against the utopian aspirations of
his early liberal optimism, that Latin America's entry into global
networks of exchange had been tending not toward social equilib-
rium and equality, but instead toward conflict and asymmetry. Two
specific elements of "Nuestra América" are worth mentioning here

with regard to *Guatemala*. First, while *Guatemala* believed that creole elites would continue to place civic interests over private gain, "Nuestra América" rails against these same elites on the grounds that they have indulged personal pleasures at the cost of national development. Cast as weak "seven-month men," creole elites have failed to become the virile and virtuous producers he had imagined more than a decade earlier. Instead of becoming yeoman farmers, they stayed in cities to become feminized and corrupt, decorating themselves with "uñas pintadas y pulsera" ("braceleted arms with painted nails"; Martí 1975g, 6:16; Martí 2001, 295). Martí also faults this class for having imitated European models of social organization instead of creating their own and, as a consequence, for having failed to include indigenous and African American people as citizens of their republics. The main message of this essay is that this imitation should be replaced by a more just and accurate response to local circumstances:

> The frock coats are still from France, but the thought now began to come from America. The youths of America roll up the sleeves of their shirts, sink their hands in the mass, and make it rise with the yeast of their sweat. They understand that we have imitated for too long, and that salvation is in creating. *Crear* is the password of a generation. If our wine is made from bananas, and if its taste turns out bitter, it is still our wine! (299)

The passage, with its message of autonomous production by Americans for Americans, operates on both metaphorical and material planes. Creoles can continue to buy French frock coats, but they must *think* as Americans. Shifting this metaphor, shirt-sleeves must be rolled up to produce bread. Martí is talking about the production of ideas here, but his referents hail from the world of commodities. That he is interested in the asymmetry of the world created after the image of commodities becomes clear when he exhorts his readers to produce wine from bananas. This metaphor for reinvigorated production is especially interesting given the classic example of Ricardian trade advantage, in which the political economist held that Britain should specialize in producing textiles, and Portugal in producing wine, to create the greatest benefit to each country in exchange.

In Martí's example, frock coats continue to come from France, but now Americans produce their own wine instead of importing it. This metaphor works to displace the logic of the global division of labor insofar as it eschews the logic of sheer advantage. If the commodity lottery tells Latin America to grow bananas (or coffee or sugar) for export and to import processed commodities from industrialized countries, "Nuestra América" rejects this model in favor of greater autonomy in the realm of production. A new value system also comes into view; no longer solely measured by advantage vis-à-vis already more powerful nations, value becomes associated with that which is "ours," or produced in Latin America. It is for precisely this reason that "Nuestra América" has been considered a precursor to the economic model that emerged in the twentieth century to replace free market liberalism: import-substitution industrialization.[26]

While *Guatemala* expresses liberal euphoria with respect to opportunities afforded by the global market, "Nuestra América" marks a sobered turn away from free-trade ideologies. In both cases, Martí exhorts male Latin American subjects to *produce:* in the first case, to produce for the global market; and in the second, to produce for the region as a whole. On a symbolic level, the model of autonomous regional production envisioned by this later text overcomes the logic of dependency under the global commodity lottery. In doing so, however, it does not overcome all of the contradictions inscribed within the liberal export republic, but instead takes them in new directions. Martí still tends to assume in "Nuestra América" that it will be creole elites—and more specifically, creole men—who will lead their countries into a more productive and just future. And at the same time, the question of material inequality in Latin America, while addressed as a fundamental problem, is not overcome: production for exchange, simply because it takes place within a national or regional, instead of global market, does not necessarily lead to a more equal distribution of wealth.[27]

The juxtaposition of *Guatemala* and "Nuestra América" is instructive in another manner, for in both América's wealth—symbolic and material—awaits realization. The time in both texts is the future, willed into being through a rhetorical formulation. The future envisioned by *Guatemala* is no longer a possibility in "Nuestra América"; this latter text remains optimistic, however, that a new future is possible: "a worker's America" sows "the seed of new America" (Martí 2001, 301). Martí had ended *Guatemala* with a similar organic metaphor, writing that with this book he hopes he has "sown . . . my plant" ([1878] 1975c, 7:158). The writing examined in this chapter is perhaps less like a plant, however, than a promissory note, holding out hope for a different, more productive future.

Chapter 2

CONSUMPTION
Modernismo's
Import Catalogues

Chapter 1 investigated the capital fictions surrounding the production of export commodities in late nineteenth-century Latin America. As regional economies become more integrated into global networks of exchange, fantasies of production had to compete with a new aesthetic sensibility. With the emergence of the literary current known as Spanish American *modernismo,* the export reverie's focus on commodity production was eclipsed by this current's sustained focus on commodity *consumption.* The Cuban poet Julián del Casal's sonnet "Mis amores" (My loves [1890]) exemplifies the aesthetic sensibility cultivated by Spanish American *modernismo* and its obsession with the pleasures of consumption:

> Amo el bronce, el cristal, las porcelanas,
> las vidrieras de múltiples colores,
> los tapices pintados de oro y flores
> y las brillantes lunas venecianas.
> (2001, lines 1–4)

> I love bronzes, crystal, porcelains,
> stained glass of multiple colors,
> tapestries painted in gold and flowers
> and brilliant Venetian mirrors.[1]

Recalling the texts studied in the previous chapter, Casal's sonnet marks an enormous shift in style and form. Whereas earlier poems had almost always articulated Americanist or national projects, Casal's sonnet is decidedly cosmopolitan in character. And while previous lettered projects had envisioned citizens dedicated to the common good, Casal's poem projects a selfish "I" who loves not the *patria*, or even a woman, but a collection of superfluous objects. Casal is often contrasted with his contemporary and compatriot José Martí, and this contrast is warranted.[2] While Martí always insisted on the productivity and utility of writing (a preference that can be seen in a text like *Guatemala*), Casal embraced the "useless" beauty of art. Furthermore, while Martí excoriated luxury as feminizing and morally corrosive in texts like "Nuestra América," Casal clearly "loved" the excessive, sensuous dimensions of material objects.

The contrast I am drawing refers to a larger shift in late nineteenth-century literary projects, from a civic-republican tradition toward a project of artistic autonomy.[3] In the case of Casal, this search for autonomy was guided by an elitist (as opposed to republican or democratic) version of "art for art's sake" inspired by contemporary European artistic trends such as symbolism and decadence. Martí's insistence on the utility of literature within the *polis* is completely reversed in Casal to reveal a vision of art as beautiful, but utterly useless. In a word, literature is itself a luxury to be enjoyed by the poet and his readers, nothing more, nothing less.

"Mis amores" functions as a list or catalogue of material objects, arranged within a "high" literary form: the sonnet. The poem takes shape around bronzes, crystal, and tapestries; even its rhyme pattern is driven by names of objects (*porcelanas* and *venecianas*) and the descriptors (*flores* and *colores*). The linguistic innovation constantly attributed to *modernismo* is, in this and other cases, driven by the qualities of specific commodities. In the next two stanzas, the poem goes on to name a set of cosmopolitan artistic forms (German ballads, Spanish *castellanas*), listed as if they were themselves collectible objects. The poem culminates in an image of a sumptuous bed of "sandalwood and gold," one of Casal's frequent references to objects hailing from the exotic and luxurious "Orient" (2001, 12).

Casal's sonnet is an example of what this chapter calls "the modernist import catalogue," an aesthetic mode of representing imported commodities in fin-de-siècle Spanish America. Importantly, none of Casal's objects of desire—save the sonnet itself—could have been produced in Cuba at the end of the nineteenth century. Instead, they would have been brought from Europe in exchange for the island's main export crop: sugar. From the vantage point of the world economy, Cuba—still a colonial possession of Spain—was a vast sugar plantation, where slavery had been abolished only two years earlier, in 1888. While Casal was himself the son of a ruined sugar planter, sugar *never* appears in his poems; nor do the people of sugar culture—(former) slaves, plantation owners, and the like—ever appear. Instead, inspiration and desire emerge from a distinct but no less legitimately "Cuban" experience of modernity: the restricted and private consumption of imported luxury goods. But Casal's elision of local realities, while often dismissed by critics as "inauthentic," "artificial," or "escapist" (in contrast, for example, with José Martí's Americanist poetry and prose) is by no means exterior to the material and ideological framework consolidated during the Export Age. To the contrary, as I argue in this chapter, the sonnet's erasure of the local only works to intensify the strange beauty of the objects it enfolds.

In "Mis amores" Casal writes as a poet, but he writes also as a proto-consumer, whose desires are incited and constrained by Cuba's intensified insertion into global circuits of commodity exchange. Casal's sonnet was shaped by his reading of numerous European literary texts, themselves made available to lettered elites through expanding networks of the import/export trade. In what amounts to another, frequently invoked incarnation of the modernist import catalogue, Casal's literary influences are often named in list form. Among the prized books the Cuban author kept in a steamer trunk were those by Baudelaire, Flaubert, Gautier, Heredia, Huysmans, Leconte de Lisle, Loti, Maupassant, Rimbaud, and Verlaine (Armas 1981, 50–51; Montero 1993, 77). Critics have drawn up similar lists for the other pioneering *modernistas* such as the Nicaraguan writer Rubén Darío and the Colombian writer José Asunción Silva— adding here and subtracting there to account for the metropolitan texts that inspired a new literary aesthetic in Spanish America. This *intellectual* consumption was buttressed by another kind of consumption, to which critics have paid less attention. I am speaking here of the consumption of material objects, which ranged from books in trunks to the porcelains and crystals circulating through Casal's sonnet.

Yet with a few exceptions, commodity consumption has not been a main point of inquiry in studies of *modernismo*. On one hand, this is because the vision of art proposed by *modernismo* and absorbed by later Spanish American aesthetic discourses helped forge a lasting opposition between "artistic" and "commercial" concerns, an opposition inscribed into the very founding of Latin American literary studies. As a corollary, consumption itself has generally been subordinated to production as a category of sociocultural analysis. As Arnold J. Bauer and Benjamin Orlove have noted, import consumption has usually been treated as an anecdotal counterpart to the "real" story of export production in late nineteenth-century Latin America, followed by the (often failed) quest for industrialization (1997, 1). From this vantage, import consumption at best plays a supporting role in the creation of modern Latin American social structures and imaginaries. At worst, in pointing to the region's material and cultural dependency, import consumption has been viewed persistently as a lamentable, inorganic, or artificial activity, the negation of national autochthony. *Modernismo*, in turn, has become nearly synonymous with these very characteristics, to no small degree because of its embrace of European ideas and goods. But to dismiss *modernismo* as an import is to lose out on the ideological significance of this current, and of import consumption itself, in the making of Latin American modernities.

In the following sections, I explore how authors associated with *modernismo* pioneered an aesthetic language of commodity consumption in Export Age Latin America. Focusing on a corpus of texts by Darío, Silva, and Casal, I explore how these authors developed signifying practices through which imported objects might be desired, cherished, and indeed "loved." I am most interested in the persistent appearance and reappearance of the list or catalogue of imported goods in early *modernista* texts. The catalogue, literary critic Janell Watson has shown, is a form that grew out of the commercial inventory to become a key expression of fin-de-siècle aesthetics in France, as a means for accounting for material abundance and excess in texts by Balzac, the Goncourts, and Huysmans, among others (1999, 109). In Spanish America, *modernista* artists "imported" the catalogue form from French authors to list and describe an ever-expanding array of commodities becoming available to peripheral consumers and artists alike. In this manner, *modernistas* were simultaneously consumers and producers; their embellished lists—appearing in texts ranging from sonnets and "prose poems" to advertisements for French perfumes and journalistic descriptions of department store displays—were simultaneously rooted in commercial and aesthetic vocabularies. In the readings that follow, I show how this modernist form sought to amplify the symbolic and aesthetic potency of different sets of imported commodities. I stress at the outset that I am not concerned so much with how this representation contributed to the autonomization or formalization of the artistic object in Spanish America, a central theme in existing studies of *modernismo*.[4] Instead, I am concerned with the autonomy *modernista* texts ascribed to certain objects themselves, as part of an emerging discourse of commodity fetishism on the periphery.[5]

Speaking (through) Commodities: Artist and Bourgeois

In 1886, the young Nicaraguan poet Rubén Darío arrived in Valparaíso, Chile, looking for work as a writer. This trip inaugurated a mobility that would match the transamerican and transatlantic dimensions of Spanish American *modernismo*, the literary current Darío named and founded. The maritime route that took Darío to Chile, and later to Buenos Aires, Paris, and Madrid had been already established by the expanding web of shipping routes that carried goods and people to far-flung regions of the globe during the last quarter of the nineteenth century. On arriving at his first port of call, Valparaíso, Darío got a job writing for the newspaper *Excélsior*. He later moved to Santiago, where he found work as a writer for the newspaper *La Época*. Experiences in both cities provided the metaphorical raw material of Darío's landmark *Azul* (1888) the book credited with launching not just a literary current but also a zeitgeist centered on the experience of modernity in Spanish America.

According to convention at least, *Azul* sought inspiration in a host of new sensations, experiences, and objects offered by modern life. The field of inspiration was not limited to Latin America, but to the world at large. Given the material conditions of the Export Age, characterized by the flow of people, goods, and ideas among nations, it should not be surprising that the thrust of *modernismo* was not national or local, but decidedly global and cosmopolitan. Angel Rama, for example, has called *modernismo* a movement led by cosmopolitan "internationalists," a subject-position that can be distinguished from both an anterior model of nineteenth-century writer-statemen, and a subsequent model of the twentieth-century national(ist) writer (1985a, 36). In his later poem *Cantos de vida y esperanza* (Songs of life and hope), Darío described *Azul* as at once "very eighteenth century and very ancient and very modern; audacious, cosmopolitan; with strong Hugo and ambiguous Verlaine and an infinite thirst for illusion" (1965, 113). To be modern, Darío intimates, meant to open oneself onto the world, mix and match influences from far-flung locales, and raid the closets of history in the creation of something defiantly "new."

At the center of this new aesthetic stands the consumption of European styles, referents, and objects in the production of a new Spanish American aesthetic. Art, in turn, is self-consciously generated through images of fantasy and illusion. In the fairy-tale-like story "El velo de la Reina Mab" (Queen Mab's veil), for example, inspired by a poem by Percy Bysshe Shelley, a queen places a blue veil over the eyes of a poet to initiate him into a world of dreams. Blue, the color of art in Darío's book, acquires material form in the shape of a diaphanous, dream-inducing veil, "as though it were made of sighs, or of the glances of pensive blonde angels. And that veil was the veil of dreams, the sweet dreams that make one see life all rose-colored" (2006, 293). This passage forms a key example of what critics have maligned as *preciosismo* (preciousness) or *cursilería* (affectedness) in Darío's style, which is discomfiting as much for its excessive sweetness as for its seemingly uncritical appropriation of European referents in a non-European social context.

Azul locates art in the realm of (European-inflected) fantasy and dreams, a characteristic that has made this book a primary example of the "escapist" nature of Spanish American *modernismo*. For *Azul* famously abandoned the representation of day-to-day realities in favor of the world of fairy tale and myth. This escapist stance, far from being ideologically insignificant, forms the core proposition of *Azul*. And reaching far beyond the sphere of art, the escapist stance rehearsed in this book provides compelling insights into the fantasies inspired by import commodity consumption in late nineteenth-century Spanish America.

A key example of these fantasies is already present in the volume's opening text, "El rey burgués" (The bourgeois king). On the surface an allegory of the degraded fate of art in bourgeois society, this text also tells a double story about the commodity form, at once rejecting the world of rationalized production as dreary and deadening, but also mining the marvelous world of *consumption* as a potent site of aesthetic inspiration. Appealing to the faraway time and place of myth, "El rey burgués" tells the story of a "poor poet" who arrives at the sumptuous palace of a king in search of food and shelter. Coming before the king's throne, the poet announces that he is a visionary. The bourgeois king of the title will have none of this; handing the poet a mechanical music box, he dismisses the poet with the laconic sentence, "Piece of music for crust of bread" 224). Because the poet-prophet is made of flesh and needs to eat, the bourgeois king is able to force him to crank out mechanical waltzes in the palace gardens in exchange for his daily bread. This contract proves fatal for the poet: quickly forgotten among the bourgeois king's vast array of possessions, he is literally left out in the cold to die, dedicating his dying gasp to his unrealized artistic ideal.

As a fable of the place of art in modern(izing) society, "El rey burgués" provides a critique of commodification summed up by the statement, "El arte no viste pantalones ni habla burgués" ("Art doesn't wear trousers or speak bourgeois"; 1965, 19), first uttered by the poet to the bourgeois king and then repeated by the omniscient narrator as the silenced poet dies in the palace gardens. The term "bourgeois," it should be noted, was not widely used in Spanish

America in the late nineteenth century. It was *modernismo,* and perhaps even Darío's story, that put the term in greater circulation.[6] According to the story, to speak "bourgeois" is to speak the language of the universal equivalent, what Marx called *warensprache,* or the language of commodities (1976, 143). It is through this language that a vast array of different social products—ranging from sacks of wheat to, in this case, the labor of the poet—can be rendered equivalent by the mechanism of price. For Marx, the acceptance and routinization of the fantasy that labor can be made equivalent to all other commodities lies at the heart of the commodity fetish in bourgeois society. In Darío's rendition of a similar problem, the "king" of the story is stripped of his aristocratic trappings and revealed for what he really is: a bourgeois who flattens human creativity through a spurious logic of equivalence. In the process, the fabled order of artistic patronage is replaced by modern contract labor. I say fabled because the European model of artistic patronage (i.e., that of the Renaissance) had never existed in Spanish America, or at least not in the way imagined in the story. By the same token, the bourgeois labor contract Darío's text excoriates had not become predominant in late nineteenth-century Spanish American societies, either in the world of writers or in Spanish American societies at large. And yet it is not necessary for Spanish American historical conditions to match European ones—a logical impossibility—for us to realize that Darío is attempting to locate, with the vocabulary available to him, some kind of shift occurring in late nineteenth-century society, one increasingly dominated by the logic of the commodity form.

Darío's story has rightly been read as an allegory of the incipient professionalization of writing in Spanish America, a process by which the writer became a paid worker and the written work a commodity. Darío, along with Martí, is one of the first Spanish American writers to have earned a living almost entirely as a writer. Nearly all of the texts comprising *Azul,* including "El rey burgués," were first published in the Santiago newspaper *La Época,* and the owner of this newspaper, Eduardo MacClure, is nearly always cited as Darío's model for the bourgeois king. From the perspective offered by Darío's story, the poet is forced to work for a living as a journalist, cranking out mechanically produced texts for the benefit of the newspaper owner. Contradictorily, this critique itself appears in commodified form in the newspaper. The birth of autonomous, anticommercial literary discourse, that is, went hand in hand with its embourgeoisement, a process toward which the writer can only show ambivalence.[7] This ambivalence stems at least in part from the fact that the poet does not object to commodification per se, but rather that *art*—considered a special good by *modernismo*—should be incorporated into its equalizing logic. "Even the shoe-maker" criticizes his poetry, the objectified poet of "El rey burgués" complains, suggesting that the protection of art from the commodity world would end this indignity. The logic of the commodity for the shoemaker is fine, the story seems to say, so long as it keeps away from the poet and his works.

"El rey burgués," then, can legitimately be read as a contradic-tory critique of the incipient professionalization and commodifica-tion of writing in turn-of-the-century Spanish America. The story of the commodity it tells, however, is accompanied and undercut by a second story, to which far less attention has been paid. If the first commodity story provides a critique of bourgeois relations of pro-duction and exchange, the second takes a distinct point of depar-ture: the wonder-filled, dream-like realm of luxury consumption, a world that is just as legitimately a product of bourgeois modernity as the realm of commodity production. The bourgeois king, we are told, has a palace filled with the most exquisite things. At first, the narra-tor of the story (whose voice is separate from that of the "poor poet") takes an ironic stance toward these objects, sarcastically naming lilac bushes, swan-filled ponds, and an alabaster staircase flanked by marble lions as measures of "good taste" and "refinement." This tone continues as the narrator tells us that the bourgeois king is a lover of grammar books, the novels of Ohnet, and academic criticism—not real art. Numerous rooms, in turn, exhibit japonaiserie and chi-noiserie, simply "for the luxury of it" (2006, 222). The thick sarcasm disappears, however, once the omniscient narrative voice begins to describe the individual objects decorating one of the salons:

quimeras de bronce con las fauces abiertas y las colas enroscadas,
en grupos fantásticos y maravillosos; lacas de Kioto con incrusta-
ciones de hojas y ramas de una flora monstruosa, y animales de
una fauna desconocida; mariposas de raros abanicos junto a las
paredes; peces y gallos de colores; máscaras de gestos infernales
y con ojos como si fuesen vivos; partesanas de hojas antiquísimas
y empuñaduras con dragones devorando flores de loto; y en con-
chas de huevo, túnicas de seda amarilla como tejidas con hilos de
araña, sembradas de garzas rojas y de verdes matas de arroza; y
tibores, porcelanas de muchos siglos, de aquellas en que hay guer-
reros tártaros con una piel que les cubre los riñones y que llevan
arcos estirados y manojos de flechas. (1965, 18)

bronze chimeras with open jaws and coiled tails, in fantastic,
wondrous groupings; lacquers from Kyoto with inlaid leaves and
branches of a monstrous flora; animals of an unknown fauna;
butterflies with rare wings upon the walls; many-colored fish and
gamecocks; masks with hellish grimaces and eyes that seemed
alive; pikes and halberds with ancient blades, their handles embla-
zoned with dragons devouring lotus flowers; in vessels of porcelain as thin as eggshell, tunics of yellow silk, as though spun from
spider webs, with embroidery of red cranes and green rice plants;
and vases of great antiquity, with designs of Tartar warriors in
kidney-length coats of shaggy fur, bearing tensed bows and quiv-
ers of sharp arrows. (2006, 222)

What the bourgeois owner might see only as japonaiserie and chi-
noiserie acquire a wondrous and mysterious cast when isolated by
the narrator's gaze. In this descriptive moment, the allegorical structure of the text is suspended. The character-types of the story—bourgeois and poet—recede into the background, immersing the reader
in a landscape of inanimate, yet strangely lifelike objects. The progression of the story's plot is also suspended, as the narrative voice
moves into the deep folds of egg-shaped sculptures holding spider-
web-spun tunics and wildly gesticulating masks.

Darío's thick and languorous description of the objects
assembled in the bourgeois king's salon forms another instance
of what I'm calling the modernist import catalogue, this time in
prose form. This mode of description is one of the most distinctive

stylistic features of *Azul*, at the heart of what critics have often called Darío's "precious" aesthetic (Rama [1970] 1985b, 98). As in the case of Casal's sonnet, objects hail forth in a list, metonymically linked to accumulate on the page. Darío's prose version of the catalogue allows for much more description and embellishment, as subclauses, syntactically linked through semicolons, imagine a small and independent world within each individual object.

Darío's text, while openly critical of the commodity relations instated by the bourgeois king, is nonetheless entranced by his material possessions. As a consequence, we get two very different approaches to the commodity form, and the objectification it entails. Whereas the male poet's envelopment by commodity relations must be resisted, enlivened objects provide the material grounds for aesthetic inspiration. Once we step into the silent salon, Darío is no longer concerned with the transformation of humans into things. Conversely, the author begins to pay attention to the wondrous and life-like properties of strange objects. These mirror-images of the commodity fetish, in turn, express themselves within distinct spatial coordinates: the court where the bourgeois forces a contract on the poet (a space not described in the story); and the silent, de-peopled salon, where the narrator's voice is allowed to linger over the assembled objects.

Paradoxically, while the waltzes the poet is forced to crank out are mechanical and debased (the negation of art), the handcrafted, though authorless, luxury objects offer themselves up as screens for embellished linguistic representation in the text. It is precisely their radical separation from their contexts of origin that they can be resignified and accorded worth by the narrator. Not only does this narrator introduce the reader to strange objects like *tíbores* (Chinese vases) and *partesanas* (halberds); he sees into them and in writing realizes their full aesthetic potential. This is not the only moment in *Azul* in which Darío's prose delves into the mysteriously enlivened world of objects. Indeed, much of the rest of his book seems to create whole stories around the individual objects found in the bourgeois king's salon. In "El sátiro sordo" (The deaf satyr), a bronze statue comes to life; "El velo de la Reina Mab" (Queen Mab's veil), is written about a queen who lives inside "a carriage made of a single pearl," enlarges a precious object, and creates a world inside of it (1965).[8]

In his celebrated essay "Paris, Capital of the Nineteenth Century," Benjamin notes that the bourgeois interior emerged as the dialectical counterpart to the office, the place where calculations are made. The interior, in contrast, provided a "dreamworld" where the commodity character of objects could be suppressed: "The private person who squares his accounts with reality in his office demands that the interior be maintained with his illusions. . . . In shaping his private environment he represses both. From this spring the phantasmagorias of the interior" (1978, 154). For Benjamin, following Marx, it is the (male) bourgeois who initiates the split between fantasy and reality in the world of commodities, first by suppressing the social conditions of production through exchange, and then by carrying this suppression over into the private space of the interior. I read Benjamin here as gesturing toward a kind of bourgeois consumption in which the "phantasmagoric" character of objects hails from their extraction from and rearrangement within a wider net of social relations. Rife with affective and aesthetic dimensions, these assembled objects begin to take on a life of their own.[9] Benjamin's analysis is helpful in that it reminds us that the phantasmagoric, otherworldly character assigned to objects decorating the bourgeois interior hails from the suppression of their origins in social processes, carried out on spatial and temporal planes. This suppression becomes particularly acute in "El rey burgués," in which the overt condemnation of the process by which commodities are produced and rendered equivalent occurs alongside the aestheticization of commodities in the sphere of consumption.[10]

The decorated nineteenth-century Parisian salon, Benjamin writes, functions as a private "box in the world theater"; it is a place that is both open and closed to the world outside (154). And in order to gauge the meaning of Darío's version of this salon, within its historical site of enunciation—Chile in the 1880s—we must go out into the world created by transnational trade.

Import Consumption as "Compensation"

One might argue that there is little unique about Darío's descriptive and enumerative style, since it transposes into Spanish a literary style already pioneered by French authors, as evident from his citation of the Goncourts, decadent brothers who made an art form of the catalogue of objects.[11] But the precise meanings attached to different goods changes when they are transported to the raw-material-exporting periphery. Hence the import catalogues of *Azul* offer much more than an imitation of a style more appropriately or organically developed elsewhere, and instead provide insights into the cultural dynamics of import consumption in late nineteenth-century Latin America.

An initial approximation to the meanings of import consumption in late nineteenth-century Latin America can be gauged from a Brazilian engraving from 1867, which visualizes the increasingly cosmopolitan nature of production and consumption in late nineteenth-century Latin America. The top frame of the engraving reads "What the Brazilian packet takes to France," and depicts a ship laden with sacks of coffee, barrels of sugar and tobacco, and bags of gold. The bottom frame, in turn, depicts "what the packet, as compensation, takes back to Brazil": heaps of French clothing, soaps, perfumes, and pomades. Here the political economy of the Export Age is put on visual display: uniform sacks and barrels leave Brazil, to come back as an assorted array of specialized consumer commodities. The "compensation" resulting from this exchange is coded in economic terms: so many units of sugar and coffee for so many hoop skirts and bottles of perfume. At the same time, the circular voyage touches on the deeply symbolic meanings attached to commodities themselves under the nineteenth-century (neo) colonial division of labor. Uniformly "raw" or "natural" products are traded for "elaborated" or "civilized" goods. In keeping with the tenets of Ricardian advantage studied in the previous chapter, Brazil should specialize in the production of those commodities it might produce most efficiently for the world market. This specialization came at a cost, however, since the basic principles of liberal

O QUE O PAQUETE DO BRASIL LEVA PARA A FRANÇA.

O QUE EM COMPENSAÇÃO O MESMO PAQUETE TRAZ DE LA' PARA O BRASIL.

European imports as economic and symbolic "compensation." An engraving from 1867 depicts the exchange of Brazilian agricultural and mineral commodities for European manufactures. The caption reads: "What the Brazilian packet takes to France" *(above)* and "What the same packet brings back to Brazil as compensation" *(below).*

political economy had already stipulated that manufactures were worth more than "raw" materials (no matter how much labor had been invested in their production process prior to their export). As a corollary, the ideological framework of classical political economy assumed that manufacturing societies were intellectually superior and temporally more advanced than those dedicated to the production of natural products, a belief deeply internalized by nineteenth-century Latin American elites. As the Peruvian political economist Luis Esteves remarked, "There is no country on earth that does not wish to become industrial"; for only "barbarous" nations remained content with specializing in "unfinished products" [*materias brutas*], to which they were unable to give form and shape (1882, 34). As these nations struggled to become "civilized" (manufacturing) nations—a progression precluded by the very doctrine of specialization—they would have to *import* manufactures produced elsewhere, ranging from soap and clothing to intellectual products like books. Hence the double sense of the word "compensation" used in the legend to the Brazilian engraving as both payment and redress of a lack.[12]

Long before the arrival of *modernismo* onto the scene in the late 1880s, access to European modes of consumption had figured as a pillar of liberal ideologies in Latin America. As early as 1841, Spanish America's most famous defender of liberalism, the writer and future president of Argentina, D. F. Sarmiento described recently arrived textiles in the Chilean port city of Valparaíso as "exhal[ing] the smell of civilization" ([1841] 1887, 130). This potent smell would only intensify as societies became increasingly if unequally integrated into global circuits of production and exchange, resulting in an elite commodity culture defined by its access to the sumptuous objects of "civilization." As cultural and literary critic Beatriz González Stephan remarks, paraphrasing Claude Lévi Strauss's famous dichotomy, bourgeois cosmopolitanism in Latin America involved the bringing together of the "the raw and the cooked" (2003, 236), or raw material production alongside the consumption of finished European goods.

The ideological assumptions that were embedded within the raw/elaborated schema had important ramifications for literary production. For with the emergence of stagist theories of commercial development in the eighteenth century, manufacture (and its attendant global division of labor) came to be seen as a prerequisite for what David Hume termed "luxury" in his essay "Of Refinement in the Arts" (1777). Whereas "luxury" had connoted corruption and feminization in earlier religious and republican vocabularies, the eighteenth century witnessed the revalorization of this term.[13] For early theorists of liberal society in Europe, commerce brought with it a flourishing of luxury and the arts (interchangeable terms for Hume): "The same age, which produces great philosophers and politicians, renowned generals and poets, usually abounds with skillful weavers, and ship-carpenters" ([1777] 1898, 301). Conversely, according to this logic, societies *without* skillful weavers and ship-carpenters are likely to be bereft of great philosophers and poets. This, at least, was how the Argentine statesman and writer J. B. Alberdi viewed Latin America's predicament in 1872. How is it possible, he asks, for a region unable to produce "satin, velvet, Breton lace . . . crystals, porcelains, mirrors, statues, engravings, etc." to produce the kind of books that appear in "the most cultured Europe"? ([1872] 1898, 246). Alberdi's rhetorical question has played out over and again in discussions of Latin American cultural production. In what we might call the "absent base" theory, a lack of modernization leads to a lack of cultural sophistication. What is left to Latin American subjects in such a situation? The answer for Alberdi: to import the products the region could not produce for itself.

If, in the Paris studied by Benjamin and others, consumption becomes an aesthetically pleasing refuge from the calculating world of production, on the neocolonial periphery bourgeois consumption acquires added significance as a refuge from the lowly place accorded to the region under the global division of labor. In another reference to import consumption as *compensation* for this lowly position, a Chilean university rector sums up late nineteenth-century thinking about import consumption: "We are primitive producers, but civilized consumers" (qtd. in Bauer and Orlove 1997, 113). In very straightforward terms, the elite Chilean speaker cleanly separates export production from import consumption at the same time he links the two in a global circuit: Chileans produce raw materials for the world market, a mode of production that marks the nation as the backward and uncivilized counterpart of Europe. Access to civilization must occur through the consumption side of the economy in the form of the most sophisticated and exquisite goods Europe has to offer.

Import consumption, in this neocolonial context, becomes a sort of obligation for peripheral subjects in the quest for civilization. It should not surprise us, then, that *modernismo* chose to found a modern artistic discourse deeply embedded in the pleasures of import consumption. Darío wrote and published *Azul* after having moved from Nicaragua to Chile, a country at that moment undergoing a major economic boom surrounding the export of nitrates to Europe. In concert with Darío's use of the term "bourgeois king," the Chilean ruling class was at once aristocratic and bourgeois. During the second half of the nineteenth century, landowning creoles who traced their lineages back to colonial times intermarried with an emerging class of bankers, merchants, and mining magnates (many of them recent European immigrants) to form what historians have called the Chilean oligarchy.[14]

Emerging Chilean class formations were fully modern in that they were articulated through an expanding web of global capital. In like manner, the consumption of luxury goods must be seen as effects of a global(izing) *bourgeois* culture and not some archaic "aristocratic" leftover of a not-yet-modern social formation, as has been frequently assumed. The literary critic Françoise Perus writes, for example, that *modernismo* is "in the last instance an aesthetics of consumption" (1976, 73), but one that ultimately marks the backward, rather than modern character of turn-of-the-century Latin American societies. Calling on the pioneering Peruvian Marxist theorist José Carlos Mariátegui, who in his famous *Siete ensayos de interpretación de la realidad peruana* (Seven interpretive essays on Peruvian reality; 1928) argues that the nineteenth-century elite was characterized by the collection of rents rather than the accumulation of capital, Perus explains *modernismo*'s aesthetics as an expression of an anomalous social organization, out of step with that of Europe. This reading is problematic on two counts: first, it assumes a clean temporal divide between modes of production in Latin American and European societies (wherein the former lags a stage or two behind the latter). Against this assumption, André Gunder Frank was among the first to argue, the uneven and mixed character of peripheral economies such as Chile's were themselves *creations* of the global bourgeois order, and not simply anomalies within it (1967). The same might be said of Darío's early text, which took direct inspiration from the expanding array of luxury goods arriving in Santiago in the last quarter of the nineteenth century. During this period, Chilean elites dramatically increased their consumption of commodities of the same type decorating the interior depicted in "El rey burgués": bronze statues, oil paintings, decorative *bibelots,* flowing gowns, and Parisian carriages (objects depicted elsewhere in *Azul*). Darío experienced this opulence firsthand in the offices of the newspaper *La Época,* filled with bronze statues and tapestries, as well as in the presidential palace of La Moneda, where he attended literary meetings with his close friend and son of the Chilean head of state, Pedro Balmaceda.

Interestingly, the literary meetings hosted by Pedro Balmaceda in the presidential palace are frequently described as "bohemian," a descriptor that immediately strikes us as contradictory (Arrellano 1993, 27–32). For under which definition of "bohemian" might a meeting hosted by the son of the president in a palace make sense? We might ask the same question, of course, of the very act of import consumption, wherein elites consumed "civilized" goods in contexts they themselves considered "primitive." On the one hand, we might be tempted to chalk this up to just another of *modernismo's* failed imitations, by which a French antibourgeois artistic stance is inappropriately transported to the periphery, with somewhat laughable results. A more nuanced reading becomes possible, however, by way of Roberto Schwarz's concept of "second-degree ideology." In his classic essay *Misplaced Ideas: Literature and Society in Late-Nineteenth-Century Brazil*, Schwarz begins with the proposition that bourgeois social structures are by definition shot through with ideology, in Europe as well as on the periphery. The way Schwarz chooses to differentiate between the two contexts is to postulate that if in Europe an ideology such as universalism "corresponded to appearances and hid the essential—the exploitation of labor," in Brazil such ideologies "would be false in a different sense, so to speak, in an original way" (1992, 20). For in Brazil, where slavery rather than free labor reigned, the ideology of universalism "did not describe reality, not even falsely" (23). This failure to describe reality even falsely could be held at bay, in turn, only by the prestige of metropolitan ideals. And though Schwarz is most concerned with the ways in which universalism became an ideal that did not even correspond with false appearances in slave-owning Brazil, his concept of "second-degree ideology" is poised to shed light on a wider range of phenomena. To return to the case at hand, this concept can help us to understand how it was possible that even the most elite endeavors—housed in the very seats of state and economic power—might be described as "bohemian" by social agents.

What I find most powerful in Schwarz's analysis is that it does not stop at identifying strains of the ridiculous in such posturings, but instead works to uncover its power to either uphold or undermine ruling-class objectives. The point for Schwarz is not so much that nineteenth-century Brazilian elites imitated, but rather that selective imitation helped to reinforce the material inequalities on which both the international division of labor and national class structures were built.[15] Again, Schwarz's main examples stem from the ideological acrobatics needed to sustain slavery (an institution that had been extinguished in all but Cuba and Brazil by the 1880s), and yet his diagnosis of *inequality* as the key issue at stake in diagnoses of the imitative nature of elite culture lends itself well to the expressive dynamics of *modernismo*. If we turn back to the space of the sumptuously decorated interior, for example, we might see that its usefulness hails precisely from its physical separation from an outside world characterized by poverty, "primitive" modes of production, and inequality. It becomes a place where the elite Latin American subject (whether assuming the name of oligarch, aristocrat, bourgeois, or indeed poet) might forget about his or her relation to national production and be seduced by the prospect of civilization through consumption. It is also the place where this same subject might forget about the vast inequalities created by the market: for the interior is the place from which production and exchange are expelled, but also the process of distribution itself. In a related vein, Carlos Blanco Aguinaga has remarked that for Darío, the bourgeois "was not the worst . . . enemy of poetry" (1997, 549), but rather the unincorporated and possibly traitorous masses standing outside the palace walls.

Domestic Modernismo:
Import Catalogues and Advertising

The glittering objects transformed into signifiers of artistic disinterest by Darío and other poets were simultaneously commodities circulating within Latin American societies. And in contrast with dominant oppositions between art and commerce, writers sought inspiration in a specific corner of the commodity world: that of refined, "civilized" import consumption. This relationship becomes particularly salient when we turn to another overlooked region of *modernista* aesthetics: advertising. In order to explore this relationship, I turn to the case of José Asunción Silva, a key proponent of art for art's sake in turn-of-the-century Colombia *and* a tireless promoter of luxury import consumption. For in addition to being a poet, novelist, and essayist, Silva was also an import merchant in turn-of-the-century Bogotá, selling the most sumptuous goods to an elite enriched by burgeoning coffee exports. For most of his short adult life, Silva managed the family business, *R. Silva e Hijo* (R. Silva and Son), an unfortunate venture that ended first in bankruptcy and later, after several personal setbacks (including the death of his beloved sister), in suicide at the age of thirty-one. This tragic end has cast Silva in the mold of the tragic artist, misunderstood and unappreciated within his peripheral milieu. Silva's friend and critic Rufino Blanco Fombona could write that the "vulgar merchants, sweaty and practical" (*groseros comerciantes, sudados y prácticos*) surrounding Silva had a hand in killing the sensitive artist (1994, 69). And yet, Silva himself was also a modernizing bourgeois, dedicated to bringing "civilized" consumption to the coffee elite of Bogotá. In some ways, we might say that Silva is an amalgamation of Darío's two characters: simultaneously an artist who speaks the language of art and a bourgeois who speaks the language of commodities. This is not to say that Silva's twin identities as artist and merchant converged smoothly: Silva himself drew attention to the incompatibility between his artistic ideals and the "low material interests" (Brigard Silva 1946, 284) that forced him to practice accounting instead of dreaming up stories. This sense of artistic frustration was accompanied, however, by the import merchant's willing and even adroit promotion of imported commodities to local consumers as markers of beauty, refinement, and "civilization."

These two identities reveal themselves in a pairing of texts, both of which employ the descriptive and enumerative form I've been analyzing as the modernist import catalogue. The first comes from Silva's posthumously published novel *De sobremesa,* which tells the story of a creole dilettante dedicated, among other things, to the collection and contemplation of exquisite objects. In chapter 4, I provide a reading of *De sobremesa* as a novel about the erratic and volatile nature of capitalist expansion in Colombia during the Export Age. For now, I want to focus only on the opening paragraph of this novel, which takes place in the dim half-light of the main character's salon, after he has returned from a prolonged stay in Europe:

> Recogida por la pantalla de gasa y encajes, la claridad tibia de la lámpara caía en círculo sobre el terciopelo carmesí de la carpeta, y al iluminar de lleno tres tazas de China, doradas en el fondo por un resto de café espeso, y un frasco de cristal tallado, lleno de licor transparente entre el cual brillaban partículas de oro, dejaba ahogado en una penumbra de sombría púrpura, producida por el tono de la alfombra, los tapices y las colgaduras, el resto de la estancia silenciosa. ([1990] 1996, 109)

> Secluded by the shade of gauze and lace, the warm light of the lamp fell in a circle over the crimson velvet of the tablecloth, and as it lit up the three china cups, which were golden in the bottom from thick traces of thick coffee, and a crystal-cut bottle full of transparent liqueur shining with gold particles, it left the rest of the large and silent chamber awash in a gloomy purple semi-darkness, the effect of the cast of the carpet, the tapestries, and the wall hangings. (2005, 50)

Like Darío's description of the decorated salon in "El rey burgués," this passage zeroes in on a set of exquisite goods. No human presence is detected; instead, descriptive adjectives are reserved for objects; the imperfect verb tense, a preferred descriptive mode in Spanish, allows inorganic objects to accumulate within a silent, circumscribed space. The influence of J. K. Huysmans's decadent novel

Au rebours, one of the models for *De sobremesa,* is deeply felt. But as in the case of Darío's Goncourt-inspired salon, Silva's decorative prose warrants attention if nothing else because its meaning changes dramatically when considered in light of the material and cultural conditions governing modernization on the Spanish American periphery. It is worth highlighting again that none of the objects mentioned in this passage—save the coffee held by the Chinese cups—would have been produced in Colombia. Since the end of the nineteenth century, Colombia had become specialized in coffee production for the world market; in return for coffee exports, elites received luxury goods from Europe, in the circuit of commodity exchange outlined above. By law of the genre of the modernist import commodity catalogue, this circuit is not mentioned. This omission is even more striking in Silva's writing because, assuming the setting of the novel is late nineteenth-century Bogotá, the objects assembled in the imaginary salon would have reached the city through an extremely complicated and arduous route. Unlike Havana, a Caribbean entrepôt, or Santiago, a city within easy reach of the Pacific, Bogotá lies ensconced high in the Andes mountain chain. Lacking both water and railways, it was so remote that all imported objects—even pianos—had to be carried to Bogotá on mule-back from the low-lying Magdalena River.

Now let us turn to an advertisement Silva wrote in 1890 for one of his luxury goods stores, the Almacén Nuevo, modeled on the great Parisian department stores Au Bon Marché:

> La cortina de felpa bordada de oro caía sobre un transparente que filtraba la luz amortiguándola con el tono oscuro del brocatel de los muebles, con la madera opaca del piano y con el brillo de los marcos de las pinturas. Había en el aire del cuarto una fragancia de agua de toilette que completaba el ambiente lujoso de la pieza. Sobre el tocador un espejo triple reflejaba los grandes frascos de agua de colonia. (Qtd. in Santos Molano [1990], 1997, 972)

> The felt drapery embroidered with gold fell over a sheer curtain, filtering the light absorbed by the deep tone of the furniture's brocade, the opaque wood of the piano, and the brilliance of the paintings' frames. There was a fragrance of eau de toilette in the air

that completed the luxurious atmosphere of the room. Above the dressing table a triple mirror reflected the image of large bottles of cologne.

The similarities between this advertisement and the opening paragraph of *De sobremesa* are remarkable: each begins with an image of light filtered through a diaphanous cloth and absorbed by dark fabrics, illuminating specific objects isolated by the narrator's gaze: in the first description, delicate china cups and crystal decanters; in the second, gleaming picture frames and the dark wood of a piano. Descriptive language is used to highlight the special qualities of each luxury object, which in turn belongs to a larger group. Amassed as a set in a closed space, the collection of objects works to create an ambient effect that is more powerful than any of its single elements.

These similarities are made all the more remarkable by the fact that the advertisement for the Almacén Nuevo was written years *before* the opening to the novel *De sobremesa*. While Silva's novel was rewritten between 1894 and 1896 (after an original version was lost in a shipwreck), his advertisement was published in 1890. After these citations, each of the texts goes on to reveal something very different: the novel proceeds by opening onto an all-male gathering in the main character's home in an unnamed locale in South America; the advertisement, by contrast, ends by revealing that everything in the imaginary room had been bought "at reasonable prices, at the Almacén Nuevo, without a doubt the best furniture and fantasy store in Bogotá." And yet before the intrusion of this commercial message, the aesthetic register cultivated by the advertisement had been in essence the same as that of the novel's opening scene.

How can we account for these formal similarities, and what insights might they provide into the parallel and intersecting universes of literary production and elite consumption of imported commodities? Even though each text is written for a different purpose and for a different audience, they share recognition of the aesthetic potential latent in imported luxury goods. Their juxtaposition here shows that the aesthetic potential of luxury goods might be mobilized for the purposes of novelistic stagesetting, just as it might be mobilized to incite consumer desire. Here once more, the Spanish American artist and the proto-bourgeois consumer are united in their desire for a similar set of goods. On the coffee-exporting periphery, the contradiction between artistic disinterest and commercial interest as the dividing line between literature and advertising is not so important, to my mind, as the attempted *transcendence* of this contradiction by way of the desire incited by the objects themselves in both genres.

The arrival and circulation of imported goods to Bogotá in the late nineteenth century was no small matter, especially when judged against this city's geographical isolation and firmly entrenched reputation as a staid, conservative, and Catholic city tied to Spanish colonial traditions. While foreign luxury held its thrall over Darío's Santiago and Casal's Havana, it was firmly resisted by large segments of Bogotá's political and commercial elite at the end of the nineteenth century. In the face of this traditionalism, Silva's job as both decadent artist *and* luxury merchant became even more important: for what these two figures shared was a common desire to liberate material and sensual desire over and against moral prohibitions, to unshackle consumption from need, and attempts to free the sensual desire latent within objects.

In the case of Silva, the oft-supposed contradiction between artistic disinterest and commercial interest was superseded by a confluence between the decadent artist and merchant's role as "promoters" of luxury consumption within a field of rapidly expanding transnational commercial relations. At the same time, paradoxically, these identities converge in a disavowal of their relationship to this very commercial field: the decadent through a discourse of artistic disinterest, and the *marchand de luxe* through a language of fantasy that seeks to suppress the commodity character of objects. The contradiction between decadent and merchant, I would argue, lay in another arena, that of gender. For while the decadent artist ensconced himself in an imaginary world of *male* artistic contemplation, the import merchant operated in a milieu that was increasingly identified as *feminine*. In late nineteenth-century

Bogotá as in other contexts, the worlds of fashion, shopping, and home decoration were increasingly becoming associated with women.[16] From this perspective, we might say that *modernismo*'s distinction between art and commerce gives way to a further division between masculine high art, on the one hand, and "domestic *modernismo*," on the other, defined as an overtly feminized and commercial version of the literary current.

Silva's incursion into domestic *modernismo* becomes even more noteworthy in his sizeable corpus of advertisements, many of which have been collected in Enrique Santos Molano's biography of the poet-merchant. In one set of ads, two women characters, "Beatriz" and "Inés," exchange letters extolling the high quality of goods in "Señor Silva's" store (qtd. in Santos Molano [1990] 1997, 975). In an advertisement Silva inexplicably wrote for a competitor's store, he uses verse to entice women consumers:

> Allí las elegantes hallar pueden esencias
> que ambientes de jardines a sus vestidos den,
> pues entre muchos otros se venden los siguientes:
> Vainilla, White Rose, Verbena, Geranio y Tour Eiffel. (871)

> There the elegant ones can find essences
> that will give their dresses a garden air,
> because among many others, the following are sold:
> Vanilla, White Rose, Verbena, Geranium, and Tour Êiffel.

Worthy of note is the fact that Silva's verses are alexandrines; their seven-syllable patterns are written to fit the foreign names of toiletries. Scholars have long noted that *modernismo* revolutionized poetic language, through experimentation with verse form. In this instance of domestic *modernismo*, high aesthetic form is deployed within a gendered discourse of commodity consumption.

Going one step further, Silva's corpus of advertisements allows us to locate the origins of what I have been calling the modernist import catalogue in actual catalogues or inventories. For this we may look to one of the many front-page advertisements Silva took out in *El telegrama*, in which commodities appear as a long list composed of items ranging from *tela ordinaria* (ordinary cloth) and gold jewelery to *artículos de fantasía para señora* (notions for ladies). The shape of the list resembles the layout of both Casal's sonnet "Mis amores" considered at the beginning of this chapter, as well as the alexandrine Silva wrote for the Almacén Bohemia. The advertisement reproduced on the following page represents the barest and most openly commercial of the lists assembled in this chapter, and yet it also contains some embellishment in the different font sizes Silva employs to attract readers' attention.

Silva's gendered discourse of import consumption, in turn, coexists with and is buttressed by a return to another discourse I have already examined, that of peripheral *inferiority* in the world of production. As an example, let us turn to a slightly different text by Silva, a newspaper chronicle in which the author assumes the perspective of Mary Bell, a North American woman visiting Colombia for the first time. In what amounts to the obverse of the modernist import catalogue, Silva's narrative voice lists the unsophisticated products Mary finds on display at an exhibition of Colombian products:

> She didn't find a single national product indicative of vigor, of abundant life, of human activity applied to serious works. Many puny things made out of straw, wood or chocolate; miniscule sets of hand-made work; useless pieces of clothing; embroidery, ink and pencil drawings. . . . Not even a trace of any great undertaking, of the kind of industry that gives renown and riches to a country. (Qtd. in Santos Molano [1990] 1997, 983)

In this fictitious report, first published in the newspaper *El telegrama* in August 1891, Mary Bell confirms Colombia's inferiority in the realm of production. This inferiority is not merely material; it is intellectual and moral. The form of the catalogue, which assumes an arrangement and display of objects, is rendered ridiculous by Silva when filled with the clumsy and intellectually unsophisticated products made by Colombians. One might argue that Silva's "Mary Bell" text ironizes the gaze of the industrialized North on its Southern neighbors. This possible interpretation is complicated by the utter *absence* of irony within Silva's lush descriptions of imported luxury goods examined earlier. When giving accounts of the inferiority of

The artist-merchant's import commodity catalogue. Advertisement penned by José Asunción Silva for his import luxury goods store El Almacén Nuevo. From *El telegrama*, Bogotá (1889).

national production, however, a distancing mechanism suddenly appears: the story is told through Mary Bell, an imaginary female consumer who rejects Colombian products, in the process affirming the equation between a country's level of industry and its level of intellect. Silva's chronicle was published in 1891, the same year José Martí wrote "Nuestra América," considered in the previous chapter. In this speech, Martí railed against American male elites' corrosive and feminizing obsession with foreign goods (metonymized as "paper dress coats" and "painted nails"), urging them to turn instead toward the soil, products, and inhabitants of the region (Martí 1975g, 6:16). In Martí's utopian vision of production, American objects provide the literal and figurative raw materials of regional autonomy in the world market. Silva's Mary Bell chronicle, as a negation of "Nuestra América," reveals Latin American products as irremediably inferior. At the same time, whereas Martí's utopian vision aims to transform feminized Latin American consumers ("seven-month men") into productive "real men" (16), Silva's chronicle ventriloquizes a North American woman's voice to highlight the inferiority of local manufactures. The text deploys a foreign and feminine voice to announce the material and intellectual gulf separating Colombia from the North. From within this gulf, only import consumption might compensate for inferiority in the realm of production.

Peripheral Flânerie: Casal at the Havana Department Store

Contradictorily, this compensation comes at the cost of *affirming* local inferiority. Indeed, it was impossible for the *modernista* writer *not* to be faced time and again with the contradiction between the fantasies afforded by imported luxury goods and the local realities they attempted to ignore. The attempt to manage these contradictions, as explored below, results not in the transcendence of the gulf separating center from periphery, but rather in a disavowal of its force through the language of autonomous art. This disavowal occurs simultaneously through a separation of *masculine* artistic contemplation from the feminized realm of commodity consumption, and through the erasure of the local elements whose presence threatens to ruin artistic enjoyment.

This attempt at resolving the contradictions faced by the *modernista* writer can be traced through a journalistic chronicle by the Cuban writer Julián del Casal, whose sonnet "Mis amores" I considered at the outset of this chapter. Entitled "El fénix," it relates a trip to the newly opened Havana department store of the same name. Like other writers of the period, such as Rubén Darío, José Martí, Manuel Gutiérrez Nájera, and Enrique Gómez Carilllo, Casal worked as a journalist to earn a living. Signing with pseudonyms like "Hernani" (a nod to Victor Hugo) in publications such as *La Habana Elegante* and *La Discusión,* Casal's chronicles relate the experience of urban modernization from the standpoint of Havana's creole and Spanish sugar elite, writing of masked balls, portrait studios, literary salons, and, as we'll see, department stores. These chronicles have remained all but ignored until recently, in part because early critics shared the poet's distaste for journalism as the lowbrow counterpart of true art. Yet a text like "El fénix," as a "minor" text in the sense Julio Ramos employs to talk about José Martí's urban chronicles ([1989] 2001, 112), provides insights into different entry points into the experiences and contradictions generated by late nineteenth-century commodity culture.

"El fénix" begins by invoking the city street as an exterior frame for the fantasies of private import consumption. It opens with an evocation of the heat and dirt of Havana's center:

> Fleeing from the dust that carpets the city; from the hot wind that blows in all directions; from the miasmas that ascend from the black morass of the sewage pipes; from the trams that pass by emitting steam; from the carriages that run over the sidewalks . . . and from the innumerable calamities that float like particles in the atmosphere of our city. . . . I entered the luxurious establishment of Señor Hierro, located on Obispo street at the corner of Aguacate, attracted by the innumerable objects glittering in its interior. (2001, 321)

A series of disagreeable conditions, posed in the ubiquitous form of the list, combine to compose an urban backdrop from which the writing subject flees. Glittering objects provide instant respite from the disorderly spectacle of the street, and the grave sense of political instability hanging over the city, provoked by the instability of the sugar export economy, ongoing agitation against Spanish rule, and the immediate aftermath of the abolition of slavery. Under these circumstances, the department store offers a welcome relief.

· We will note that there is no possibility here of street *flânerie;* the writer's leisurely stroll will have to take place in a closed, semipublic space. Like the bourgeois interior outlined by Darío and Silva, the department store offers an oasis from the disagreeable elements of daily life in Havana. At the same time, as Oscar Montero has shown in his reading of "El fénix," Casal's authorial voice displays no small degree of discomfort when submerged into the overtly commodified space of the store. Crossing the threshold, Casal locates himself in a world that is just as agitated and confusing as the world outside, though more selective and refined. One of the purposes of the chronicle is to impose order on the vast array of goods. Following the organizing principle of the department store itself, Casal proposes to describe the objects found in three different departments: jewelry, home decoration, and children's toys, signaling their division in the text with asterisks.

Casal simultaneously employs the rhetoric of art, journalism, and advertising. The language of advertising crops up at different moments: in the first paragraph, he takes care to pinpoint the location of "the luxurious establishment of Señor Hierro," employing a voice similar to the one used by Silva to reveal where the objects in his advertisement could be purchased. At another moment, Casal remarks that "El fénix" is on par with the "best stores in Europe" (321), a promotional gesture directed at boosting both the reputation of the store and the self-esteem of the potential consumer. At other moments, Casal appeals to the language of high art, calling on the Parnassian poet Teódore de Banville to identify the diamond as the most "chaste and heroic stone" (2001, 322). This reference is itself ambivalent: on one hand, it serves to highlight the aesthetic value of the goods on display, a potential the chronicle will work to exploit through description; on the other, it can be read as an ironic nod to the gulf separating "pure" poetry and the profane commodities gathered together in the jewelry department. Right after this reference to Banville, Casal initiates a lush description of the sort we have seen in Darío's "El rey burgués," in which ornate objects seek expression through an equally ornate language. As he settles his agitated eye on a grouping of jewels, the tone of the chronicle settles into calm, even trance-like concentration to describe

> a gold pheasant, with a mother of pearl gullet and diamantine wings, that carries a diamond in its beak, eager to pose on the sculptured breast of a modern Cleopatra; a finely worked bracelet of matte gold, sustaining a medallion surrounded by sapphires and rhinestones on its front, in which the noble face of a Merovingian gentleman can be seen; a half moon of rhinestones, with a star of rubies, under whose gleam two doves coo, letting a pearl fall so as to kiss each other better; a daisy of white enamel, decorated with a diamond that imitates a drop from a stream, fit to glimmer in the hair of a Bernice. (322–23)

We have already seen this form—the *modernista* import catalogue—and so it is not necessary to comment on its structure. What is necessary to point out, however, in the cumulative reading of high art, commercial, and journalistic versions of this catalogue, is that while the specific objects and contexts of enunciation change—from objets d'art in Darío's "El rey burgués" to furniture in Silva's advertisement to jewelry in Casal's chronicle—the effect is largely the same. Lush description cultivates desire for beautiful things. In all three cases, the logic of the passage is to peel away distracting elements such as towns, buildings, and walls; people also disappear, so that the narrative voice might focus on the singular, often lifelike characteristics of objects. This movement is especially dramatic in Casal's chronicle, since it enacts a process by which the narrative voice moves from the agitated street into the department store, and then from the display case to settle on a sparkling golden pin in the shape of a pheasant. Description transforms the pin into an object that is not only desirable, but desires;

its exquisiteness is complemented by an agency all its own, as the pin wishes to pose on the bust of a modern-day Cleopatra.

Casal's description complicates rather than repeats the functions of the commodity catalogues considered earlier. In the imaginary salon of Darío's "bourgeois king," we will recall that the collected objects were exceedingly rare works of art, ranging from Chinese vases to eggshell-thin porcelains. And in Silva's advertisement, there was no reason to suspect that the furniture and decorations were not authentic markers of taste and distinction. In Casal's chronicle, by contrast, many of the jewels are revealed to be shiny fakes. Materials such as rhinestones, enamel, and semiprecious stones intermingle with sapphires and gold; genuine diamonds, earlier identified as Banville's "chaste and heroic stone," serve as tiny adornments available for consumption by a humble shopgirl. Yet the form employed to describe the jewels is the same as that used by Darío to describe precious works of art. Even if made of inauthentic stones, they are still considered beautiful and exclusive enough to be assigned high aesthetic value. This brings us to a potentially important insight regarding the logic of the modernist catalogue within emerging commodity culture: it is the representational form, and not the objects themselves, that is able to generate desire. For the modernist catalogue, it does not matter whether the objects are priceless works of art or rhinestone necklaces. Both sets of objects can be charged with refinement and elegance; both can incite fantasy and desire.

This potential for fantasy is reduced dramatically, however, as Casal moves out of the jewelry section and into the two other departments his chronicle proposes to cover: home decoration and children's toys. It is in these two sections that Casal's authorial voice is increasingly overtaken by irony with respect to his surroundings. Casal continues to provide the reader with long lists of goods—"japanese vases," "elegant albums with whimsical buckles," "mother-of-pearl rosaries" (2001, 323)—but his enumeration ceases to provide narratives for the goods in question. With this shift comes a closer attention to the origins of the objects: a six-cylinder organ—compared to the one possessed by a famous

Italian diva—is revealed as coming from a factory in Europe; others have been brought from the latest exposition in Paris (323). Whereas the aesthetic value accorded to imported luxury goods assumes their exotic provenance, overt mentions of the exchange process between Cuban merchants and European manufacturers creates a different effect in which, again, the fantasy potential of the objects is dramatically curtailed. And if it was possible to suppress the commodity character of jewels to elevate their aesthetic value, this becomes entirely impossible when Casal is faced with the toys in the children's section of the store. Faced with piles of miniature Noah's arks, dolls, toy soldiers, and wooden horses, the writer finds a scene of accumulation completely devoid of beauty, and from the outset ridiculed as artificial: "It is almost impossible to walk through this department without tripping" (324). In contrast with the ladies' jewels, toys possess a materiality that is opaque and somewhat menacing; they do not open themselves to receive the chronicler into their folds but instead converge as dense obstacles. We can begin to see how the author views commodities that do not fit his taste.

Significantly, it is at this moment near the end of Casal's text when the world outside (already marked as displeasing) intrudes once again, this time through the image of children on the street clamoring to get a better look at the toys inside: "From behind the iron gate that separates them from the street, children with open mouths and dilated pupils peek through, trying to fit their heads between the bars"(324). The gaze from the street is one of candor and hope, dramatized by the fact that these children—clearly poor—are unable to enter the store at all, much less acquire the objects of their desire. Casal, now in the position of the observer, casts children in the role of mesmerized consumers unable to tell the difference between fantasy and reality: the objects in the toy section "awaken the first of the heart's ambition," allowing them to "misspend the treasure of their tears" (324). This insight is uncanny because while Casal's description of jewelry had self-consciously highlighted the fantasy embedded within commodities, in the case of children's toys this fantasy is read as misguided. The shifting voices of the chronicle reveal a subject who is in certain moments seduced by the commodity fantasy and at others resistant to its lure. At the same time, there is a logic of disavowal and displacement embedded within Casal's attempt to see the "reality" behind the commodity fantasy. For while allowing social inequality to make its way into the chronicle, he disavows the fact that his own version of the commodity fantasy—deep inside the display case— is rendered effective because it hides those very inequalities from view. Further, Casal displaces social inequalities onto an opposition between unmarked categories of child and adulthood. The racial markings of the crowds outside, while an obsession of white Havana elites, are not mentioned; nor is the abject poverty of the masses in relation to the shoppers inside the store.

No wonder, then, that Casal figures his exit from the store as a descent into hell. After having achieved some degree of ironic distance from the fantasy world of the department store, he cannot help but envision his return to the street as moving from "the heights of an old Italian palace, populated with artistic marvels" and into the depths of "filthy tunnels, interminable and narrow, full of groans, screams and blasphemies" (324). The image, Casal tells us, comes to him from the paintings of Piranesi. Casal narrates his return to the unappealing "reality" of turn-of-the-century Havana through the filter of an eighteenth-century Italian painting, with the effect of making the city street seem vividly unreal and otherworldly.

Casal's reference to Piranesi's painting at the end of his chronicle is not gratuitous, for it allows the final voice of the chronicle to emerge: that of the artist who himself has traveled through metaphorical rings of hell to arrive at a place of transcendence. Once Casal can identify the street scene with an Italian painting, he distances himself from both the department store and the street. Through recourse to the ideal plane of art, Casal ends his chronicle: "I felt a great sense of satisfaction, because I did not covet any of the objects that had momentarily dazzled my eyes. I continued to prefer a good sonnet to the most valuable diamond. And I continue to prefer it. In spite of the incredulous smiles of my readers" (324).

"Mis Amores": An "Ideal" Department Store

After having strolled through the department store—the only place where *flânerie* seems possible in turn-of-the-century Havana—and crossed over once again to the "miasmic" heat and dust of the street, Casal disavows any desire for the objects in the store. The only object worthy of his desire is "a good sonnet." One interpretation of this switch is that Casal is now speaking as a true artist, ultimately more committed to art than to commodities, however beautiful and valuable these may be.[17] But given the points of articulation on which "El fénix" itself insists, another interpretation is possible: it is only in poetry that the poet can liberate himself from the twin spectacles of the imported commodity and the hellish Havana street. As a particularly compelling example, let us return to Casal's sonnet "Mis amores" (My loves), published in the same year as "El fénix":

> Amo el bronce, el cristal, las porcelanas,
> las vidrieras de múltiples colores,
> los tapices pintados de oro y flores
> y las brillantes lunas venecianas.
> Amo también las bellas castellanas,
> La canción de los viejos trovadores,
> Los árabes corceles voladores,
> Las flébiles baladas alemanas;
> El rico piano de marfil sonoro,
> El sonido del cuerno en la espesura,
> Del pebetero la fragrante esencia,
> Y el lecho de marfil, sándalo, y oro,
> En la que deja la virgen hermosura
> La ensangrentada flor de su inocencia.
>   (2001, lines 1–14)

> I love bronze, crystal, porcelains,
> stained glass of multiple colors
> tapestries painted in gold and flowers
> and brilliant Venetian mirrors
> I also love beautiful *castellanas,*

The song of old troubadours,
The sound of flying Arab steeds,
Faint German ballads
The fine piano of sonorous marble,
The sound of the horn in the forest thicket
The fragrant essence of the censer
And the bed of marble, sandalwood, and gold,
In which virgin beauty leaves
The bloodied flower of its innocence.

Like the journalistic chronicle "El fenix," this sonnet is organized into divisible parts, each of which corresponds with a different set of objects. Whereas the chronicle followed the organizational principle of the department store, placing asterisks to delineate sections dedicated to jewelry, furniture, and toys, the sonnet follows the formal rules of the sonnet: two stanzas of four lines, followed by two stanzas of three lines. The objects listed in the first stanza might very well have been found in the furniture section of the department store: bronzes, crystal, porcelains, stained glass, tapestries, and mirrors. But whereas the journalistic chronicle constrained Casal's ability to highlight the aesthetic value of decorative objects, because their commodity character was all too evident, the commodity form becomes invisible in the sonnet. Filtered through poetic form, objects in "Mis amores" become signifiers of "pure" aesthetic value. With this, the material side of objects recedes, and their ideal side is amplified. If we move to the next stanzas of the sonnet, the poetic "I" goes on to declare love for immaterial artistic forms, such as *castellanas* (a term that also means "Castillian women") and German ballads. We will note that even the most immaterial of Casal's "loves," however, acquires a thing-like status; the sonnet, after all, follows the basic contours of the import commodity catalogue in its impulse to categorize, enumerate, and list objects.

And yet there are important differences between the formal possibilities of the sonnet and those of the chronicle. We will note that as the sonnet progresses, Casal's list of "loves" becomes more immaterial, spectral, and erotic. This was exactly the opposite of what occurred in Casal's journalistic chronicle in which the vulgar materiality of the commodities became more pronounced as the writer moved from jewelry to furniture to toy departments. The department store, while at the outset full of aesthetic possibilities, eventually produces disillusion in the observer. The sonnet, by contrast, preserves and indeed amplifies the mysteries held within material objects. In this regard, the image provided by the final stanza of "Mis amores" is most intriguing, in which the sandalwood, gold, and marble bed is invested with the erotic energy of a past sexual act. The body of the deflowered subject, whom we assume to be a woman (though this is not clear), is represented only as a trace of blood. Sexual desire is generated not through the act itself, but rather through the sublimation of the feminine body into the bed, now a sexual fetish in the Freudian sense.

With this turn to the trace of virginal blood, "Mis amores" gains a degree of distance from the immediate realm of market exchange represented in "El fénix" and in doing so is able to reroute the erotic charge of commodities into a more ambiguous and aesthetically potent direction. But this distance gained by the sonnet should not be viewed as an achievement of artistic "purity," but rather as a particular refraction of social relations in late nineteenth-century Havana. As yet another instance of *modernista* commodity fetishism, this refraction of the material world simultaneously illuminates and mystifies. On one hand, the form of the sonnet allows the poet to provide special insights into the erotic charge of the commodity, tapping into a source of libidinal desire whose potential is not exhausted by the act of commercial exchange. To return to the image of the bed in "Mis amores," Casal provides an intriguing image of the commodity as a halfway point between the organic and the inorganic, between presence and absence, and between materiality and trace. But by the same token, this poem, especially when juxtaposed against Casal's textual foray into the department store, reveals a further mystification of the imported commodity by way of aesthetic representation. We will remember that at the end of his chronicle, Casal notes that he continues to prefer a "good sonnet" to the "most valuable diamond." Why is this so? It is certainly because the sonnet allows the speaker to achieve a certain distance from the commodity universe that has just been revealed, at bottom, as ugly. The precise way in which "Mis amores" makes objects beautiful is thus of great significance. If in the department store, the authorial voice is never allowed to truly take leave of Havana, the sonnet bears no geographical markers save those assigned to artistic forms. Likewise, whereas the chronicle could not avoid the presence of women shoppers inside the store and poor, racially marked children outside jostling to get a look at the merchandise, the sonnet allows the artist to contemplate a set of objects in peace, without the disturbance of any human subjects (just the trace of virginal blood on a gorgeous bed). Woman, the consumer par excellence in the department store, is thereby removed from the sonnet. In the chronicle, the writer's need to maintain his distance from the crass world of the commodity-on-display was already expressed through a heavy dose of irony, an irony that disappears totally when the poet speaks of the objects he "loves" alone and in private. In this way, the sonnet, in its removal of social referents from its purview, does not attain independence from the commodity world so much as engage in its remystification. If poetry functions for Casal as an "ideal museum," to invoke the title of one of his collections of poetry, "Mis amores" functions as a kind of ideal *department store,* transplanting objects into a linguistic universe whose contents and borders are controlled by the poet.

José Ortega y Gasset, in his prologue to Rubén Darío's *Prosas profanas,* wrote that "a stanza is an enchanted island" (qtd. in Jitrik 1978, 25). The Spanish philosopher meant to call attention to the autonomous, self-contained qualities of poetry, but his statement takes on a different meaning when we consider the poetics of the commodity developed by *modernismo.* Enchantment, beauty and wonder are not properties solely of poetry, but also of the imported commodities that *modernista* poetry envelops, holds, and transforms.

II. BUST

Chapter 3

MONEY I

Financial Crisis and the Stock Market Novel

> *By God, may this abundance that*
> *surrounds us not be fictitious!*
> —Julián Martel, *La bolsa*

So Rich, and So Poor

According to the economic laws through which Latin American countries were incorporated into the global commodity lottery at the end of the nineteenth century, a nation was rich on the basis of its natural resources. While dormant, this wealth could be "awoken" by the magical touch of human labor, and then through exchange on the global market. Following liberal doctrines of trade advantage, nations that specialized in the production of those commodities it could produce most efficiently for the world market were destined to become wealthy and prosperous. In chapter 1, I showed how liberal visionaries predicted Latin America's "raw" commodities would be exchanged for more valuable manufactures, setting off a chain reaction toward industrialization, in the process creating widespread wealth and political stability. One of these texts, "Las riquezas de Bolivia," for example, proclaimed Bolivia "one of the richest lands of this rich land of America" and promised a glorious future once this country's metallic wealth was incorporated into global circuits of exchange (1872, 39). The Cuban writer José Martí's pamphlet *Guatemala* (1878), in turn, envisioned a republic enriched both materially and morally by the incredible expansion of coffee exports. Yet, in most cases, the wealth promised by these texts failed to materialize: Bolivia and Guatemala today remain among the poorest nations of the Western Hemisphere. And even the most successful of the export republics—Argentina, Brazil, and Chile—were subject to volatile cycles of financial boom and bust, in the course of which national wealth seemed to disappear altogether, almost overnight. Hence the resulting paradox: How might a region so rich in commodity wealth be so poor?

The roots of this contradiction are already present in the Latin American "commodity map" considered in the Introduction. In this map, the geopolitical construct of Latin America is represented as a continuous and self-contained storehouse of primary or "natural" commodities. The labor needed to produce commodities is erased, an appearance Marx refers to as commodity fetishism. Moreover, the mystification internal to the commodity relation becomes even more blinding on a world scale, as Latin America appears cut off from the global circuits through which specific modes of production emerged over the course of the nineteenth century.

As a representation of export-oriented economies, the commodity map is mystifying in yet another manner, for in representing Latin America as a collection of commodities, it cannot register the ghostly and transcendental properties of *money,* the measure through which all commodities are rendered commensurable as values.

The arrival of money onto the scene signals what Marx called the "transubstantiation" of individual and concrete commodities into an abstract and generalized form (1976, 197). Hence the Latin American commodity map points to the origin of wealth in "raw" commodity form, and in doing so erases not just the labor needed for the production of those commodities but also the process by which commodities are transformed into money and back again in the process of accumulation.

A similar absence characterizes the nineteenth-century engraving considered in the previous chapter. This engraving depicts the circular voyage of Latin American export products, as they leave the continent as so many sacks of coffee and tobacco, to return, as if by magic, as an assortment of European consumer commodities. In this engraving the circuit of international wealth is again rooted in commodities. But what the engraving leaves out, in its representation of commodities exchanged for commodities (as in barter), is the process through which these objects are rendered equivalent through the abstracting lens of money. The invisible relation that allows coffee sacks to become uniform in shape as they are readied for export and allows inflated hoop skirts to seemingly kick up their frills on return ships home, is money, the most shadowy, mystery-filled realm of capital. Behind the commodity fetish, that is, stands an even more blinding form of value: the money fetish. The constant, back-and-forth transformation between commodity and money forms within capitalist exchange is by no means a straightforward affair; instead, the transformation of commodity into money, and money into commodity in the process of circulation carries within itself the possibility of short-circuits and crises. This is not least because money functions as a measure of value (in Marxian terms, "socially necessary labor time"), at the same time as it functions as a lubricating medium of exchange that always seeks to detach itself from its productive base. The more that capitalist exchange expands across spatial divides (through the world market) and across temporal boundaries (through credit), the greater the possibility that money will fail to accurately represent value, leading to all kinds of disruptions and short-circuits in exchange, namely, the periodic full-scale crises that have littered capitalism since its eighteenth-century inception.

These crises of money are especially important when we turn to late nineteenth-century Latin America and its noted history of financial instability. While the region had experienced financial crises since the Independence struggles of the early nineteenth century—financed to a large degree by loans from British bankers—the period between 1870 and 1930 brought unprecedented financial instability to the region. With increasing market integration and liberalization, the Export Age ushered in recurring cycles of financial boom and bust. Cities and regions were dazzled by the "dances of the millions," a powerful metaphor that emerged during this era to capture the illusory and fantastic appearance and disappearance of national prosperity during a cycle of boom and bust. At different moments, coffee or sugar turned into vast profits, "danced" before the delighted countenances of national bourgeoisies, and then vanished into thin air. At the same time, the promise of unrealized agricultural wealth in countries such as Argentina and Brazil provoked frenzied cycles of loans by British banks to national governments. These loans—issued for the most part to finance public works projects—fomented speculative bubbles of unprecedented scale. Euphoria-inducing periods of financial boom, however, were inevitably followed by painful periods of bust, in which credit dried up, national treasuries went bankrupt, and foreign debts skyrocketed.

While the previous two chapters focused on the fantasies associated with commodity production and consumption, respectively, this and following chapters examine the mischief unleashed by money, a form of value imbued with illusory and indeed *fictitious* power. In the present chapter, I focus on the narratives and storylines that stepped in to account for one of the most dramatic cycles of boom and bust experienced by a Latin American country during the Export Age: the Baring Crisis of 1890, in the course of which Argentina, flying high after a huge influx of loans from British banks, suddenly went bankrupt in a stock market crash of unprecedented proportions. After outlining the general contours of the Baring debacle, I turn to study a literary genre that emerged to explain the mischief wrought by "fictitious prosperity": the realist stock market novel. Between 1890 and 1900, a rash of stock market-themed novels was published in Argentina, forming a genre that emerged as a formalized response to upsets in the financial sphere. I center my analysis on the paradigmatic example of the genre, Julián Martel's *La bolsa* (The stock exchange [1891]), as an early attempt by creole elites to reckon with and account for the dramatic *failure* of peripheral capitalist economy. *La bolsa* presents itself as an outraged condemnation of the financial sphere, a position most often accepted at face value by critics. On closer examination, however, Martel's novel itself becomes a vehicle for economic ideology in Export Age Latin America. As a product of crisis, the stock market novels highlight the collapse of fantasies and illusions about capitalist modernization, but in the process creates new ones, namely, belief in the possibility of a more "normal," less crisis-prone (and less financialized) form of capitalism in Argentina. *La bolsa*'s novelistic critique of "fictitious prosperity" and the contradictory solutions to crisis it imagines are the subject of what follows.

A Tale of Boom and Bust:
The Baring Crisis of 1890

The growth of the Argentine economy in the 1880s was, by all accounts, spectacular. For decades, Argentine liberals had struggled to consolidate a liberal state with doors open onto flows of European capital and immigrants. The Constitution of 1853 had sacralized liberal principles of free trade and private property, but it wasn't until the 1880s that the country became fully (if unevenly) integrated into transnational circuits of capital. The transition began in earnest in 1879, when the Argentine state initiated a bloody campaign against the remaining indigenous tribes on the vast pampas to make way for white settlement and export agriculture.[1] Decades of strident calls for European immigration to work these tracts of land and to improve the national "race" were finally heeded: between 1880 and 1910, Argentina's population more than doubled with the influx of masses of Italians, Spaniards and Eastern Europeans.[2] Ranching and agriculture—Argentina's two main sectors of economic production—boomed with increasing European demand for export products like wool and wheat. Encouraged by these developments, European and especially British capital flocked to Argentina. In the space of a decade, British investment in Argentina increased six-fold, from 25 million to 150 million pounds (Ferns 1977, 397). In 1889, this figure represented over *half* of the overseas investments of Great Britain, the world's richest banker and strongest imperial power (Richmond 1989, 11–12). British banks, led by the Baring Brothers, made loans to the Argentine state as well as to provincial governments to support public works projects. These included ports, roads, bridges, and railways, the structures of modern communications designed to increase exports to Europe and act as a stimulus to national industry. Argentine bonds were floated on the London stock exchange, setting off an intense round of speculation on both sides of the Atlantic. Echoing the liberal visionary D. F. Sarmiento's predictions in his essay *Argirópolis* (1850), Argentina was revealed as a country with the potential to become as wealthy and productive as the United States. Investor confidence in Argentina grew to an all-time high, as publications like the *South American Journal* enthusiastically remarked that "no country in the world offers greater advantages to foreign capital" (qtd. in Ferns 1977, 393). How could a country with such abundant natural resources, land, and labor *not* succeed?

Thus began the loan frenzy of the 1880s, by far the most intense round of foreign investment a Latin American country had ever experienced. The period also marked, according to the historian Luis Sommi, the most extreme period of laissez-faire liberalism the country had yet seen, guided by "a new generation of large capitalist landowners allied with foreign capital" (1957, 25). Such high levels of foreign investment dramatically altered life in Argentina. Private companies began to build railroads, ports and bridges to shorten the temporal and spatial distance between Argentine and European markets. The daily rhythms of life were altered most visibly in the capital city of Buenos Aires, where a construction boom permanently altered the city's physical landscape. In his book *El noventa* (1935), the politician and writer Juan Balestra remembered this period as one in which Buenos Aires, "begins its ascent to become the second Latin capital of the globe." In this interpretation, Buenos Aires was becoming second only to Paris, the undisputed capital of the nineteenth century, to become the capital of Export Age Latin America. Balestra writes that the Spanish-style houses of the creole oligarchy were sold and "given over to speculation," as the rich relocated to sumptuous mansions in neighborhoods like Recoleta. Interior decoration, one guided by "virtue" and "utility" gave way to the luxury and ostentation (qtd. in Sommi 1957, 46). Cafes, theaters, department stores, and luxury shops of all kinds provided a proliferating array of goods and services to the urban elite. As a counterpart of this opulence, slums multiplied to the south of the city to house a burgeoning, mainly southern European immigrant proletariat.

At the center of this vertiginous growth stood the Buenos Aires stock exchange, an increasingly important clearinghouse for capital in Argentina.[3] In the triumphalist and self-congratulatory tone that dominated the 1880s, Argentine capitalists viewed the stock market as "the center where the vital pulsations of the country are manifested"; in the words of a report released by the Cámara Sindical in 1887, "it is from this Stock Exchange that the resources that have transformed the Nation have emerged, banks, railways, bridges, ports, public and private credit, all of it is made here, and from Buenos Aires to the ends of the Republic, there is no improvement [*progreso*] that does not find form, capital, and protection under our asylum" (*La bolsa de comercio* 1954, 147).

While the report cited above highlights the productive capacity of the stock market, generating ports and railways, this institution was just as noted for its delightfully magical aspects. With the financial boom, the vagaries of the stock market began to alter the rhythms of everyday daily life in Buenos Aires, as "everyone"— ranging from stockjobbers and bankers to society ladies and their servants, according to commentators of the era—followed the rising and falling values of national currency, *cédulas* (land mortgage bonds), and shares in joint-stock companies. Francisco Ferreira relates that "[t]here was no Herculean task [*obra de romanos*] for whose realization a corporation was not formed in twenty-four hours, with millions and millions in capital" (1890, 16). Land became the site of particularly intense speculation, and there was no parcel, arable or not, that didn't find a buyer, since prices only went up. Newspapers dedicated whole pages to notices of land auctions, which became the favored reading of the public (Balestra, qtd. in Sommi 1957, 43). In the growing stock market bubble—one of the first of its kind in Latin America—speculation became an end in itself: the point of buying *cédulas* was not to get involved in the production of commodities (say, to plant wheat and export it), but to buy it for resale at a higher price. The only bad deals were the ones that didn't get made.

But then, in July 1890, the president of the Argentine National Bank informed Baring Brothers that the state would be unable to meet its quarterly obligations. The ensuing crisis shook the London Stock Exchange, almost bankrupting the venerable house of Baring. This eventuality was only avoided when a consortium led by the Bank of England stepped in as a lender of last resort. The Argentine state had no such luck and was held to paying an astronomical hard currency debt. Full-blown panic ensued on the Buenos Aires stock exchange as individual investors tried, to no avail, to sell off now worthless securities. The entire national economy, dependent on an intricate web of transatlantic credit relations, came to a complete standstill. Political turmoil followed on the heels of economic meltdown; a coup toppled the laissez-faire government of Miguel Juárez Celman.[4] The Argentine state defaulted on its loans and was forced to concede its most valuable asset—railways—to its British creditors. Argentina's remaining debt obligations were then transferred to another set of foreign banks (led by the North American firm J. P. Morgan). The destabilizing effects of the Baring Crisis spilled over into other countries of Latin America, contributing most notably to the Brazilian stock market crash of 1892, known as *Encilhamento* (literally, saddling-up).

A country once predicted to become as wealthy as the United States was in the course of a few months bankrupted, its credit ruined, its railways confiscated, and with few prospects for getting out of debt. The Baring Crisis of 1890 was not the first time the Argentine state had gone bankrupt, nor, unfortunately, would it be the last.[5] What was new about the crisis of 1890 was its intensity and scale. From a position of soaring hopes and aspirations— magically turned into money by the stock market—the country's elite was suddenly forced to stare bankruptcy in the face. The sheer calamity of this event provoked desperate attempts on the part of modernizing elites to explain how the mess had been created in the first place. The moment of euphoric speculation thus gave way to a more sobering, somber moment, demanding answers to a set of urgent questions: How had this happened? What were the signs (for in hindsight, there were always signs)? And most important, who was responsible?

The Stock Market Novel

One of the most significant responses to the Baring Crisis came in the form of a realist novel, Julián Martel's *La bolsa* (The stock exchange [1891]). The novel, which focuses on the rise and fall of a speculator named Dr. Luis Glow, was published in serial form in the Buenos Aires newspaper *La Nación* a year after the crash, as the country was still reeling from its effects. Martel was the pen name of José María Miró, who before the Baring Crisis had worked in the same newspaper as a journalist. In marked contrast with the fantasies of export production and import consumption studied in previous chapters and with the optimistic assessments of Argentina's growth in the 1880s, *La bolsa* represents the disappearance of national wealth into an invisible and abstract void. In its opening pages, a relentless wind blows over the city of Buenos Aires, thrashing everything in its path. Gusting from the southeast, the wind, anthropomorphized as alternately capricious and cruel, twists palm trees, batters "for sale" signs, and even shakes the bases of equestrian statues of patriots in the city's main square. The wind comes to stop only at the stately doors of the Buenos Aires Stock Exchange, the principal setting of the novel. Here the relentless movement does not stop, however, but now takes the form of the agitated businessmen and speculators rushing about on foot and in carriages to close another day of business. In what is possibly the best-known passage from Martel's novel, a throng of hucksters and beggars line the exchange. Most prominent among them are those "parasites of our riches that immigration brings to our shores from the most remote regions," including "filthy Turks," "idiot Bohemians" with crying children, and a cast of shrieking newspaper hawkers, peddlers of falsified oil paintings (1891, 35). This disorder forms the inverse of the fantasies of "progress" and "civilization" examined in the past two chapters and intensifies only as the narrator's gaze moves into the interior of the stock exchange. This space is one defined by physical contamination, through the "promiscuity of types and promiscuity of languages" circulating in the main hall (39). It is also a space of abstraction and mystery. The bodies of speculators sway to and fro, as if moved by invisible "electric currents" (1891, 40). All eyes are fixed on the blackboards of the Exchange, which throw "sinister" shadows onto the back walls.

At the height of the 1880s boom, the stock market was viewed as a space of production, whence according to a report from 1887 "all the resources that have transformed the Nation have emerged, banks, railways, bridges, ports, public and private credit" (*La bolsa de comercio* 1954, 147) After the crash, however, the wealth generated by the stock exchange disappears into an uncontrollable windstorm. While the moment of boom allowed for a confidence in this institution, the moment of bust creates deep anxieties surrounding the invisible and abstract forces through which wealth is generated and destroyed. Understanding the precise mechanisms through which seemingly solid wealth *disappears* from the nation's borders becomes a matter of utmost importance.

The stock market, Martel's omniscient narrator relates, is home to "inexplicable phenomena that repeated themselves every day, and whose cause was a mystery" (1891, 64). One of the main objectives of *La bolsa* is to explain these phenomena and discover the causes behind national financial calamity. After visualizing the trajectory of the uncontrollable windstorm rushing over the city, *La bolsa* proceeds to tell the story of Dr. Luis Glow, the son of an English immigrant, as he gets rich on the stock market, only to lose everything—including his life—in the ensuing crash. Glow is accompanied in his rise and fall by his beautiful and fashionable wife, Margarita, as well as by a host of unsavory and corrupt business associates, ranging from corrupt government officials and immigrant swindlers, to the German-Jewish banker Filiberto Von Mackser, the object of one of the most overtly anti-Semitic portrayals in Latin American literature. Glow's prosperity, the novel notes from the first chapter, is not meant to last: after depicting the free-flowing, easy money of the stock market boom, the novel follows him down the "maelstrom" of the stock market crash. All of a sudden, Glow's easily gotten wealth disappears, leaving him not only penniless but heavily in debt. Unable to raise money, he settles accounts with the only thing he has left: his own life. The last image of the novel is that of a female monster devouring Dr. Glow, as she proclaims "Soy la bolsa" ("I am the Stock Exchange/bourse," 242).

In Argentine literature, Martel's *La bolsa* is considered one of the most important works of the "Generation of 1880," a group of writers whose works coincided with the consolidation of liberalism under the governments of Juan de Roca and Miguel Juárez Celman. Working in genres ranging from the studiously frivolous "causerie" (Lucio V. Mansilla) to the naturalist novel (Eugenio Cambaceres), authors of this generation provided a wide-ranging set of literary responses to rapid modernization. Previewing the tone employed in the stock market novel, these texts were often denunciatory. In López's *La gran aldea* (The big village [1884]), for example, nouveau-riche immigrants and luxury-addicted women are viewed as antisocial elements who threatened to destroy order: the final image of the novel is that of a baby burning in a mansion after her mother has left for the theater. Cambaceres's *En la sangre* (In the blood [1887]), in turn, used a Lombrosian framework to diagnose the criminal tendencies of Italian immigrants through the memorable figure of Genaro.[6] These representations, as several critics have shown, already show a questioning of Argentina's liberal project: Sarmiento and Alberdi's dream of hardy, frugal immigrants from northern Europe is countered by depictions of the racially *inferior* elements arriving in Argentina from the southern and Eastern margins of Europe. Similarly, the liberal dream of "civilization" through increased commerce with Europe, mainly through the export of wheat and cattle products, had resulted in all kinds of uncontrollable excess. As a culminating subgenre of the Generation of 1880, the stock market novel would continue to identify sources of danger to the nation as it careened into an unstable and unequal modernity. In the stock market novel, however, dangerous elements such as luxury and immigration would be subordinated to the stock market as the chief representative and indeed cause for instability and disorder. With the crash of 1890, the invisible and yet materially palpable forces of *finance capital* could be identified as the chief danger facing the nation, from which other undesirable outcomes had sprung. Hence in the opening of *La bolsa*, immigrant bodies are cast as the physical counterparts of the invasive and violent financial wind whipping through the streets of Buenos Aires. Similarly, the luxury of the mansions, stores, and theaters of Buenos Aires is framed by *La bolsa* and other novels of the period as a symptom of a much larger problem: the free-flowing, but ultimately illusory wealth generated by the stock market.

Martel was not alone in turning to the novel to explain the mysteries of the stock market. Between 1890 and 1900, a rash of novels about the Baring Crisis was published in Buenos Aires, in what is known as the "cycle of the stock market."[7] The name given to these novels, that of the "cycle," is fitting, since it represents a specific moment in the financial cycle, in which Argentine elites no longer speculated in stocks and bonds, but in a metaphorical kind of speculation, producing stories about the calamity that had just occurred. In addition to Martel's *La bolsa,* novels organized around the speculative fever leading up to the crisis include Manuel Bahamonde, *Abismos* (1890); Segundo I. Villafañe, *Horas de fiebre* (Hours of fever [1891]); Carlos María Ocantos, *Quilito* (1891); Eduardo de Ezcurra, *Buenos Aires en el siglo XX* (Buenos Aires in the twentieth century [1891]); Alberto del Solar, *Contra la marea* (Against the tide [1894]); Eduardo Gutiérrez, *Lanza, el gran banquero* (Lanza, the great banker [1896]); Pedro G. Morante, *Grandezas* (Grandeur [1896]); and José Luis Cantilo, *Quimera* (1899).

Aside from *La bolsa,* the only two novels of the cycle that remain widely available are Villafañe's *Horas de fiebre* and Ocantos's *Quilito,* both of which follow the same generic contours as *La bolsa.* Told from the perspective of an omniscient narrator, their linear plots are focused on a single male speculator whose rise and fall coincides with that of the national financial edifice. In *Quilito*, the eponymously named character is a spoiled and luxury-addicted young creole who wins then loses big in the stock market; rather than face a life of hard work after the crash, he commits suicide. In *Horas de fiebre*, Alfredo personifies "[la] fiebre de especulación que consumía a todos" ("[t]he speculative fever that consumed us all" [1960, 16]). This mention of consumption, in turn, prefigures Alfredo's demise; after going bankrupt, he learns he has tuberculosis and kills himself. Formally, all three novels bear a striking resemblance to the spiky movements of a stock market graph, in an overlay between economic and literary apparatuses of representation.[8]

Like the financial crisis itself, the stock market genre was not confined to Argentina, but also made an appearance in Brazil and Chile, countries that also experienced severe reversals of fortune at the turn of the century. In Brazil, the Viscount of Taunay—a novelist and erstwhile stock market speculator—published *O encilhamento* (The saddling-up [1893]), a novel that focused on the Brazilian crisis of the same name that had been spurred by the Argentine debacle. In Chile, the period of financial boom and bust surrounding the country's nitrate export economy was chronicled in Ventura Fraga's *Krach!* (1903), a phonetic rendering of the English word "crash." And a great portion of Luis Orrego Luco's well-known *Casa grande* (Big house [1908]) takes place around the stock market crisis.

The Argentine stock market novels are also contemporaries of Zola's much better-known *L'argent* (Money [1891]), the French naturalist's study of the speculator Siccard's scheme to sell shares in a company designed to colonize Palestine for Christians.[9] The Argentine novels are chronological predecessors of Frank Norris's *The Pit* (1903), which revolves around Curtis Jadwin's attempt to corner the Chicago wheat exchange. Zola's *L'argent* has frequently been cited as a model for *La bolsa,* and much discussion of the novel has revolved around the extent to which Martel's version corresponded with the program of French naturalism.[10] This line of inquiry, which tends to place the Argentine novel in a derivative and/or incomplete position versus the European "original," has the additional disadvantage of overlooking the ideological and aesthetic significance of *La bolsa* within its historical conditions of enunciation. Long before the publication of *La bolsa,* Latin American authors had been concerned with the mysteries of financial speculation, a preoccupation that, as Richard Rosa has shown, manifests itself in particular ways in nineteenth-century Latin American literature (n.d.).[11] Hence even though it is true that Martel read Zola's *L'argent* and seems to have borrowed liberally from it, I will maintain that its treatment of the financial crisis deserves attention for the window it gives us onto the global financial system from the vantage of one of its peripheries. Just as finance capital traversed the globe, so too did the stock market novel; in each case, this travel occurred under different circumstances, and with wildly different effects. Before we take leave of the relationship between the putative European "original" vis-à-vis its Latin American "copy," we might note that *L'argent* ends with the ruin of Siccard, but not of the financial system as a whole. The same ending is repeated in Norris's *The Pit,* in which the ruined main character disappears from the scene, but trading goes on just as before.[12] In the Latin American stock market novel, by contrast, the calamity is so great that the entire system comes crashing down, and with it the social universe depicted by the novel. In this context, the only end possible is, to return to the ending of *La bolsa,* engulfment by a monster.

Fiction and Fictitious Capital

Ricardo Rojas, one of the founders of modern literary studies in Argentina, calls Martel "one of the principal founders of the Argentine novel" and hails *La bolsa* as a faithful "portrait of Buenos Aires society in the crisis of its puberty," written from a position of "civic sadness" (1925, 680). Heralded by Rojas and other early critics as a truthful and disinterested account of the crisis, it was later criticized by commentators on these same grounds. The novel's over-earnest didacticism, forced plot measures, and overbearing narrative voice transformed the novel into a *novela de tesis (romàn a thèse).* Marked as severely flawed in aesthetic terms, the novel has nonetheless persisted within discussions of Latin American and Argentine literature on the basis of its historical and ideological importance, especially as the "anti-immigrant" novel par excellence (Fishburne 1981; Foster 1990; Viñas 1971), or as marking a more general crisis of Argentine liberalism in the late 1880s (Niemeyer 1998). Beyond literary studies, *La bolsa* is invariably mentioned as capturing the climate of freewheeling financial speculation at the end of the 1880s.

La bolsa, then, is often judged as an inferior piece of literature, but one that nonetheless highlights different elements of fin-de-siècle Argentine culture. And while viewed as ideologically misguided in its racism, the sincerity of the critique of financial fraud and corruption is rarely questioned. I will return to the question of race and racism in *La bolsa,* but for now I want to question the straightforwardness and/or naiveté assigned to this narrative. For to accept the sincerity of *La bolsa* as an antifinancial tract is to overlook the novel's own inconsistencies and contradictions in the realms of economic and literary representation and with this, the fictions about capital that the novel itself generates. If on one hand, the novel denounces the financial sphere as a place where truth is manipulated and distorted through speculation, the creative representational techniques employed by Martel open the novel itself to the same critique. That is why, given the great lengths to which *La bolsa* goes to represent a false, manipulated, and indeed "fictitious" social reality created after the image of financial speculation, this realist novel ultimately rests on foundations of credit and belief that are just as shaky and illusory.

Employing a set of tropes that date back to Britain's eighteenth-century "financial revolution," *La bolsa* and other stock market novels highlight finance capital as an illusory and indeed fictive form of wealth.[13] As we have seen in the opening pages of Martel's novel, illusion has trumped all sense of reality: invisible wind currents move to their own accord, fantastically drawn church spires come in and out of sight, and numbers appear on the blackboard of the exchange as if drawn by a disembodied arm. References to the theater, to masks, and to deceptive appearances abound in the novel, as false wealth allows people to pretend to be who they are not. The French aristocrat Fouchez, for example, emigrates to Buenos Aires, forms a puppet theater, and then goes on to become a swindler on the stock market; once the crash hits, he dons a disguise and escapes on a steamer back to France. All of the spaces depicted in the novel—from Glow's office to the theater to the boulevards where the rich parade their wealth—are coded as spaces of deception and dissimulation. This falsity, in turn, is coded as

distinctly feminine in its excess and danger. This old trope, which
runs back to reinventions of the goddess Fortune to "Lady Credit"
(L. Brown, 2001; 109–15) in eighteenth-century Europe, animates
La bolsa as the "siren song" of wealth, which culminates in the male
speculator's engulfment by a female monster. Orientalized referents combine with feminized ones to reveal the stock exchange as
"[la] cueva de Ali Baba" ("Ali Baba's cave"; [1891], 83).[14]

La bolsa's pervasive references to excess illusion, theater, and
imagination in the economic sphere (and in the social sphere at
large) serve as the primary object of the novel's critique: the form
of value Marx felicitously named "fictitious capital." In volume 3 of
Capital, Marx uses this term to refer to credit monies not backed
by actual commodities, but rather by a promise to produce them
at a later date. This capital is rendered fictitious through its relationship to temporality; because it has not yet been produced, its
realization depends on collective belief in its eventual realization
(1991, 525–42). Before Marx, Simonde de Sismondi had called this
type of value "immaterial capital," which he further defined as "the
capitalization of the future," and "the exchange of reality against a
hope" (qtd. in Perelman 1987, 181–82).

The fictitious and immaterial qualities of credit hail directly, in
turn, from the inherently representational qualities of money itself.
In the first volume of *Capital,* Marx undertakes a painstaking analysis of the duality of money as both a measure of value and a medium
of exchange, functions that allow accumulation to take place at the
same time as they open the possibility of grave disturbances in the
sphere of circulation. In its role as measure, money is the "universal equivalent," the ideal third term through which the value of all
commodities can be represented (1976, 184); as medium, money
lubricates the whole process of exchange by streamlining the vast
number of transactions occurring at different moments and in different locales. "Circulation bursts through all the temporal, spatial,
and personal barriers imposed by the direct exchange of products"
(209), to "sweat money from every pore" (208). At the same time,
however, while money circulates through the economic system as a
representative of value, allowing money to beget money, it cannot

stand on its own as value. Money, that is, is a measure and medium of value, but it itself is not value. As the process of exchange speeds up and expands to incorporate more and more transactions across time and space, value and its representational form can diverge from one another, to create great profits but also potentially wide disturbances within the sphere of circulation itself.

The divergence between value and monetary representations of value are nowhere more visible—and potentially explosive—than in the modern credit system.[15] The creation of this system, Marx recognized, was absolutely necessary to the functioning of capital accumulation on a global scale. Along with permitting long-distance trade, the credit system lends enormous flexibility and velocity to exchange by permitting not only already-realized values to circulate in the marketplace, but *future* ones as well, on the basis of their expected realization at some later date. Why wait for a crop to grow when its expected yield can be lent as capital in the here and now? Land on which a railroad is predicted to be built can similarly be sold in anticipation of its future value. David Harvey, following Marx's discussion of fictitious capital, writes that capital, constantly reaching its limits in the production process, finds a temporal and spatial "fix" in the form of credit (2006a, 267–68). Fictitious capital reaches across time and space to increase the rhythm with which surpluses can be created. As in the discussion of money above, the inherent advantage built into this sped-up process of accumulation, however, is also its inherent disadvantage. The increasing separation between commodity production and credit greases the wheels of commercial transactions and absorbs money that would otherwise have nowhere to go. But this very proliferation allows the value of fictitious capitals to reach what Marx termed "insane heights of distortion" (269), hence creating the conditions for a speculative bubble to emerge. So long as the cycle is reproducing itself, fictitious values can be the basis for the generation of real wealth: stocks and bonds bought and sold on the stock exchange become profits plowed back into the system. The utter ease with which this reproduction of wealth takes place is astounding, and frequently cast in today's parlance as investor "euphoria." The problem with fictitious capitals becomes apparent, however, once *belief* in their ability to yield profits is shaken, setting off a chain reaction in which fictitious capitals evaporate. This is the other, inevitable, side to the temporal relation established by fictitious capitals as discussed by Marx: once the bubble bursts, the very illusory power that had motivated speculation in the first place can now be identified not only as fiction, but as an unfulfilled promise, or a lie.

La bolsa emerges from the latter side of the temporal divide between the proliferation of fictitious capitals and their evaporation in the course of the crash of 1890. Fictitious capitals had evaporated, leading Martel to judge that the whole period of speculation had itself been a giant fiction. The term "fictitious" is used in *La bolsa* to describe speculative capital as both illusory and false. And on a larger level, the term "fictitious" brings us into the realm of literary production, allowing us to examine the imaginative apparatuses at the heart of *both* aesthetic and monetary economies.

In the first part of the novel, set in the midst of heavy speculation, Glow has a brief moment of prophetic realization, expressing concern that the entire country has been seduced by "fictitious abundance." With the crisis, however, the fantasy of wealth is revealed as the traumatic reality of poverty. In tracing the failure of national promises to mature in the realm of production, *La bolsa* gestures toward a second meaning of "fictitious" as not only illusory but fraudulent. In a key scene in *La bolsa,* Dr. Glow, with some prodding by his associates, agrees to participate in the creation of a fake joint-stock company. The idea, as presented to Glow, is to raise money by selling shares in a construction company that promises to build a new city. Money is to be generated, then, on the basis of a false promise: that of a "fictitious city" (*ciudad ficticia* [1891], 69). The plan is presented to Glow by the French swindler Fouchez, who relates that the scheme involves buying a parcel of land close to Buenos Aires, then building flimsy houses, "to allow people to think that they form the basis of an important *future* population." The French *future,* italicized as a foreign word, highlights the temporal element that is key to the fraud. After the foundationless houses are built, the plan involves hiring hundreds of vagabonds to masquerade as "bakers, shopkeepers, shoemakers" in order to give the settlement "the appearance of life and movement" (70). After generating (false) belief in the project through advertising, its founders would float shares on the Buenos Aires stock exchange, and cash them in before dissolving the company. The articulation of this plan gives Martel a chance to stage fictitious capital as a lie knowingly perpetuated by individual speculators; it also sets the stage for the "correct" moral response to such fraud. Presented with this project, Glow—whom the omniscient narrator assures us is at bottom a healthy man corrupted by the stock market— enters into one of his periodic but always short-lived fits of civic outrage. Shadowed by a statue of the Roman citizen Cicero in his law offices, Glow immediately objects that the scheme is robbery. Ciceronian virtue is cast aside, however, as Fouchez assures Glow that this type of business deal is "the order of the day," accepted by the business community at large when money supplies exceed legitimate opportunities to employ them (71). In the same chapter, the narrator shows how Glow himself is duped into investing in a fake chartreuse factory by an acquaintance in a fake mustache, a scheme that will contribute to his eventual bankruptcy. Here the novel seeks to illustrate that in a climate of heavy speculation, any distinction between fraudulent and legitimacy is rendered moot, since all investments, even those in a fake construction company, will provide yields, at least for a time. With the crash, however, those taken in by the swindle will be left with nothing.

The plan to sell shares in a "fictitious city" allegorizes the process by which use-values (houses, land) are rendered sheer exchange-values under heavy regimes of speculation. It is not coincidental that this plan involves the settlement of land: in the bubble of the 1880s, land itself became an instrument of specula- tion through the *cédula,* or land mortgage bond. Land, we should remember, was what Argentina had in plentiful supply under theo- ries of trade advantage. This natural advantage became even more evident after the bloody army campaigns of the late 1870s and early 1880s forcibly removed indigenous peoples from the pampas. In this case as in others, a period of real violence—referred to in the Marxist tradition as "primitive accumulation"—serves as a support for speculative financial ventures. It was precisely after the Argentine state had extended its territory through dispossession that British investors became excited about the nation's possibilities for economic growth. The promise was that the country would become a major exporter of agricultural products to Europe. This happened, but with a side effect that is present wherever capital is invested: speculation. Real production, that is, occurred in tandem with the financialization of land values—both in Buenos Aires and in rural areas. This made it so that, for a time, commodity production was wholly unnecessary to turning a profit. The stock market crash, however, revealed the baselessness of speculative wealth. Railways, farms, buildings, and whole cities had been conjured in the imagination but had not actually been built, making it seem, in hindsight at least, that Argentine speculators had been running a con game of vast proportions. Buenos Aires, under the sway of speculative wealth, itself took on the aspect of a "fictitious" city.

In *La bolsa* as well as in other stock market novels, the ability to diagnose the "fictitious" foundations on which modern Argentine society had been built is accorded to the omniscient narrator, a key element of nineteenth-century realism. The presence of the narrator is especially forceful in *La bolsa,* as a voice of truth and virtue in the midst of the widespread duplicity and falsification represented in the novel. This narrator knows exactly who is lying in the moment of utterance, and who, by contrast, is telling the truth (Viñas 1971, 83). Similarly, the narrator can tell noble intentions—such as the creole speculator Ernesto Lillo's desire to lift his poor mother from poverty—from evil ones; most notably, a Jewish-led conspiracy to dominate the earth's financial system. As an example of this narrative will to clarity and control, the omniscient voice identifies speculation as the "tinsel cape that speculation and administrative abuse had thrown over the shoulders [of the nation], a cape that sooner or later had to fall forever, taking with it—like the tunic of legend—the bits of flesh of those who had worn it" (1891, 34). This voice knows—indeed, has always known—that fictitious capital is fake, corrupt, and false. Going back in time, to the agitated moment of speculation, the novel itself pretends to tear away the tinsel cape, and reveal a gold-like truth.

And yet, this stern, all-knowing narrator condemns the excesses of fictitious capital *in a novel,* which as a system of representation bears parallels to the object it critiques. This contradiction is similar to the one identified by Richard Rosa in his reading of the Puerto Rican novelist Zeno Gandía's *El negocio* (The business [1920]), in which "Narrating the business transaction means exposing oneself to the same type of rhetoric, dissimulation, fraud, swindle, and deceit that characterizes its object" (2007, 96). As representational apparatuses, both fictitious capital and *La bolsa* as a novel about fictitious capital rely on credibility (or credit) for their effectiveness: in the first case, the credibility of the security; and in the second, the credibility of the omniscient narrator in his narration of events, motives, and actions. Like the *cédulas* circulating in the stock market, *La bolsa* is composed of a stack of papers that asks to be accepted at face value. This is problematic to say the least, since the entire novel is dedicated to showing how it was possible for the value of papers such as *cédulas* and bonds to have been manipulated and inflated through representational practices. Moreover, the narrator—as a disembodied and invisible presence—mimics the unsettling wind-like, vaporous quality of fictitious capital the novel takes as its object of denunciation.

Several critics have explored historical and formal connections between literary production and credit-based forms of wealth such as paper money, stocks, bonds and debentures. Marc Shell argues, for example, that literary and monetary economies are homological in that both rely on forms of credit: "Credit, or belief, involves the very ground of aesthetic experience, and the same medium that seems to confer belief in fiduciary money (bank notes) and in scriptural money (created by the process of bookkeeping) also seems to confer it in literature. That medium is writing" (1993, 7). Patrick Brantlinger notes, in turn, that "[m]oney and fiction, both representational systems relying on credit, are also often interchangeable" (1996, 144). The novel, a genre that rose to prominence together with the rise of credit-based forms of wealth in eighteenth-century Britain, has long been linked with precisely the kind of runaway imagination that Martel's novel rejects.

While going to great lengths to show us the ways in which value had been manipulated and distorted on the stock exchange, the narrator of *La bolsa* demands trust in his singular perspective. In this way, the novel rejects fictitious capital as an illusory form of wealth just as the novel embraces *literary* fiction as a mechanism for telling "the truth" by way of a stern omniscient narrator. It is in this vein that Brantlinger has called fictional realism "the most hypocritical of all literary modes" (1996, 87), repudiating the bourgeois money economy while relying on its same structures of belief. In *La bolsa,* to believe that the social universe condemned in the pages of the novel is false, we are required to believe that the narrator's words are *not* false. Or as Derrida remarks in his reading of Baudelaire's short story "Counterfeit Money," we are asked to take the narrator "on credit" (1992, 100). And yet the common reliance of both money *and* literature on apparatuses of representation opens the possibility of counterfeit forms of value: "So what can . . . the title 'Counterfeit Money' mean? What does it give itself for, that is, what does it make itself out to be? How can or should we take it? Its place and its structure as a title leave a great indetermination and a great possibility for simulacra that open the field precisely to *counterfeit money*" (85). In similar fashion, Martel's novel, by providing a critique of fictitious capital *in a work of fiction*, opens the field to fictitious capital. And yet Martel, clearly a less playful author than Baudelaire, seems to want us to take his narration at face value, thereby suppressing the novel's parallels with fictitious capital. This suppression, I argue below, is absolutely crucial to what I see as the novel's ideological significance: its attempt to repair or restore belief in the ruined financial system.

A Literary Supplement

The process through which *La bolsa* set about repairing trust and belief in the economic sphere is highlighted through its genesis and publication. As noted, the novel first appeared in serial form in the leading Buenos Aires newspaper *La Nación* just months after the crisis, signed under the pseudonym Julián Martel. *La Nación* was founded by the venerated liberal intellectual and army general Bartolomé Mitre. Some critics have maintained that Martel's critique of speculation coincides in part with the editorial position of Mitre's newspaper, which opposed the laissez-faire policies of Roca and Juárez Celman that favored an emerging financial sector (Niemeyer 1998, 133). And yet, as we have already seen, it was only *after* the stock market crash that Miró/Martel was able to articulate this critique, suggesting that *La bolsa* was not the product of a fixed ideological opposition, but rather of contingent historical events. Critics have long noted that José María Miró had covered the stock market as part of his reporting duties, and many suggest that he gambled and lost money to financial speculation (even that he had done so to impress a woman).[16] What is clear is that once the stock market collapsed, Miró the reporter assumed the identity of Martel the novelist, and immediately came to denounce the excesses of speculative wealth.[17] Martel, a surname used in French and Spanish, comes from the Latin word for "hammer"; the choice of pseudonym is fitting on two levels, corresponding at once with the wrath and utter lack of subtlety of his narrative voice. The adoption of a literary pen name was common practice in Latin America as elsewhere, and as such does not warrant attention. What does warrant attention is the fact that the author of a novel that insists so adamantly on tearing masks, capes, and fake mustaches from its characters should alter his own identity in telling his fictional story. There is of course nothing automatically duplicitous in assuming additional identities, in writing or in any other realm of social life. The truth-value of literature and other symbolic forms never lies in their sheer documentary capacity, but rather in their ability to recombine and represent social life in illuminating ways. And yet in the particular case of *La bolsa,* we are faced with a narrator who insists on banishing artifice while asking us to disavow our knowledge of the artifice of novelistic form. We are asked to knowingly suppress our knowledge of the doubleness of the narrative voice and to accept its transparent sincerity.

The heavy-handed insistence on sincerity is not simply an effect of literary naïveté or lack of skill, as is frequently argued. Rather, I want to suggest that it has a compelling ideological function, one that can be glimpsed only if we reconnect the novel to its immediate context of enunciation. Just as we are asked to forget that Martel the novelist was once Miró the reporter and perhaps speculator, the reader is allowed to forget/disavow his or her own participation in the gigantic swindle represented in the novel's pages. The transformation of Miró the reporter into Martel the novelist was accompanied by an even more significant transformation in the form of the knowledge offered by the newspaper itself. With the publication of *La bolsa,* newspaper space once given over to eagerly followed stock quotes, land deals, and financial analysis was suddenly given over to a *fictional* account centering on those same indicators, but now cordoned off from the rest of the news page with a thin horizontal line typical of *folletínes.*

Nineteenth-century newspapers had long dedicated space to serial narratives, and so the appearance of fictional forms in the pages of *La Nación* wasn't new. What is noteworthy is that the newspaper, in publishing *La bolsa,* allowed for a complete about-face in the representational forms through which economic "reality" could be expressed. For whereas the newspaper's earlier function had been to present truthful and transparent information about trading (reporting on the arrival of loans, the formation of joint-stock companies, and the ever-rising price of *cédulas*), the crash revealed the wealth accepted as real to have been an illusion. As a consequence, doubt was cast on the supposedly objective information that had been relayed by *La Nación* and other newspapers in the lead-up to the crisis. *La bolsa* itself intimates that newspapers had been complicit in fomenting belief in the growing bubble. In the opening scene, the "promiscuous" crowd includes a reporter who "distills" the conversations he overhears at the stock exchange to produce "sensational" reports with information that could make or break speculators (1891, 38). Aside from Martel's possible implication of Miró the journalist as a producer of "sensational reports," the citation above questions the newspaper as an institution operating on the basis of transparency and objectivity. Martel's denunciatory novel, from this standpoint, could appear as a normalizing mechanism within the newspaper itself, at least a temporary one, with the ability of reconstituting truth (or at least the *possibility* of truth) for readers. In order for this to happen, the division between fiction and reality had to be reaccommodated: a corrosive form of fiction that had masqueraded as reality—fictitious capital—was countered by a special kind of fiction, one with access to the "truth" behind the economic collapse. In the course of a crisis, what was accepted as reality is revealed to be a fiction; and in the case of *La bolsa,* a fictional genre is charged with reestablishing a principle of reality in the social universe. On a metatextual level, *La bolsa* might be read as a giant retraction of the supposedly truthful information published in *La Nación* just months earlier. That this retraction took the form of a novel attests to the fact that apparatuses of economic representation (like the newspaper report) were in such disrepair that only a fictional genre such as the novel might go back in time to sweep away the lies and reinstate a principle of truth. We might go as far as to say that the novel stepped in as a kind of backup system for representation of the economic sphere in a time of widespread doubt and disbelief.

That the novel itself marked a new moment in economic representation in the aftermath of crisis can be gauged from the very positioning of the text in the pages of *La Nación.* During its run, the serialized novel at the bottom of the newspaper page, speaking of the past but uncontaminated by its lies, positioned itself to tell the real story behind the news. Formalized literary discourse appears as contained, even as it forms part of the newspaper, revealing a larger dialectic between literary and journalistic discourses at the end of the nineteenth century, as at once discrete and mutually dependent.[18] On the one hand, the fact that literary and journalistic discourses were not wholly separate at the turn of the nineteenth century makes it possible for the *folletín* to become a site of economic knowledge. Because of this closeness, the novel is able to continue the production of economic knowledge begun earlier in *La Nación,* now with a modified claim to truth and objectivity and from a wholly different perspective. On the other hand, the incipi-ent *distinction* between literary and economic discourse made the novel an apt vehicle for post-crash reflection. The novel offered a form of representation that was safely outside of the daily opera-tion of the financial sphere, in a way that journalistic reportage, economic essays, and advertisements were not. In part, this was because incipient discourses of literary disinterest, most famously under the rubric of *modernismo,* were casting art as poised against economic "interest." The pretense to artistic disinterest is explicitly postulated in a key scene in *La bolsa,* in which a poet descends from his clichéd garret to see the Buenos Aires elite, drunk with speculative wealth, parade through the streets in their carriages and finery. The poet, struck by a prophetic vision, suddenly sees a "maelstrom" open up, splitting carriages into thousands of pieces and engulfing "magnates" and "prostitutes." This prophetic vision, which calls directly on Edgar Allan Poe's *Maelstrom,* lends special authority to literary discourse; the "poor poet" ignored because "he isn't a trader" *(bolsista),* is the only one able to see the com-ing crash (1891, 152). This patina of disinterest, in turn, shines over the novel as a whole through the voice of the narrator, who claims a similar visionary role in separating truth from falsity, and virtue from corruption.

And yet, as suggested earlier, the truth offered up for examina-tion by *La bolsa* did not result from sheer civic or aesthetic disin-terest, but rather from a much more contingent set of factors, chief among them the time sensitivity of fictitious capital itself. Contrary to the image of the visionary poet, whose poetic disinterest allows him to predict the market crash, the novel itself can articulate this perspective only after the fact. This temporal distinction between "before" and "after" contributes to parallel shifts in literary form (from reportage to the novel), authorial identity (Miró to Martel), and, most importantly, moral response (from agitated optimism to serene outrage). The shift toward a vocabulary of morality per-forms an ideological function, for it allows the novel to restore the *possibility* of truth and virtue within the very sphere it condemns. This emphasis on morality also allows Martel and other authors to blame the crisis on specific individuals and behaviors, as explored in the next section.

Narrative Solutions

The Baring Crisis forced the Argentine nation into painful and traumatic bankruptcy; in the midst of this outcome, one of the ideological tasks of *La bolsa* was to identify and secure remaining sources of value with which the nation might initiate its process of recovery and regeneration. As noted above, the course of any financial crisis is marked by the evaporation of fictitious capitals. Credit monies freeze, and market agents are suddenly forced to pay their debts. Because of the widespread climate of disbelief, neither securities nor commodities will be accepted as payment: only hard cash will do. Marx describes this process with a wonderful religious metaphor: the credit system, he writes, is "essentially Protestant" in its *faith* in abstract and invisible forms of capital; once crisis hits, however, Protestants once again become Catholics, insisting on the material embodiment of wealth as cash. In this way, "the credit system does not emancipate itself from the basis of the monetary system any more than Protestantism has emancipated itself from the foundations of Catholicism" (1991, 592). In times of financial boom, "Protestants" are willing to accept an abstract and distant God in the form of stocks and bonds; when the crisis follows on the heels of doubt, "Catholics" want to touch, feel, and see their God in the form of hard cash. The irony here, of course, is that hard cash, much like the icons of Catholic faith, is itself a fetish. Yet for a bourgeois economy, "hard cash" becomes the embodiment of true value in the aftermath of crash, at least until Catholics gather the courage to become Protestants again, signaling the beginning of a new round of speculation.

La bolsa performs an adjustment in belief similar to the one outlined by Marx in that its condemnation of the financial world is itself the *product* of crisis, and as such part of an ideological project aimed at restoring confidence in the economic sphere. From the ashes of falsification, the novel promises truth from the tinsel torn from the flesh, a new form of "gold" materializes in narrative form.

Through this premise of true value, *La bolsa* emerges as a kind of therapy for financial crisis, not simply because its mechanisms of plot and narration allow for a better understanding of the mischief wrought by fictitious capital, but because the novel itself allows the reader to experience the crisis from the position of moral and epistemological certitude. To return to Marx's metaphor, it allows former "Protestants" to become chastened and now-repentant "Catholics." At the same time, the novel positions itself as exterior to the corruption of the financial world, even as it positions itself as a new site of economic knowledge. As a backup system for an ideological system in severe disrepair, the novel—from a position of literary and civic *disinterest*—poses its own "solutions" to crisis.

Solution One: Jewish Lies and British Truths

One of the ideological solutions to severe economic crisis proposed by *La bolsa* is a racialized understanding of fictitious capital, which posits British Protestants and Argentine Catholics in a face-off against a third term: "the Jews."

The liberal Argentine state was founded on racialized notions of citizenship. Beginning in the 1870s, the state launched a wide-scale immigration scheme to "improve" the Argentine race. Already in the 1840s, thinkers such as J. B. Alberdi and D. F. Sarmiento had railed against the perceived ineptitude of Spanish *creoles* and *mestizos* in the realm of commerce and urged the swift incorporation of European immigrants. The Desert Campaign of 1879 was waged in the name of the irredeemable "savagery" of indigenous peoples, who needed to be removed to make room for productive white settlers. In liberal imaginaries, the ideal immigrant was from northern Europe; in reality, the vast majority hailed from Europe's southern and eastern margins.

By the 1880s, creole elites sounded alarms that the nation had attracted immigrants from the wrong parts of Europe. *La bolsa* marks the peak of anti-immigrant hysteria in Argentina, joining its critique of the dangers of finance to the dangers of unselective immigration, and depicting southern and eastern Europeans as "parasites" of national wealth. It is because the stock exchange operates in the vaporous realms of fictitious capital that this novelistic attempt to track its movements focuses on visible bodies, inscribed with racial and sexual difference. Fictitious capital as a form of value, then, becomes inextricably linked to categories of race, gender, and sexuality, particularly through the contaminatory figure of the Jewish banker. A key element of the extreme reductionism of *La bolsa* is its identification of a Jewish conspiracy to control Argentine finances, as exemplified through the machinations of the banker Von Mackser (a baron's title bought from an impoverished German aristocrat). Revealed by the all-knowing narrator to be an envoy of the Rothschild dynasty (a name that, as Werner Sombart notes, came to denote the "Jewish influence" over the financial world at the end of the nineteenth century; [1911] 1951, 99), Von Mackser functions as the very personification of fictitious capital. Depicted as effeminate, duplicitous, and disloyal, the Jewish banker represents the excesses associated with financial speculation (Martel 1891, 53).[19]

La bolsa's reliance on fantasies of the Jews as agents of and metaphors for money is, of course, not unique to the Argentine context but instead forms part of a much wider repertoire of intersecting discourses of race, nation, and capitalism in Europe and the Americas.[20] Indeed, as Dr. Glow remarks, in one of the moments of the text in which the protagonist's voice is not contradicted by the omniscient narrator, the problem of the Jew is the problem of modern society at large, characterized as "the deaf, silent, slow invasion; the silent, subterranean, frightful conquest of modern society" (121). Glow, while himself held in the thrall of speculative money, is accorded the authority to identify the real threat to Argentina in "the Jews." As the son of a British immigrant father and creole mother, Glow bears a solidly "white" racial identity, the truth of which is externalized in his "hermosa cara de hombre del Norte" ("handsome face of a Northern man," 117), a loving description that reveals Glow as the ideal immigrant subject, and transforms his financial corruption into a secondary feature of his persona. While the effeminate, disloyal, and parasitic Jewish banker operates as a stand-in for the fraud and duplicity of the financial world, Glow represents a different kind of racial "stock," a term whose etymology in English points simultaneously toward the abstract realm of securities as well as to the biological realm of reproduction and breeding. Whereas Von Mackser is biologically and ontologically associated with the excessive and contaminatory qualities of fictitious capital, Glow represents a biologized form of value. The place of "the Jews" in *La bolsa* is that of embodied referents for fictitious capital: racially compromised, morally corrosive, and eternally mobile. This scapegoating allows Glow to be cast as a victim of the financial crisis he helped to create.

Martel's somewhat predictable symbolization of the problem of finance as a Jewish problem is rendered even more contradictory by the fact that it seeks to preserve a fantasy of British investment capital as productive and stable in contradistinction with an unstable, mobile, and parasitic "Jewish" kind. Since Independence and especially during the last quarter of the nineteenth century, Argentina had formed part of what many historians have called Britain's "informal" empire, exercised through trade arrangements and loans. British immigration, on the other hand, was small in comparison with financial investment—50 million pounds on the eve of the crash (Ferns 1977, 397). The project of Argentine modernity was literally and figuratively in debt to British capital, as Roca himself recognized:

> I have always had the greatest affection for England. The Argentine Republic, which will one day be a great nation, will never forget that its present state of progress and prosperity is due, in great part, to English capital, which does not fear distance and which has flowed into Argentina in substantial quantities in the form of railroads, streetcar lines, settlements of colonists, the exploitation of minerals, and various other enterprises. (Qtd. in Burns 1983, 139)

This statement, issued by Roca at the height of the "loan frenzy" of the 1880s, heralds British capital as fearless, loyal, and, above all, productive, instantly transforming itself into railroads, streetcars, and settlements. After the crash, Martel's response to the breach between expectation and reality is that the finance capital that had arrived to Argentina must not have been "British" at all but "Jewish." This even though the crash of 1890 was known as the "Baring Crisis," after a bank that in European imaginaries had long been identified as "Christian" in contradistinction with the Rothschild group. Underscoring this point, Philip Zeigler writes as the first sentence in his chronicle of the House of Baring: "[t]he Barings were not Jews" (13).[21] The putative "Jewishness" or "Britishness" of finance capital is of course not the point. To the contrary, the point is that *La bolsa* holds on to the possibility of making this kind of distinction.

The Baring Crisis dramatically increased Argentina's dependence on the British empire, and yet *La bolsa* never points blame in the direction of "non-Jewish" British banking interests in Argentina. Quite the contrary, this is an attachment that is celebrated, even after disaster strikes. Dr. Glow's associate Ernesto Lillo—coded as the least corrupt character of the novel—announces gratitude toward the British, who "are bringing their capital [to Argentina] with a confidence (*confianza*) that honors us" (1891, 45). *La bolsa*, in this way, allocates blame for the crisis while preserving the bonds of affection between British bankers and the Argentine nation. This narrative resolution prefigures the strategy undertaken by the Argentine government to appease its creditors in the aftermath of the Baring Crisis. First, the state turned over all of the nation's gold reserves in partial payment; when this ran out, instead of declaring a moratorium on payments, the state authorized the sale of millions of hectares of public lands along with the majority of the nation's railways (Sommi 1957, 78). In the meantime, wages declined and thousands of workers became unemployed. The aftermath of 1890 obeyed a general rule of financial crisis in the "rapid concentration of capital" among creditors; what is specific in this case is that the redistribution flowed from Argentine to British capitalists (Sommi 1957, 83).[22]

In the reductive terms offered by *La bolsa*, there are two kinds of capital: one that is "British" and productive, and one that is "Jewish" and parasitic.[23] Even though it was Glow in the novel, and British bankers in reality, who had played the biggest hand in the creation of the stock market crisis of 1890, Martel asserts belief in a racially "pure" and nonexcessive form of capitalist expansion that may assert itself once again after its "Jewish" charge is expunged. The identification with Britain as a model for "honorable" and productive investment is of course totally irrational, given the fact that British loans, and the speculative behaviors of Argentine creole and British speculators, had sparked the bubble in the first place. The split, schizoid character of Glow—who simultaneously plays the stock market while pointing a righteous finger at "the Jews"—corresponds with the split, schizoid quality of Argentine modernity itself: forced to recognize the volatility and excess of the financial system with the crash, the country nonetheless depends on that very system for survival. Hence the illusion cultivated by *La bolsa* that foreign capital, as long as it is the good, productive, "British" kind, can continue to offer Argentina opportunities for stable, lasting growth. This contradiction follows the logic of the Derridean pharmakon, in which the poison (British loans) is repackaged and then identified as a cure (Derrida 1991, 118).[24] With this fantasy, we see that at this moment in history, it is already impossible for even the biggest critics of finance capital to imagine a future for the nation without foreign investment. Along these same lines, it is less preposterous at this moment in Argentine history to blame the Jews than to critique the distribution of global financial power.

Another, secondary, function of *La bolsa*'s anti-Semitic and pro-Anglo fantasy is the total occlusion of a different order of racialized violence: that perpetrated against the country's indigenous inhabitants in the name of European "civilization" throughout the 1870s. During this intense round of primitive accumulation, the state acquired vast reserves of land by brute force; it was this land, transformed into an instrument of speculation, that fueled the financial bubble of the 1880s.[25] Primitive accumulation, usefully renamed "accumulation by dispossession" by David Harvey (2006c, 43), is a constant and ongoing practice that becomes especially significant on the colonial and neocolonial peripheries of capitalism. Here, the most naked and brutal forms of violence not only temporally coexist with but also make possible the rapid rise of the financial sector, a movement we generally do not see in stock market novels of the period.

The violence that occurs *before* abstraction is erased from novels like *La bolsa,* just as it is most often erased from histories of finance capitalism in Argentina and elsewhere.[26]

Solution Two: Refounding the Oikos

In *La bolsa*, Woman functions as a symbolic "companion" to the male Jewish banker and a source of danger to the male Anglo–Creole subject.[27] The novel ends with Dr. Glow, in the throes of a nervous breakdown, imagining himself being devoured by a female incarnation of the stock exchange. For a moment, the woman beckoning him seems like "la criatura más hermosa que habían contemplado sus ojos" ("the most beautiful creature his eyes had ever seen"). Once he is locked in her embrace, however, she grows "asquerosas patas provistas de largas uñas" ("disgusting paws with long fingernails"), and her breast sprouts long, thick hair (1891, 242).

Just as preexisting anxieties surrounding race could be channeled toward explaining the financial crisis, so too could those surrounding gender. Aided by positivist medical discourse, the rapid modernization of the 1880s was frequently encoded in gendered terms, as traditional "angels of the home" found their negative counterparts in images of prostitutes, adultresses, and temptresses.[28] In the course of financial crisis, Martel's novel shows, femininity—and women's bodies—became available as metonyms for the excesses of the financial system itself. The association was not new. As J. G. A. Pocock has shown, for example, credit and finance in eighteenth-century Britain was widely perceived as the encroachment of contingency and fantasy into the polis, a transformation often equated with "the ascendancy of the passions and the female principle" (1985, 114). Laura Brown, in turn, has shown that authors such as Daniel Defoe invented "Lady Credit" as the hysterical mistress of Britain's financial markets, characterized by instability and volatility (2001). These associations appear throughout *La bolsa* and other stock market novels. At the same time, metaphors centering on sexual reproduction gesture toward problems in the monetary economy: the scene inside the stock exchange had been characterized by the "promiscuous" mixture of bodies and languages, and male speculators heed the "siren call" of the market. These metaphors hail from associations between the instability of the stock market and that attributed to women, but also from the stock market as a site of uncontrollable libidinal desire. Sex and money become inextricably tied as systems of (re)production. Because of this reproductive principle, the stock exchange is so frequently associated with women's bodies. In Spanish, the name given to the stock exchange, *bolsa* (like *bourse* in French), is a feminine noun whose original meaning is "purse." Marc Shell has shown that purse plus its monetary contents has been linked with the female womb in Western culture since medieval times (1995, 30). And ironically, although Argentina's very name signifies metallic wealth, the "purse" is empty of silver and will not reproduce more; instead, it consumes creole men.

The link between heterosexual reproduction and stock market speculation is not only metaphorical in *La bolsa*, however, but carries over to the novel's imagining of the individual household as the foundational unit of bourgeois society. The etymology of the word "economy" hails from the Greek *oikos*, or domestic household. In *La bolsa* as in other stock market novels, the domestic household stands in metonymic relation to the economy as a whole. Short circuits in the national economy are allegorized by short circuits in the sex-gender system. These short circuits, in turn, are provoked by out-of-control female desire, signified to a large degree by women's unquenchable desire for luxury. This feminine threat, posed by wives, is all the more dangerous because it resides not outside, but within the *oikos* itself. If in patriarchal society women function as objects of exchange and reproduction, *La bolsa* works to show that this basic mechanism of masculine sociability is compromised and in need of repair.

Describing a party held by Glow and his wife Margarita, the omniscient narrator weighs in on the ornamental appearance of the young women of Buenos Aires. Observing "physiognomies reddened with poisonous ingredients" (1891, 139), the implicitly male observer laments "the artifice of the dressing room, which has begun to introduce itself among us" (140).[29] Whereas the male *modernista* writers studied in the previous chapter had celebrated luxury while attempting to avoid its feminized and commercialized connotations, the stock market novel identifies female consumption as a threat to the cohesion of the republic. Anxieties about women's consumption is of course not unique to stock market novels, but rather runs through *fin-de-siglo* Latin American literary production, in texts ranging from López's aforementioned *La gran aldea* (Argentina, 1884) and the Uruguayan novelist Lola Larrosa's simply titled *El lujo* (Luxury [1889]) to the Puerto Rican writer Carmela Eulate Sanjurjo's *La muñeca* (The doll [1895]). What is significant about the denunciation of feminine luxury consumption in *La bolsa* and other stock market novels is that it identifies *domestic* economy as a site of intervention into the political economy of the nation. Women, the narrator of *La bolsa* urges, must stop "decorating" their flesh, and he exhorts them instead to "read good books," or study "the science of the domestic sphere" (1891, 140). Home economics is offered as a solution for stabilizing the *oikos,* and, in larger terms, the national community it metonymizes. This stabilizing mechanism works by reigning in "feminine" energies in the stock market *and* by reasserting male control over women's desires.

Even though Dr. Glow is devoured in the end by a hairy female monster calling herself "la bolsa," this character is given a chance to reassert masculine order in the home during a key scene of the novel. When Glow learns of his impending ruin, Margarita urges her husband to hide his remaining assets in her name or to simply refuse to pay his debts. "I've become convinced that the world only pays homage to money, from wherever it comes. . . . Even the most honorable poverty inspires disdain" (1891, 162). Mirroring the fantasy of the Jewish conspiracy, Margarita's defense of money serves as a foil to Glow's own interestedness, which he is able to disavow when faced with his feminine other. Glow, after all, is the one who abandoned his lawyer's practice to speculate; he is the one who agrees, after some coaxing, to mount a fake company. But on the night he faces off with his wife, Glow counts himself among the class of men who keep their word, and "the honor of commercial contracts" (164). His wife, on the other hand, misunderstands the word "honor," "an elastic . . . and little-understood word for people of [her] sex" (163). Even though a few chapters later, Glow agrees to another fraud—a rigged horse race—this character is still allowed to identify female duplicity as the real threat to social order. Though Glow is unable to complete his moral regeneration, the novel suggests that it is only through a reordering of the relation between masculine and feminine principles, and between husbands and wives, that the social order might be stabilized in the future.

In *La bolsa,* we are faced with two powerful ideological solutions that succeed in avoiding the actual mechanisms through which financial crisis had been generated in the first place. If the fantasy of the Jewish conspiracy allows a restoration of belief in the very British capital that had sparked the crisis, the fantasy of female excess allows for a restoration of belief in the mainly male agents who, if able to withstand the feminine temptations of the market, might engage in "honorable" business practices in the future. In this way, the production and reproduction of value might be set on its correct course once more. It is thus that the simplicity of Martel's narrative, legitimately criticized on aesthetic and political grounds, becomes a potentially effective vehicle for economic ideology.

Remembering, to Forget

Through parallel fictions of race and gender, *La bolsa* attempts to envision a more "normal" trajectory for capital accumulation for Argentina, free from violent surges and deflations in value proper to the financial realm. What this and other novels of the genre studiously ignore, however, is the fact that capitalism tends *by its very nature* toward instability, volatility, and crisis. The possibility of "fictitious capital" is not simply a product of deviance and corruption; it is inherent within the very concept of capital itself, which can take the form of credit if conditions for its proliferation are ripe. What John Kenneth Galbraith calls "the extreme brevity of financial memory"

(1990, 13) can assert itself only on the basis of the spurious belief that the market has gone back to "normal." The most solid forms of value—land, railways, export crops—can once again become instruments of speculation. But before this can happen, people need to *believe* in the soundness of the larger economic system. Paradoxically enough, the stock market novels, precisely in their *condemnation* of the financial system, position themselves to reestablish this belief by insisting that if certain moral, sexual, and racial adjustments are made, the national economy can be set on its feet again.

This kind of thinking not only ignores the real causes for crisis; it actually creates the ideological conditions under which crisis can happen again. Once people with property believe in the solidity of the system again, they can go on as before. This is the very definition of recovery. Capitalists can reestablish their confidence in themselves, much in the way *La bolsa* reestablishes confidence in poor Dr. Glow, who in another incarnation will surely be set loose into the market again (provided, of course, that British bankers continue to bless Argentina with loans).[30]

The performance of sincere moral outrage in the face of financial calamity did not convince everyone, and to close I turn to a bit of advice from the Brazilian novelist Joaquim María Machado de Assis. Writing in his newspaper column in the aftermath of the Brazilian crisis of 1890, Machado relates that the week's news has revolved around never-ending financial troubles. With characteristic irony, he pleads ignorance to the mysteries of stocks, bonds, and debentures that so preoccupy Rio de Janeiro's upper classes:

> Finance, finance of finance, everything is finance. Wherever I turn, I face the incandescent question of the day. I know the vocabulary, but I still don't understand all of the ideas to which the words correspond; and, regarding these phenomena, it's enough to say that each one has three truthful explanations and one false one. It's best to believe everything. (1996, 134)

While Machado pretends not to understand the mechanisms through which financial crisis is produced, this is an ignorance that, in the case of Latin America's most astutely disingenuous writer, should never be taken at face value. And indeed, the point of Machado's commentary is not to demonstrate his lack of knowledge of financial matters but quite the opposite. For Machado knows that the mysteries of finance reside not in any objective truth, but rather in the manipulation of perception and *belief*. It is thus that each story of financial crisis might hypothetically have at least three "true" explanations. This assertion is immediately undercut by the suggestion that a fourth explanation might be false. With characteristic deviousness, Machado exhorts us to "believe everything," at the same time as the very framing of this assertion encourages us to believe nothing. The biting irony offered by this newspaper column turns out to be a much more subversive strategy for responding to crisis than the sincere outrage offered by the realist novel. While *La bolsa* attempts to subdue the fictitious elements of money, Machado falls prey to no such illusion. Instead, he shows that the financial system—constructed as it is over the shaky edifice of perception and belief—continues to be subject to all kinds of manipulations. The realist stock market novel wants us to believe that the "fictitiousness" of wealth is an aberration under capitalist economies and that it can be banished. This very act of banishing, as we saw, relies on the introduction of new fictions: in the case of *La bolsa* and other examples of the stock market genre, these fictions are repackaged through the realist novel. Machado, on the other hand, recognizes a permanent element of fiction in narratives about money. The truth of money, that is, is fiction. This truth is not grasped by banishing its fantastic elements, but rather in preserving chimera as its state of normalcy.

Chapter 4

MONEY II
Bankruptcy and Decadence

> *Without exception,*
> *international debts and loans*
> *have summoned the specter of*
> *bankruptcy across the continent.*
> —César Zumeta,
> *El continente enfermo*

A Tale of a Ghost Bank

I begin this chapter by telling the story of a ghost that ran across the Colombian nation at the end of nineteenth century: the ghost of Colombia's First National Bank, el Banco Nacional. By 1894, this National Bank had become virtually insolvent, emitting far more paper currency than it could secure in metal reserves. When the National Bank's untenable financial situation became known, the country's small business elite demanded its liquidation. And so, in 1894, a law was passed to liquidate the bank. But it kept operating, and another law was passed to liquidate it. Finally, on January 1, 1896, the Banco Nacional officially ceased to exist. But then, and this is where the ghost story begins, the bank continued to print and circulate money. As related by economic historians Alejandro López Mejía and Adolfo Meisel Roca, in the years following the bank's liquidation, the institution printed an additional 2,999,000 pesos in bank notes, "in spite of the fact that it no longer existed" (1990, 75).

The prospect of a bank that doesn't exist printing millions of pesos in paper notes opens up a host of ontological questions: How can a financial institution continue to operate "in spite of the fact that it no longer existed"? Alternately, how can an institution that prints a precise quantity of banknotes, $2,999,000 to be exact, be said not to exist? But the story doesn't end here. The printing went on well beyond the $2,999,000 to reach many more millions in pesos, in what became the worst crisis of hyperinflation in Colombian history. While remaining in a state of nonexistence, the undead bank printed and printed paper notes until *it ran out of paper*. And so at one point, in 1899, during the infamous War of the Thousand Days, the bank began to print peso notes on paper that had been designated for chocolate wrappers: one side of the note read "República de Colombia," with the denomination in pesos, and on the other, "Chaves Chocolates" (Bergquist 1986, 200). (The reader might refer to chapter 1 to see an 1880s advertisement for Chaves Chocolates.) It is not difficult to grasp the problems this banknote causes: hyperinflated to the point of worthlessness, and with the unwilling endorsement by the chocolate company, it cannot be taken seriously, not even by itself.

But this financial situation was no laughing matter, as runaway inflation, coupled with the destruction of civil war and crippling foreign debt, left Colombia in total financial ruin at the beginning of the twentieth century. The Conservatives who won the War of the Thousand Days decided to put an end to this money madness once and for all. Not by liquidating the bank: this had been done before, and not made any difference. Instead, the new government ordered the destruction of the printing presses at the national mint. The money monster, frequently referred to as *la bestia negra* (the black beast) in anti–paper-money tracts of the era, was finally dead.[1] Or so it seemed. Because everyone knows you can't burn a ghost.

Money is at bottom a system of representation built on belief and trust. But in the financial anecdote I've been recounting, these representational qualities are stretched to an extreme, to the point where the banknote itself becomes unbelievable, and hence unviable as an instrument of exchange. As indicated in the ghost tale of the undead bank and its hyperinflated paper children, belief comes under such strain that it is difficult, if not impossible to repair. Elements of this breakdown in belief are already present in the chocolate wrapper cum banknote. As far as I have been able to gather, no specimen of this note remains; it is just as well, since its absence lends it an even more unreal, ghostly quality. The very act of imagining the juxtaposition of "República de Colombia" and "Chaves Chocolates" on a hyperinflated, near-worthless note is a useful exercise in furthering the story I have been telling in this book. As I have argued until now, the dream of Latin American modernization was predicated on the production of export commodities for the global market; in return, countries would import foreign manufactures in the hopes of sparking industrial production in their own countries. At the end of the 1880s, Colombia was producing more coffee than it ever had for the world market, and as the presence of the chocolate factory attests, some industrialization was beginning to occur. But in the case of the absent banknote, the dream of domestic production was overtaken by the uncontrollable proliferation of the money form.[2]

The result is a challenge to belief in the capacity of money to represent value in a stable manner. How to restore belief, for example, in a national financial system such as that in late nineteenth-century Colombia, in which the representational properties of money have wholly overrun any principle of reality, to such a degree that currency itself baldly admits its own fictionality? Early banknotes in Latin America (from the 1870s onward) had frequently depicted allegories of agricultural and industrial production as visual referents for the nominal value of the money. In Colombia, for example, a one-peso banknote issued by a private bank in 1881 shows a woman picking coffee as a reference to the commodity production that sought to assure the value expressed on its face.

In the case of the paper money issued by the National Bank at the end of the century, however, the accidental appearance of the chocolate factory disrupts the intended vision of production, transforming the note into, essentially, "funny money." The very existence of the chocolate factory attests that some kind of commodity production is going on, but this production is literally eaten up by the voraciousness of the money form. On a larger scale, the banknote's own dream of a smooth transition between commodity

Late nineteenth-century Colombian banknote showing a woman picking coffee. From Hernández Gamarra (2006).

and money as forms of wealth breaks down entirely. An even more serious crisis of belief pertains to the legitimacy of the *state* that issues such money. Ultimately the "República de Colombia"—and not the Chaves chocolate factory—promises to make good on the endorsed value of the banknote, a possibility that becomes more remote with each banknote it issues. Paradoxically, at the same moment the state exercises its power by issuing legal currency, it attests to its own insolvency. Symbolically and materially, the state performs the spectacle of its own bankruptcy.

By the end of the nineteenth century the Colombian state was bankrupt, a fate it shared with many other Latin American countries. As I showed in the last chapter, the Argentine nation went bankrupt in the Baring Crisis of 1890, a process that ended with expensive refinanced loans and the loss of nearly all of its railways. Yet even worse fates were suffered by countries that had never enjoyed high rates of investment from abroad but were nonetheless caught in endless cycles of boom and bust, dependent on single export commodities, interest on debt, and unstable currency regimes. Colombia, together with the countries of Central America, Mexico, Venezuela, Peru, and Bolivia, had all suffered economic catastrophe, with little hope for recovery. The situation was one akin to what Walter Benjamin, writing of the crisis of hyperinflation in 1920s Germany, would identify as conditions under which precipitous decline, and not rise, becomes the norm, and "rescue alone [is] extraordinary, verging on the marvelous and incomprehensible" (1978, 70).[3]

Under increasingly desperate circumstances such as these, which kinds of narratives are possible? As an initial approximation to the emergence of such narratives in Export Age Latin America, we can turn to the words of the Colombian political economist and avowed liberal Miguel Samper, who wrote in 1884 that national treasury reports "almost always recorded good figures" while at the same time as the binding of the volume containing them "sometimes serves the function of a tombstone" (qtd. in Deas [1982, 328]). Here we are faced with the inversion of optimism regarding "young" countries: death and decay set in before the future imagined had a chance to flower.

Bankruptcy, Suicide, Decadence: José Asunción Silva

In 1896, the same year as the Colombian National Bank was to have been liquidated for the first time, the writer and import merchant José Asunción Silva shot and killed himself in his family home in Bogotá. He was just thirty-one years old.[4]

I introduced Silva to the reader in chapter 2 as a double-sided figure: as an artist who helped to consolidate a new aesthetic language under the guise of Spanish American *modernismo,* and as an import merchant who used a similar language to promote merchandise in advertisements for his store. Now I want to take the story in a different direction. For if the commodity fantasies forged by Silva the merchant-artist corresponded broadly with a short moment of elite optimism and enjoyment, his suicide corresponds with a darker moment, one marked by crisis and bankruptcy.

Three years before his suicide, Silva had lost nearly all his property and personal possessions in a highly acrimonious and public bankruptcy scandal. At one point, some fifty-odd creditors were after him to pay outstanding debts taken out against his import business, *R. Silva e Hijo*. The bankruptcy had itself been brought about by a combination of factors: wildly fluctuating prices of coffee affected credit flows and payments, and the paper money regime discussed above made it difficult, if not impossible, for an import business to stay afloat, since commodities had to be purchased in Europe with hard currency, then sold to customers who paid in near-worthless national currency. And then there were Silva's legendary habits of personal consumption: according to a biographical essay by the contemporary Colombian novelist Fernando Vallejo, who has studied Silva's personal accounting ledgers and business correspondence, the artist-merchant continued to order French suits and Egyptian cigarettes for himself even as he sunk deeper and deeper into debt. In a typically sardonic manner, Vallejo proposes that we recast Silva the literary icon as Silva the debtor: "They taught us in grade school that he was a forerunner of *modernismo.* Yes, and of the Latin American debt as well" (1995, 92).

Inevitably, Silva's credit ran out, and his numerous foreign and local creditors demanded that he settle his debts. It is even said that Silva's grandmother was among the angry band of creditors, and that she went so far as to accuse her grandson of hiding assets to avoid payment.[5] His desperation mounting, Silva wrote what is rumored to be a 103-page letter to the man who had cosigned on his loans, Guillermo Uribe Uribe, an old family friend and business associate, to defend his character and credit against the ruthless onslaught of bankruptcy.[6] All to no avail. As in the case of the monetary hyperinflation that would overcome the Colombian nation a few years after Silva's death, insolvency has the effect of generating more and more paper, the value of which stands in inverse proportion to the debt it attempts to cover.

Bankruptcy is a figurative death, marking the inability of the social actor to continue in his or her transactions. Suicide, on the other hand, *is* death. And here, of course, Silva's story is quite different from that of the Banco Nacional: whereas the bank could go

on printing paper long after its official demise, Silva's suicide articulates a grim finality to economic failure, beyond which no further
representation is possible.

In the decades following his death, Silva was transformed
into a legendary figure in his native Colombia and beyond. To no
small degree, this legend turns on Silva's bankruptcy and subsequent suicide. For early critics such as Rufino Blanco Fombona,
Silva was the victim of a provincial bourgeois milieu unable to
understand his *alma de selección* (select soul; 1994, 69). Concha
Meléndez writes that Silva's short, tragic life was waged as a battle
between "Mercury and Apollo," resulting in the triumph of the former ([1938] 1988). Silva's nephew, Camilo Brigard Silva, wrote in an
articled entitled "El infortunio comercial de José Asunción Silva"
his uncle's "extraordinary artistic sensibility" was unsuited to the
management of "low material interests" (1946, 284), a conflict that
could be resolved only through suicide. Through interpretations
such as these, Silva is transformed into one of the first martyred
saints of literary autonomy in Spanish America, as a man whose
fine artistic inclinations were dashed by the brutal cash nexus of
modernizing society. The effect of such a reading is to bring questions of art and political economy together in order to enforce a
strict separation between them: bankruptcy is relevant to a reading of Silva in purely negative terms, as an obstacle to his development as an artist. Contradictorily, bankruptcy constitutes the core
of Silva's identity as a tragic literary figure at the same time as this
very condition is dismissed as a meaningful category for the interpretation of his literary works. That is, insofar as bankruptcy figures
as a sheer *obstacle* to literary production, the artist and his works
are effectively removed from the wider economic context in which
bankruptcy occurred in the first place.

The narrative of disinterest surrounding Silva is particularly
contradictory in light of his enthusiasm for advertising studied
in chapter 2, a commercial practice he pioneered in turn-of-the-
century Bogotá by experimenting with full-page promotions in
El Telegrama and writing experimental ads in verse and episto-
lary form. The narrative of disinterest is also contradictory when

we turn to monetary matters, not only because Silva borrowed money from anyone willing to lend it to him, but also because—as a prominent liberal businessman—he became involved in debates surrounding the paper money regime implemented by the government of the *Regeneración*. In 1887, he published in the Bogotá newspaper *La Nación* two polemics defending the need for free currency exchange (*libre estipulación*), on the grounds that the free flow of credit "is indispensable to all civilized societies" (4).[7] Even more significantly, a reading of Silva that pits the "spirit" of the poet against the "low material interests" paints a fantasy picture of the commercial world of late nineteenth-century Bogotá as somehow solid and stable, when in reality one of its chief defining features was its unpredictability and volatility. The monetary world Silva inhabited was not simply cold and heartless; it was rife with ontological mysteries of the most troubling kind. In short, it was a world haunted by ghosts.

In Colombia and indeed in Latin America, José Asunción Silva is one of the first literary figures to be positioned in body and spirit against the commercial economy in the name of aesthetic value. In traditional readings of Silva, bankruptcy and failure need to be passed over to get to the "real" story of literature. Yet the story of literature, as I've been arguing throughout this book, is wrapped up in the story of economics, even—especially—when it claims the contrary. Moreover, while more recent critics have approached the question of literary modernity from the perspective of professionalization (the ability of the author to make a living from writing, which Silva was not able to do), this approach is apt to overlook how failure itself might have something to tell us about other aspects of peripheral capitalist modernity, such as bankruptcy.[8] Without questioning the ultimate silencing effect of bankruptcy and suicide on Silva, the narrative of literary disinterest and artistic spirit that envelops him to this day is perhaps even more silencing, since it assumes that Silva had little to say about the mysteries of money that resulted in personal and national economic failure. But as I argue, to interpret Silva's bankruptcy as either proof of his artistic disinterest or as sheer obstacle to artistic production occludes the ways in which art might speak through bankruptcy.

The productivity of bankruptcy within artistic discourse is confirmed, paradoxically enough, by the very staging of Silva's suicide. In a carefully staged scene of pathos, the lifeless body of the artist, shot through the heart with a revolver, is often conjured alongside two objects: first, a wallet containing Silva's last ten pesos in paper money; and, second, an open copy of the decadent Italian writer Gabriele D'Annunzio's novel *Triunfo della morte* (1894).[9] What I find most compelling about this scene, beyond its notes of utter desperation, is its conjuring of a European decadent literary text to provide death as the ultimate answer to a near-worthless Colombian ten-peso note. And as I show in the following pages of this chapter, Silva's attraction to decadence, the fin-de-siècle European literary current concerned with decay, decline, and death, can be understood only in light of the extremely precarious economic conditions of the periphery. As such, I will look at decadence as a guiding concept for understanding bankruptcy and failure in late nineteenth-century Spanish America, and I will do so through the decadent novel Silva left behind as an additional component of his suicide scene: *De sobremesa,* written and rewritten in the days following his suicide, and not published until 1925.

Largely dismissed by critics as an unfinished and/or incoherent work until very recently, *De sobremesa* reinvents decadence from a Spanish American perspective, to provide a poetics of bankruptcy on the periphery of global capitalism. The majority of the novel takes the form of the diary of a rich South American poet as he travels through Europe, reading philosophy, contemplating paintings, and collecting life experiences. Hence at first glance, *De sobremesa* seems to have very little to tell us about the economic conditions that dogged Silva until his suicide. Decadence is, after all, a literary current that actively eschewed all aspects of bourgeois culture in favor of the solitary pursuit of aesthetic experience, a proposition *De sobremesa* seems to accept. I define decadence initially as a European fin-de-siècle movement that began to backtrack on the bourgeois promises of infinite progress and social health.[10]

Associated with authors such as J. K. Huysmans and the Goncourts in France, Oscar Wilde in Britain, and Gabriele D'Annunzio in Italy, decadence is most often approached as a marking rejection of bourgeois notions of health, productivity, progress by way of a fascination with sickness, sterility, and decline. The movement also corresponds with a vision of art as solitary pursuit of fleeting aesthetic experience, limited to only the most hyperrefined and neurotic male aesthetes.

At the same time, Silva's novel might seem to tell us little about *Spanish American* society, since it borrows a French aesthetic sensibility to depict a social reality that was nothing like that of France at the end of the nineteenth century. The great majority of the novel takes the form of the European diary of its South American protagonist; the references to art and literature are European (ranging from Spinoza and Nietzsche to pre-Raphaelite painters), as are the fashionable accoutrements with which he decorates his person and living space. Like Silva himself, his protagonist is enamored of European furniture, paintings, and jewelry, and by exotically Oriental stimulants such as Egyptian cigarettes and Cantonese tea. In chapter 2, I discussed how it has been common to approach Spanish American *modernismo*—the wider rubric under which decadence is normally placed in this region—as an "import," as if importing were not a structural and hence organic feature of the region's modernities. The same has been true, for the most part, of approaches to decadence, which early critics viewed as an artificial response to local realities. The logic went (and to some extent still goes) something like this: decadence assumed the existence of a society *old* enough to enter into decay in the first place. The problem of Latin American countries was that they had not yet matured; how, then, could literature register their decline? But once we turn to the realm of political economy, images of decline and death ran rampant to describe currency debacles, national bankruptcies, and interminable cycles of boom and bust. Under such conditions it is more than coincidence that at the same moment in which the economic history of the "young" countries of América was being consigned to the crypt, a literary sensibility obsessed with sickness, death, and decay garnered the fascination of turn-of-the-century authors such as Silva.[11]

Moreover, decadence (as an offshoot of Spanish American *modernismo*), has frequently been criticized for its reliance on European—especially Gallic—referents. *De sobremesa* takes place almost entirely in Europe; Manuel Díaz's Rodríguez's *Idolos rotos* (Broken idols [1901]) and *Sangre patricia (*Patrician blood [1902]) are both organized around voyages between Venezuela and France; and Abraham Valdelomar's novellas *La ciudad de los tísicos* (The city of consumptives [1911]) and *La ciudad muerta* (The dead city [1911]), while set in Peru, are full of either European or markedly Europeanized creole characters. One of the main objections to this Europhilia, as examined in chapter 2, is that it employs foreign models to describe local realities, resulting in a literature that is artificial and/or inappropriate. But this line of reasoning assumes that decadence becomes inappropriate only once it is imported to a new context, when in fact the entire style is rooted in the cultivation of the artificial as an aesthetic principle. Further, even if we accept the charge that Spanish American decadents "imitated" a European style in a non-European context, this gesture itself becomes meaningful in that it posits a concrete *relation* between center and periphery within a larger world system. As I wish to show in my reading of *De sobremesa*, Europe emerges as a site of contradiction for the male creole subject, the passage through which produces sickness, crisis, and failure.

Framings: *De sobremesa*

The premise of *De sobremesa* is the following: José Fernández, a rich creole aesthete, has returned after a long stay in Europe to his South American home (the particular country is never named). The novel opens with a frame narrative, in which José Fernández is gathered with a group of male friends in his luxuriously appointed salon. This is the after-dinner conversation alluded to in the title. The conversation revolves around José Fernández himself, and the strange nervous disorder he has acquired while traveling in Europe. Seeking answers to his malady, his guests ask him to read from his European diary; José Fernández obliges, and the rest of the novel takes the form of his first-person reflections as he moves between Paris, spas in Switzerland, and London, searching for some purpose to which to dedicate his life. Two such possibilities for meaning and direction reveal themselves to José Fernández in the diary: first, a grand scheme to modernize his country; and, second, the pursuit of Helena, a ghostly feminine muse. These two great pursuits, however, are undercut by José Fernández's own mental instability, and his movements are punctuated by frequent and debilitating nervous crises. In an attempt to understand these crises, José Fernández visits the best European psychiatrists, professionals who are unable to properly diagnose his malady. And so, he returns home to the unnamed locale in South America, to the private salon where the novel begins and ends. He has neither found Helena nor initiated his grand modernization scheme; the explanations behind these twin failures are contained in the diary he reads aloud to his friends.

When it was finally published in 1925, *De sobremesa* was surrounded by doubt and suspicion, when not outright dismissal. Early critics attacked Silva's novel (even friends like Baldomero Sanín Cano) as a flawed piece of work, a judgment explained by the fact that the novel had been cut short by the author's suicide. As a means by which to compensate for these imputed flaws, critics looked to the novel in an autobiographical vein, to provide clues about Silva the man. But how could the antihero of *De sobremesa*, an admittedly insane and immoral character, reflect the life of the tragic national poet? More recently, critics have begun to reinterpret this narrative imbalance as meaningful in its own right, as, for example, a master work of ironic citation (González 1994, 1997), or as a novelistic refraction of "anomalous" *fin de siglo* sexualities (Molloy 1997; Montero 1997). Building on these recent readings, I want to turn attention to the ways in which imbalance and anomaly express the contradictions of peripheral capitalist development in turn-of-the-century Colombia. Specifically, I am interested in exploring the striking similarities between José Fernández's imbalanced psyche and the imbalance of peripheral political economy, which instead of reaching balance or surplus, runs in the other direction, toward crisis and bankruptcy.

At first glance, the imbalance José Fernández suffers is not financial in character: unlike the bankrupt Silva, his fictional alter ego is fabulously rich.[12] Indeed, unlike Silva at the time of writing *De sobremesa*, José Fernández does not work to make a living or worry about debt: instead, he draws income from pearl fisheries in Panama and gold mines in the Andes, dramatically removing him from the grave financial woes experienced by Silva. As I'll argue, however, even though this character is rich, his psyche provides a metaphor for economic imbalance and crisis, creating a link between the unquiet masculine self and the wildly oscillatory fortunes of peripheral economies. This metaphorical relation to political economy, in turn, is rendered compelling by the novel's own insistence on economic categories like production, consumption, and exchange in codifying José Fernández's strange nervous disorder.

As noted, the novel opens with a frame narrative, in which a group of men sit together in the aftermath of a scene of consumption, the digestion of a dinner. The novel's fixation with consumption is already present in its first paragraph, a description of José Fernández's luxurious salon:

> Recogida por la pantalla de gasa y encajes, la claridad tibia de la lámpara caía en círculo sobre el terciopelo carmesí de la carpeta, y al iluminar de lleno tres tazas de China, doradas en el fondo por un resto de café espeso, y un frasco de cristal tallado, lleno de licor transparente entre el cual brillaban partículas de oro, dejaba ahogado en una penumbra de sombría púrpura, producida por el tono de la alfombra, los tapices y las colgaduras, el resto de la estancia silenciosa. (1996b, 229)

> Secluded by the shade of gauze and lace, the warm light of the lamp fell in a circle over the crimson velvet of the tablecloth, and as it lit up the three china cups, which were golden in the bottom from the traces of thick coffee, and a cut-crystal bottle full of transparent liqueur shining with gold particles, it left the rest of the large and silent chamber awash in a gloomy purple semidarkness, the

effect of the cast of the carpet, the tapestries, and the wall hangings. (2005, 50)[13]

I cited this opening paragraph in chapter 2 as a key example of the modernist import catalogue, a discursive form where an imaginary interior is filled with flowing descriptions of sumptuous and rare objects. In my previous analysis, the above passage served as the basis for a discussion of an advertisement Silva produced for his luxury goods store in 1890, in which he rehearsed a very similar style of description. The main function of the modernist import catalogue, I argued, was to forge a fantasy of refinement and civilization on the periphery through the consumption and display of European commodities. In *De sobremesa,* however, the fantasy of refinement at the heart of the modernist import catalogue quickly turns in on itself, since excessive consumption is immediately identified as one of the sources of José Fernández's nervous disorder. Fittingly, it is a local doctor in attendance who first identifies José Fernández's malady as linked to "el lujo enervante y el confort de esta casa" ("enervating luxury, the refined comfort of this house"):

> They are the vices you say you're inventing, those Jewels in whose contemplation you spend your time fascinated directly from Canton, the coffee Rovira sends you, chosen bean by bean; the tobacco from the Orient and the cigarettes from Down Under, the Russian kummel and the Swedish krishabaar, all the nice touches of the princely life you lead, and all those little dainties that have replaced the poet in you with a pleasure-seeker who by dint of pleasure is headed Fast for depletion. (58)

If we compare this passage with the languorous description of the decorated interior that opens *De sobremesa,* a very different inflection is given to consumption. Luxury produces not refinement but *over-refinement* resulting in nervousness, emasculation, and even "hysteria." In the diagnosis offered by the doctor, the ingestion of "exotic" substances—Chinese tea, American tobacco and coffee, and Russian liqueur—render the male subject's organism unfit for production and reproduction; instead, his system runs toward depletion. José responds by affirming his identity as a decadent aesthete who eschews "bourgeois" productivity in favor of a life dedicated to sensation. Not only poetry fascinates him, but "everything": "all the arts, all the sciences, politics, speculation, luxury, pleasures, mysticism, love, war . . . the very sensations that my senses demand be ever more intense and exquisite" (55–56).

This commitment to decadent principles of consumption and aesthetic sensation over and against bourgeois productivity opens onto the aesthete's diary. With the opening of this diary, the modernist interior opens onto the locales where objects decorating his salon might have been collected. At the same time, the physical interior opens onto the *psychic* interior of the subject. The diary José Fernández opens provides a window onto the mysterious nervous illness he suffers, which not coincidentally is linked to his trip to Europe.

When the diary begins, we already know that José Fernández suffers a nervous disorder. But nothing prepares us for the utter disorder of the diary itself, whose multiple voices and registers constantly threaten, as Gonzalez writes, to "overflow" (*salirse de cauce;* 1994, 280). The unevenness we might expect from any diary is aggravated to an extreme, however, by the fact that José Fernández is himself driven by contradiction and crisis. Some days he fancies himself a serious intellectual, who reads Spinoza and studies pre-Raphaelite paintings; other days, he disparages himself as a ridiculous *rastaquouère* (an uncomplimentary name literally meaning "hide ripper" given to nouveaux riches Latin Americans traveling in France), or as an effeminate dandy "pirouetting" through Parisian salons and spending hours on his toilette. In like manner, while some days he embraces his identity as a hypersensitive and nervous fin-de-siècle aesthete, on other days he imagines himself a virile captain of industry. These oscillations find their formal counterpart in the unevenness of the diary entries themselves, which change in tone, length, and language depending on José Fernández's state at the time of recording his thoughts. His shifting identities and moods are not accommodated comfortably; instead, they culminate in periodic nervous fits. Transcribed belatedly, these fits provide the outermost limit of the psyche, beyond which no further representation is possible. He reports on October 25, for example, that "these have been ten days of mad activity, with nothing to show for it" (2005, 212); in the next entry, dated January 16, he relates the arrival of another nervous crisis: "I spent ten days out of my head" (213).

It must be noted at this point just how much José Fernández, as a subject overrun by crisis, differs from the earlier heroes of nineteenth-century romantic and realist Spanish American novels, who even in the midst of crisis and failure had nearly always retained their claim to masculine integrity and virtue. Here we might think of Efraín in Jorge Isaacs's *María* (1867), a paragon of stability in the context of the epileptic fits suffered by his Jewish convert cousin. José Martí's *Lucía Jerez* (1885), a novel sometimes studied with *De sobremesa* for its modernist sensibilities, nonetheless creates a morally upright male protagonist in Juan Jerez, a lawyer who stands by in horror as his cousin Lucía picks up a gun to kill her perceived rival. Even corrupted characters like Dr. Glow in Martel's *La bolsa* (1891) offer the possibility of redemption once it is established that the real agent of corruption is the female monster of the bourse.

José Fernández, by contrast, transforms the male protagonist into a roving sign of crisis and illness. Sylvia Molloy has productively approached José Fernández's illness as a case of male hysteria (1997). As a male hysteric, José Fernández confounds expectations that woman, or another feminized other—the male Jew, as in *La bolsa*—should personify crisis. What is perhaps new about Silva's protagonist with respect to his Latin American forebears is that he himself becomes a roving sign of crisis: It is not the Jew, the woman or any other Other: instead, the problem resides within himself; there is no outside. And here the fact that the novel takes the form of a first-person diary acquires importance as a literary form through which crisis is not *externalized* as in *La bolsa,* but interiorized on the level of subjectivity.

A rebours, De sobremesa, and the Psychic Structure of Boom and Bust

One of the major innovations of *De sobremesa* with respect to earlier Latin American texts is, then, that it imagines a male subject who is dominated by unruly *desire* rather than virtue, and whose resulting crises and breakdowns can no longer be displaced onto others but are instead internal to himself. At the same time, the specific dimensions of José Fernández's character are innovative with respect to its French decadent model. It is common practice to note that Silva's novel was inspired to a large degree by the "breviary" of decadence, J. K. Huysmans's *A rebours* (*Against Nature*, [1884] 1998), a novel dedicated to describing the aesthetic experiences of the nervous and over-refined Des Esseintes. The last of an inbred line of aristocrats, Des Esseintes retreats to a self-imposed solitary confinement in a chateau on the outskirts of Paris. The chapters of *A rebours* are not organized around events but around Des Esseintes's contemplation of books, paintings, and objects. In one memorable instance, he buys a tortoise whose carapace he encrusts with jewels, an exquisite rarity he enjoys until the poor creature collapses beneath the sparkling dead weight; in another, he reads medieval manuscripts; in yet another, he outfits a dining room as the interior of a ship, complete with portholes and mechanical fish.

Legend has it that Silva got his copy of *A rebours* on his first and only trip to Paris in 1885, as a gift from none other than Stéphane Mallarmé. Silva brought Mallarmé a hothouse orchid (of the kind that grow in Colombia), and the master of French symbolism gave Silva the novel. (In a twist that resonates with the story of peripheral economic failure I'm telling, Silva's annotated copy of *A rebours* was confiscated in the course of his bankruptcy.) Like other writers of *modernismo,* Silva was enthralled with Huysmans's novel and used Des Esseintes as a model for José Fernández in *De sobremesa*: like his French forebear, José Fernández is nervous, overrefined, and dedicates himself to a life of luxury.[14]

But in other ways, José Fernández cannot help but be different from his French model, with differences that become crucial to an adequate appreciation of the uniqueness of *De sobremesa*'s interpretation of decadent aesthetics. First and foremost, while Des Esseintes speaks from Europe, José Fernández speaks from the periphery, and must *travel* to Europe from a self-consciously extrinsic position. There is thus a temporal and spatial displacement involved in the peripheral articulation of decadence, reflected in the very form of *De sobremesa*: the frame narrative takes place in an enclosed space in South America and opens onto the diary that recounts the protagonist's European travels. While Des Esseintes's only travel consists in moving from Paris to its secluded suburbs and back again, José Fernández's travel is inter- and cross-continental. If for the European subject to become a decadent means to retire from society to quiet solitude, for the peripheral artist it means *joining* European society. And if Des Esseintes languishes for most of the novel in his chateau, searching for ever-more rare experiences that fail to excite him, José Fernández lacks this ennui. Instead, he is always on the move, a mobility whose most important referent is his unquiet mind. Instead of the quietly intense boredom suffered by the French decadent, José Fernández experiences psychic reversals so severe that they border not only on hysteria, but on manic cycles of euphoria and depression. Alternately, while Des Esseintes operates on a principle of slow decline (for which inbreeding is the ultimate referent), José Fernández operates according to a principle of boom and bust.

Throughout the diary, José Fernández suffers what we might identify as *cycles* in which the character alternates between calm and agitation; euphoria and depression, punctuated by frequent crises. Of strong musculature (yet another trait that distinguishes him from Des Esseintes, who is physically a weakling), he nonetheless falls prostrate when his nerves are jangled. All of this resonates with the metaphors economic historians have long used to describe the unstable trajectories of Latin American economies as they integrated into global circuits of capital throughout the nineteenth century. To ground the possible similarities between the up-and-down movements attributed to the individual psyche in *De sobremesa* and to the overall economy in economic history, we might turn to José Antonio Ocampo's classic *Colombia y la economía mundial (1830–1910)* (Colombia and the world economy), a book whose table of contents powerfully registers the circular and repetitive logic of boom and bust. A chapter on export-led growth throughout the nineteenth century includes the following subheadings: "First bonanza (1850–57), fluctuations [*vaivenes*], contradictions and global recession (1858–69); bonanza (1870–73); recession and crisis (1874–77); bonanza (1878–82); severe depression and recovery (1883–92); bonanza (1893–98); severe depression" (1984, 9). What *De sobremesa* offers, I argue, is a representation of a psyche whose up-and-down movements function as a small-scale model of national economic dysfunction. Conversely, we might say that economic life in late nineteenth-century Colombia was so unstable that its ultimate referent was the psyche itself.

The Chimera of Production:
The Decadent's Export Reverie

José Fernández's psyche, I have argued, operates on a principle akin to economic boom and bust, or cycles of accumulation followed by sudden reversals or depletions. This is important because it allows the male creole protagonist—perhaps for the first time in Spanish American literature—to operate as a roving sign of crisis. Unable to balance himself out, though always trying to do so, he emerges in the diary as a male sign of crisis. And as I argue here, this character also emerges as a sign of insolvency. Again, the engagement with insolvency is metaphorical and not literal: as already noted, José Fernández is a supremely wealthy owner of gold mines and pearl fisheries, economic activities that sustain a lavish life of leisure and transatlantic travel. At the same time, however, the instability of José Fernández's psyche plays itself out within a specific set of material conditions. That is, the specific contours of Spanish American economies and polities are never far from the novel's reach, and indeed become important elements of its plot.

The most compelling instance in which metaphorical and real economy intersect comes at a specific moment of the diary, when this subject decides, once and for all, to abolish excess and to become *productive* as an economic agent. Significantly, this productivity is phrased in familiar terms, passing through the dream of modernization studied earlier in this book as export reverie.

Let me set up this episode. While in Paris, José Fernández finds his mistress in bed with a woman; enraged, the diarist attempts to kill her. But the weapon he carries—a small jewel-encrusted dagger—is more of an ornament than a weapon, and this attempt at reasserting phallic power fails. In the aftermath of this attempted crime, José Fernández flees to Switzerland. And it is here, in Switzerland, the land of Rousseanian republicanism and Protestant asceticism that he swears off his attachment to luxury and courtesans as *wasteful* and perverse. Standing atop the Alps, a vision suddenly appears before his eyes. A plan appears to him, "clear and precise as a mathematical formula." First, he notes, he will sell his gold mines, in order to then invest the earnings in U.S. markets. While his capital is working on its own, magically reproducing itself with help from the Astor family, he will travel through the United States "studying the inner workings of American civilization, looking into the wherefores of the fabulous development of that land of energy" (2005, 90). Afterward, he will return to his own country, surveying each province one by one, "researching their needs, studying the best crops for the soil, the potential means of communication, the natural resources" (91).

José Fernández's articulation of this plan reads as a stunning parody of nineteenth-century political and economic discourse. For one, it stages Simón Bolívar's "delirium" atop Mount Chimborazo, in which the Liberator is possessed by the "God of Colombia" and sees a glorious national future unfold. It also cites Andrés Bello's famous "Silva a la agricultura de la zona tórrida" (Ode to tropical agriculture, 1826), as José Fernández promises to locate all unexploited sources of wealth, "from the plantain extolled by Bello in his divine ode to the lichens that cover the polar ice caps" (93). In calling on these poetic and civic referents, his plan unfolds as a parody of the optimistic and hopeful strains of nineteenth-century liberal discourse, which I have named export reverie. Once production has gotten underway, José Fernández notes that he will dedicate himself to straightening out the nation's *financial* health: "In two years . . . I will have hatched a rational finance plan, which is the basis of all government." With this plan in place, the country will, *finally,* become rich: "The country is rich, formidably rich, and has untapped resources; it is a matter of skill, of simple calculations, of pure science, to resolve the problems of the day" (91).

The day will arrive, then, when the country's deficit will become a surplus (*superávit* [1996b, 261]) to be invested in railways and bridges to promote even more transatlantic commerce. Aided by consultations with famed European economists, the country will grow rich, industrialize, and attract waves of immigration. These themes, of course, are not new to Latin American literature; what is fascinating is that the discourse of "progress" I studied in chapter 1 as export reverie had become so codified by the time Silva was writing that it could take on the form of parody. This is without a doubt because by the 1890s, in the midst of devastating economic busts across Latin America, the hopes and dreams of modernizing creole liberals had been dealt severe blows.

José Fernández's fantasy seeks recourse in the outward signs of modernity desired by turn-of-the-century elites: railroads, steamships, Hausmannized boulevards, and opulent department stores. At this point, the plan begins to take on an overly dystopian character, as he toys with the idea of establishing a conservative dictatorship "like that of García Montero in Ecuador or that of Cabrera in Guatemala. . . . Under that dark regime, with its dungeon gloom and inquisitorial evils, the miracle of the transformation I dream of will come to pass" (2005, 96). With this recognition of the necessity of violence to create an economic "miracle," José Fernández's plan breaks from the optimistic platitudes of export reverie to reveal the potentially dark underside of liberal modernization in the neocolonial periphery.

But the real defeat of the modernization plan parodied in *De sobremesa* comes by way of the novel's temporal structure, through which we already know from the beginning that José Fernández has failed at every project he has attempted to undertake. From the opening scene, we know that after his return from Europe, he became neither a captain of industry, nor a political leader, nor a prolific author, but a dilettante. As if to highlight the eventual failure of José Fernández's grand scheme, the novel switches temporal planes after the Swiss episode, bringing the narrative back to the "present" in America: "I was mad when I wrote this, wasn't I?" (2005, 98). While the author has gone to great lengths to make the reader answer "yes," José Fernández's friends vehemently disagree. One of them responds that this moment represents "the only time you've been in your right mind" and imagines what became of the wealth earmarked for modernization. It was spent on luxury: "Truffled goose liver pâte, dry champagne, tepid coffee, green-eyed women, japonaiserie, and wild literary schemes" (2005, 99). At the very moment he is being chastised by his friend for having squandered his fortune, José Fernández is served his third cup of tea, a stimulant he is unable to stop consuming.

While on one hand this scene serves to poke fun at the simple-mindedness of the local bourgeoisie (they can't understand that the megalomaniacal excess of the plan is an extension of José Fernández's mental imbalance), it also points to the failure of this subject to become productive. Once again, consumption plays an important role as both a sign and cause of this failure. For as the doctor makes clear, luxury is consumed at the price of national development; whether or not the narrator and/or author's attitude toward this outcome is positive or negative, the dialogue sets up an explicit causal chain between the production of domestic wealth and its consumption through foreign luxury items.[15] The scene itself enacts this unevenness, through an imbalanced character, whose imbalance is placed in a context of a dream of production and excess of consumption.

Silva's Swiss scene comments on the imbalanced relationship between production and consumption in Latin America, but it also demonstrates that what is "irrational" is not just luxury consumption but "virile" economic production itself. In this way, José Fernández's plan shows that what is insane is living according to modernization schemes that seemed doomed to fail. For as Silva was writing, generations of Latin American *letrados* and states-men had attempted to do just what José Fernández, in his Swiss delirium, was saying needed to be done: export sectors had been expanded, loans taken, and European political economists had been consulted. These kinds of plans, implemented throughout the region in the nineteenth century, however, did not deliver on the promise of European-style modernity. Instead, by the 1890s, every Latin American country depended on unstable monocrop export regimes for income, just as they depended on foreign manufactures and consumer goods. And also by the 1890s, each country in Latin America (like Silva himself) had a sizeable foreign debt or was bankrupt. It is not just the decadent José Fernández, then, who suffers from a malaise involving an imbalance between production and consumption, but, on a larger level, Latin American economies themselves.

And it is here, in invoking the simple, foolproof measures for creating real, lasting national wealth, that the full force of Silva's parody comes through. For even during Silva's lifetime, this seemingly "simple" and straightforward plan *had* been put in place, over and over again. Accordingly, what José Fernández "discovers" as if for the first time faithfully represents the measures taken by governments to create prosperous, stable nation-states over the course of the nineteenth century. But in most cases, this grand plan had not resulted in fabulous riches; instead, it had brought economic *in*stability, paper currency, and astronomical hard-currency debt, as it had to Silva's Colombia.

In rehearsing a plan that had been put into place over and over again, José Fernández's delirium provides an insight into the impossible conditions under which modernization was to take place. For how might a renewed commitment to production be the cure when the system under which production takes place seems to guarantee failure from the beginning? Who would repeat such a plan? On the other hand, how not to repeat it?

Viewed in this light, the scene above the Swiss Alps does not represent a move toward stability for José Fernández; to the contrary, it marks the height of his delusion. In another moment suffused with irony, he assures himself that under his plan, the country's national bonds will become as secure as those of the British: "The theretofore depreciated bonds will be an investment as solid as the consolidated English ones" (2005, 95). Within the conditions established by the novel, this comes off as sheer madness. Yet the novel doesn't merely point to José Fernández's insanity as the reason for the failure of his plan. Instead, it points *to the inviability of the plan itself.*

With the Swiss episode, we see a return of sorts to the civic dream of earlier literary production as well as an attempt at returning to a vision of a stable, productive masculinity as hero of national modernization. What *De sobremesa* seems to know, however, in delivering a wry parody of the language of nineteenth-century modernization, is that these subjects were *already* driven by contradictions: they did not have to bed Parisian courtesans or spend their time contemplating beautiful jewels to reveal that they too suffered imbalance by their very positioning within an uneven and unequal world system. The delirium of *próceres* (founding fathers) and early liberals fuses with the delirium of the fin-de-siècle decadent; the effect is one of estrangement and, simultaneously, recognition. The South American decadent reveals himself as the descendant of these stern, virile, and sincere men (not only of his French model Des Esseintes); conversely, the civic and economic dreams of these foundational figures become infused with mania and imbalance, either because they were always already manic, or because their predictions had failed to come true. In short, given the material conditions of possibility governing the imbalanced male creole subject, production cannot be the solution to the crises suffered by the male creole protagonist. This is because production as imagined by earlier generations of liberal visionaries is revealed as a chimera. The foundational capital fiction of Latin America—that export-led modernization would create vast wealth for nations—disintegrates in the novel. The liberal visionary has become a decadent.

Transubstantiations: Woman, Art, Money

With his grand plan to modernize his country, José Fernández vows to ward off feminized excess in a grand effort to become a productive male subject: "Good-bye Byzantine sensualities!" (*sensualidades de bizantino*) he proclaims, "Now to live the life of a man!" (1996a, 266). But this proposed solution—production to override consumption—only creates new crises. These crises are not provoked by consumption, as his friends back home insist. Instead, in the terms offered by this book, these new crises shift from the realms of production and consumption to conjure the ghostly and uncontrollable aspects of money.

As in the Swiss mountaintop reverie, the novel's treatment of economic crisis is metaphorical, while at the same time tethered to the text's insistence on its material referents. The first step of the Swiss plan is to sell his South American gold mines to British bankers. Like the earlier lettered elites he cites, he travels to London to do so. Hence the protagonist's trajectory within Europe follows him from Paris, the city of luxury and fashion, to Switzerland, a country associated with nature and Protestant asceticism, to London, the world's financial capital. And it is here, in London, that José Fernández will suffer his most serious nervous crisis yet, provoked by the ghostly image of a woman. This woman, named Helena, is simultaneously real and unreal, and material and immaterial. An artistic muse and referent for "pure" virginal femininity, she is also a referent for *money* and its disquieting properties. Frequently associated with gold and with coins, this ghostly presence/absence periodically provokes fits in José Fernández.

José Fernández's first sighting of Helena occurs in the immediate aftermath of the Swiss reverie discussed above. At a hotel in Interlaken, his commitment to production and restraint is interrupted when he meets a courtesan he knew in Paris and falls into bed with her. Enraged that this "Delilah" has seduced him, hence foiling his "plans for a rational, abstinent life," he tries to strangle her (2005, 104). But if continued excess comes in the shape of a woman, so too does the possibility of salvation. After a three-day-long opium binge, he emerges from his room to behold a vision of ethereal femininity in the figure of Helena, a young Italian woman traveling with her father. In the patriarchal imagination of the male aesthete, she is the beautiful virgin amid the whores, who promises a pure and nonthreatening form of femininity.

As critics have discussed, Helena is represents as an aesthetic ideal for the artist in José Fernández. With blue eyes, burnished hair, pallid face, and long, delicate limbs, she appears to José Fernández as a "a young princess painted by Van Dyck," "Anne of Austria in Ruben's portrait," and a virgin by Fra Angelico (106). And then there is her name, Helena, which recalls the legendary beauty of Helen of Troy. This vision of Helena, however, is already obfuscated by José Fernández's opium-induced haze, another indication that the imbalance resides not in the women who surround him but in José Fernández himself.

From the beginning, then, Helena is not quite real. The two never speak, much less touch. Instead, the man's relationship to his muse is displaced onto two fetish objects: a cameo and a bouquet of white tea roses. Helena leaves a cameo decorated with butterflies in the dining room where José first spots her. Later that night, standing beneath Helena's hotel balcony, he glimpses her long shadow. The image recalls Silva's famous poem "Nocturno" (1892), in which the male figure of the poem fuses with the shadow of his dead love. In the novel, José Fernández tosses a bouquet of flowers to Helena's balcony; she reciprocates by tossing a bouquet of white tea roses to his feet. At this moment, he again hears the dying words of his grandmother—"Lord, deliver him from the madness that sweeps him away" (112)—and promptly faints. The next morning, José Fernández seeks Helena, but she and her father have departed from the hotel, direction unknown. José Fernández is thus left with the cameo and the (already dying) roses as proof of the angelic virgin's existence.

Momentarily stabilized by the promise of salvation represented by his new muse, José Fernández travels to London to sell his gold mines, the first step of his grand plan. After setting his plan in motion, he notes, he will do everything possible to locate Helena: "When my Business with the English bankers is concluded I will go and find her there" (114). As we have seen, Jose Fernandez is constantly changing his mind, and so the insistence that he must keep his date with the British bankers before he might look for his true love is significant. In narrative terms, the transformation of gold mines into *gold* as money opens onto the mystery of Helena as referent for value that cannot be secured by the protagonist.

While in London, José Fernández sells his mines to a pair of Jewish financiers, Blundel and Morrel. At first, the money he makes "almost effortlessly" (116) from selling his mines does not propel him toward luxury and sex, as it has in the past. Instead, the presence of Helena's cameo, and crystal box in which he has placed the white tea roses, allow his hands to remain "unpolluted by a woman's touch" (114). He does not spend wildly, only buying an occasional portrait or book, nor does he set foot in a theater or salon, instead preferring "the quiet neighborhoods of the well-to-do bourgeoisie" (116).

While in London, José Fernández convinces himself that he is a model of moderation and restraint. He reads, and works in the ministry of foreign relations, making copies of the letters leading to England's recognition of his country's independence. With great irony, this activity again inscribes José within a larger tradition of Latin American *letrados,* this time to impersonate men like Simón Bolívar and Andrés Bello, who traveled to London in the first decades of the nineteenth century to sell mines and take out the first loans for Latin American independence movements. As Richard Rosa has discussed, Simón Bolívar sold his family's gold mines to British bankers (n.d.) a tradition into which José Fernández inserts himself nearly a century later. In what seems an ironic nod to Bolívar's foundational transaction with Britain, José Fernández's holding company is called "Miranda y Compañía," in reference to the Liberator's Venezuelan teacher.

But as for the independence leaders whom we might collectively call "Miranda and company," who in addition to fighting for Independence created the first Latin American debts, things do not go as planned for the South American agent in London. After selling his mines, he begins to have nightmares about Helena, whom he feels is turning into a "morbid obsession" (119). His sexual appetite—until now held in check by his two fetish objects—once again reasserts itself. José Fernández's Jewish banker Blundell plays the role of financier-pimp and arranges for him to meet a celebrated courtesan. While *De sobremesa* is rife with recognizable fin-de-siècle stereotypes such as the femme fatale and the lascivious Jew, the crisis originates and expresses itself in the creole male subject.

In symbolic terms, the sale of the mines opens on to a sexual transaction, mediated by the very bankers to whom José Fernández made the sale. And while at first this transaction allows José Fernández to think that moderation and balance are to come, he faces an uncontrollable urge to put his contained energies back into circulation: "my very blood cried out to me, ablaze with desire; my nerves stretched out from three months' continence" (121). But for this subject, circulation always means crisis. In the apartment of his would-be lover, he spots a bouquet of white tea roses on the floor. The roses morph into a vision of José Fernández's grandmother and Helena, their two profiles merged as if on "an old medallion" (121). The courtesan, the roses, and the coin-like apparition of Helena-grandmother are too much for José, who, true to form, suffers another nervous breakdown.

While sexual in nature, the resulting breakdown also functions as an allegory of *financial* crisis. That the heterosexual economy should be deployed to symbolize financial crisis is not coincidental. As Luce Irigaray pointed out some time ago, women are the commodities par excellence in patriarchal societies, not only insofar as their exchange cements relations among men (a system of hom(m)o-sexuality in Irigaray's pun), but also in their *form*. Like the commodities analyzed by Marx, women are measured in terms of both use- and exchange-value; while use-value corresponds with the mundane, corporeal qualities of the body, exchange-value opens up the "metaphysical niceties" generated through exchange. Once a woman goes "on the market" as a commodity, her value is determined in relation to an ideal form of womanhood that will always remain extrinsic to her (1985, 176). In the scene from *De sobremesa*, it is precisely this ideal side of woman, associated with money, that provokes crisis. Put alternately, the material aspects of woman-commodity dissipate into the ghost-like aspects of woman-as-money. The noncoincidence of woman as tangible object and woman as ghost reveal striking parallels with problems of value in a transnational arena. For what happens over and again in *De sobremesa* is that the imbalanced subject is haunted by an ideal form that flashes up in moments of crisis, only to disappear to the nervous twitches of the male subject's body. Further insights into the nature of José Fernández's malady are revealed as he oscillates not only between states of euphoria and depression but becomes increasingly susceptible to ghostly visions of value that always remain beyond his grasp.

In subsequent moments of the diary, José Fernández reveals that he visits two psychiatrists, one French and the other British, who both suggest cures for regulating his system. In exchanges that are both comical and poignant, the European doctors try to tell the South American dandy how to become a more rational and balanced subject. The comments of the British psychiatrist, Dr. Rivington, are especially noteworthy in this regard. For Rivington, who is compared to Herbert Spencer, the answer is to find Helena and marry her, thereby closing the wild breach between ideal and material forms that so troubles his patient. The doctor proposes that his patient leave luxury behind, reproduce with Helena, and immerse himself in a "vast industrial venture . . . an ironworks, a factory," or "a giant agricultural investment" (2005, 130). This new plan for stabilization rests on the materialization of Helena—an abstract referent for value—followed by the realization of value in the sphere of production. But what the doctor doesn't know is that Helena *can't* be materialized; she is a referent that forever escapes José Fernández's grasp, both as woman and, allegorically, as artistic and monetary value. Moreover, the plan the doctor has outlined bears striking resemblance to the productive cure proposed by José Fernández himself, before the unpredictable appearances and disappearances of Helena begin to wrack his system. José Fernández seems to understand the futility of the plan offered by the doctor, and he breaks off treatment. In an ironic turn, he notes that though he had paid for a full course of treatment, the doctor doesn't refund the money. "I thought he would return my check, but no, he kept it, and no doubt he will use it well. All the better" (144). Read allegorically, the British doctor tells the peripheral subject how to balance himself out by transforming his chimeras into real-ity, and, once again, to *produce*. The doctor then charges him for the advice, even as his patient knows that the cure is no good: first, because he has already thought of it himself; and second, because the conditions for stabilization—the transformation of *ideals* into material reality according to a bourgeois logic of (re)production—remains an impossibility in the peripheral context from which José Fernández hails.

Near the end of the novel, José Fernández experiences his greatest crisis yet when he discovers a gravestone inscribed with Helena's name in a Parisian cemetery. He loses consciousness, for several days this time, and on waking decides that the only option left to him is to return to his home in South America, where we find him at the beginning of the novel. The solution to the mystery of Helena comes neither through production nor reproduction, but through her literal death. Along with this, the two possibilities for stabilization offered by the novel—the modernization scheme and the feminine artistic muse—have failed. Back home, the severity of the crises he has suffered without fail in Europe have waned, but so too have his illusions. The frame narrative that bookends José Fernández's travel to Europe is thus posited as a "present" governed by conditions of failure and impossibility. The silence and calm of the salon where the after-dinner conversation takes place is predicated on a figurative and real death.

Jules Barbey d'Aurevilly famously remarked in a review of *A rebours:* "After such a book, the only thing left for the author is to chose between the muzzle of a pistol and the foot of the cross" (qtd. in Huysmans [1884] 1998, 197). J. K. Huysmans chose the cross: ten years after writing *A rebours,* he joined a Trappist monastery and lived the rest of his life as a devout Catholic. José Asunción Silva, by contrast, chose the first of the two of the first options, killing himself shortly after finishing his novel. Once again, the Spanish American version of decadent aesthetics goes further than its European site of inspiration, this time with grim finality. And while we cannot reduce Silva's anguish to painful material circumstances, his novel continues to provide a rich and compelling metaphorics of the conditions of *impossibility* under which Latin American modernities emerged and, all too often, failed.

Aesthetics and Regeneration:
Or, a Gold Coin Called "Hope"

While the pathos provoked by Silva's dramatic and tragic suicide remains a touchstone for hagiographies of the poet, the resolute, if at times ironic, fatalism of *De sobremesa* did not provide a lasting response to bankruptcy and penury in turn-of-the-century Latin America. Instead, the self-consciously dead-ended route of decadence ran its course, to be replaced by a much more robust discourse concerning the regenerative power of aesthetics. I am speaking here of the post-1898 literary current known as *arielismo,* so named after the Uruguayan writer José Enrique Rodó's *Ariel* (1990), an essay that remains a touchstone in Latin American literary and cultural history. Employing the conventions of classical oratory, the essay is staged as a speech by Prospero of Shakespeare's *The Tempest* to a group of young men. Dedicated to "the youth of América," the essay preaches a message rooted in the regenerative possibilities of aesthetics and culture, shorthanded as "spirit."

After our reading of the decadent aesthetics proposed by *De sobremesa,* the turn toward a classically conceived notion of aesthetics is noteworthy, as is the invocation of *youth* as a site of cultural and civilizational regeneration. On one hand, as others have noted, this tendency marks rejection of excess conjured by *modernismo,* especially in its decadent inflections, with its return of balance, harmony, and hierarchy as guiding principles. Against "the violence of bad taste," beauty: "To give meaning to beauty is a work of mercy" (1991, 42). We will note that this sense of harmony found in aesthetics depends on the symbolic elimination of feminine excess: Prospero speaks to an all-male audience, and Ariel is a spritely unsexed being.

Rodó's essay is most often read as a response to the United States occupation of Spain's two remaining colonies, Cuba and Puerto Rico, an aggression that set off alarm bells across the continent. It is also famous for its recourse to a racial-civilizational discourse of Latin "spirit" against the crass "materialism" of Anglo-America, in which the spritely "Ariel" is posited against the hulking "Caliban" of the North. One of the *many* contradictions of the essay is that an English play is chosen for the extended metaphor. Another is that the anticolonial thrust of Rodó's essay explicitly entrusts the cultivation of "spirit" to white male elites in line with a Greco-Latin definition of culture. In so doing, *Ariel* not only falsely identifies the Latin American "we" as white and European; it does so while disavowing the material *interestedness* of this very class.[16]

Scholars have long pointed to Ariel's attempt to define regional identity vis-à-vis the "Caliban" of the North by way of a compensatory discourse of aesthetics.[17] I want to propose a slightly different reading in light of the ongoing crises of bankruptcy afflicting Latin American societies at the end of the nineteenth century. Part of what made Rodó's message so attractive to creole elites on the cusp of the twentieth century, I think, was not only that it provided a narrative of cultural identity vis-à-vis the North. Given the unstable and insolvent character of Latin American states, this discourse also succeeded in identifying a form of value that was immune to the fluctuations and crises of the marketplace. The metaphorical "money" it identified in aesthetics couldn't pay national debts, but it couldn't disappear into the winds of exchange, either.

Here it is useful to note that Rodó himself was, like Silva, a subject shaped by bankruptcy. At the height of his celebrity following the publication of *Ariel,* Rodó was hounded by creditors and usurers, his diary expressing a "sensación de angustia que no me cabe en el pecho" (feeling of anxiety that bursts from my chest; qtd. in San Román 2009, 86). This sense of anxiety extended beyond Rodó's personal circumstances to those of the nation as a whole. For if it is true that in the years before 1914 Uruguay became one of the most prosperous republics of Latin America (winning the rotating nomination to the status of the "Switzerland" of the region), it was still subject to great economic and political instability. In the course of the civil war of 1904, the last of many between the country's two main political factions, Rodó vividly evoked this sense of instability. Four years after writing *Ariel,* Rodó wrote a letter to a friend in which he despaired for the political and economic future of his native Uruguay, in the throes of the civil war of 1904: "Nada hay seguro en nuestro bendito país, ni en política, ni en cuestión económica; todo es inestable, problemático, todo está amenazado de mil peligros y expuesto a desaparecer de la noche a la mañana: incluso el país mismo . . ." ("Nothing is assured in our blessed country, not in politics, nor in economic matters; everything is unstable, problematic, everything is threatened by a million dangers and on the brink of disappearing overnight: including the country itself . . ." qtd. in Bennedetti 1966, 53). Nothing was secure, save, perhaps, the promise of aesthetic plenitude offered by *Ariel.*

But if it is the case that Rodó wanted to establish more solid grounds for value, why does he choose an airy, chimerical being— Ariel—to represent it? For Ariel, while invoking "spirit," is *not* in Rodó's essay a chimerical being. Far from it, Rodó's Ariel is figured as a touchstone of stability. As the orator Prospero speaks to the gathered male youths, he gestures toward a bronze statue of Ariel, spritely motion captured as tangible form. The solidity of this bronze statue is in turn likened to that of a *gold coin.*[18] As Prospero closes his speech, he recalls an ancient gold coin he once saw in a museum inscribed with the word "Hope." The image marks yet a new stage in the creole search to secure value in the face of disaster.

The gold coin inscribed with the word "hope" functions as the inverse of the feminine and ghostly referents for value circulating through *De sobremesa.* In order to become a stable referent for value, the gold coin of *Ariel* cannot circulate; instead it remains locked down in a museum (or even better, in the mind of the sage). This coin generates "hope" (a term that speaks to the futuristic temporality of money as a measure of value), but on more solid grounds than those offered by money that remains in circulation: for neither the gold coin nor the bronze statue of Ariel can be adulterated, transformed into paper money, or spun into the deceptive chimera of fictitious capital.

This is not to say that *Ariel* succeeds fully in its stabilizing gestures. The proposition of an all-male community through which

The artist as national currency: the front side of present-day 5000-peso Colombian banknote depicting José Asunción Silva.

value is produced and circulated generates its own specters of imbalance. Additionally, the minting of the coin of "hope" within an *aesthetic* economy protects value from fluctuation and tergiversations at the same time as it restricts its sphere of influence to the self-proclaimed temple of aesthetics. Value can be located and restored, but has to do so in the protected environment of Prospero's room or in a museum. As a cost, aesthetics can no longer purport to fix wider problems, but must accept a restricted compensatory function.

The excision between aesthetic and monetary forms of value thus has a particular history in modern Latin America, one that passes through a special kind of disillusion to arrive at the identification of value in aesthetics. The Dominican critic Pedro Henríquez Ureña, widely recognized as a founder of twentieth-century literary criticism in the region, makes this argument in *La Utopía de América* (1925):

> Our America should affirm its faith in its destiny, in the future of its civilization. In order to sustain it I do not look to the present or future development of material riches, but instead to the fact that in each of our crises of civilization, it is spirit that has saved

Poetry as national currency: reverse of 5000-peso banknote depicting a fragment of Silva's famous poem "Nocturno."

> us, fighting against elements that appear to be more powerful; only the spirit, and not military force or economic power. (1991, 45)

Nonmonetary spiritual value hence serves as an antidote to what Henríquez Ureña calls the "absurd economic organization" of the region.

Epilogue: The Poet's Currency

I began this chapter with the story of a Colombian phantom bank and its hyperinflated chocolate-wrapper banknotes, notes whose funny appearance disturbed notions of value to such a degree as to render themselves unbelievable. The wider historical context in which these banknotes circulated served as a point of departure for the poetics of bankruptcy established in José Asunción Silva's post-humously published novel *De sobremesa*.

Now I wish to close by making reference to another banknote, one whose appearance, I hope, will strike the reader as strange and unsettling in light of the discussion I have developed. This banknote, again from Colombia, depicts none other than José Asunción Silva, on a five-thousand-peso note designed to commemorate the hundred–year anniversary of his death. On the front of this banknote, Silva's face appears on the right, in the midst of luxuriant tropical foliage and fauna, depicted in art nouveau style. On the back, a woman in a long, flowing gown stands in a grove of trees under the light of a huge full moon in an illustration of Silva's famous poem "Nocturno," about a love lost to death. To the woman's right, directly under the moon, an urn appears on which the poem is engraved. This poem, which one critic has called part of Colombia's *intangible patrimonio espiritual* (intangible spiritual patrimony; Cobo Borda 1988, 36), fuses with the value of the money form. Such a fusion makes sense only to the degree that aesthetic and monetary forms of value are recognized as fundamentally different, with the former as the disinterested supplement of the latter. Money and art are separated, that is, so that they might come together in a stabilized relation on the banknote.[19]

With this banknote we are faced with Silva's involuntary endorsement of national currency from beyond the grave. And while not as strange as the chocolate wrapper-cum-banknote, the choice is contradictory to say the least: this is a man who, after all, went *bankrupt* amid national financial disaster around the same time as the repeated failures of the Banco Nacional.

It is just this history of private and public failure that has to be erased so that the note may be accepted with a serenity matching that of the poet's own visage. Once we remember this history, however, Silva's visage has an unintended estranging effect. For Silva, while alive, knew something about the history of Colombian political economy that the banknote must efface to be taken at face value.

Were we to read the banknote alongside of the delirium of *De sobremesa* and its fundamental *disbelief* in the possibility of national solvency under conditions that to a large extent remain in place today, the banknote takes on different meaning.[20] Were we to imagine, for example, that instead of "Nocturno," the bank note were to state José Fernández atop the Swiss Alps, promising good things to come, or this same subject chasing the ghost of Helena, it would take on another meaning entirely. But, in fact, the poem "Nocturno," a poem about shadows, already introduces an element of stability into the note. Hence even in regulating an image of Silva as disinterested poet, a stable signifier of literary value, the banknote itself conjures the shadows that emerge whenever money remains in circulation, especially in a context characterized by over a century of monetary catastrophe.

Walter Benjamin once wrote: "Nowhere more naively than in [banknotes] does capitalism display itself in solemn earnest. The innocent cupids frolicking about numbers, the goddesses holding tablets of the law, the stalwart heroes sheathing their swords before monetary units, are a world of their own: ornamenting the façade of hell" (1978, 87; see also Shell 1995; and Rosa n.d.). If alive today, Benjamin might well have added poets to the list of characters holding forth against the hellfire. And nowhere more than in peripheral, poor nations do the gates of monetary hell threaten to swing open, enveloping those valiant guards who, either purposefully or against their will, attempt to keep them closed.

Chapter 5

EXPLOITATION
A Journey to the Export Real

*Where to escape, where to seek
protection? Women and little
children, eyes wide with terror,
ran into the gang's gunfire before
finding shelter. "Long live Colonel
Funes! Down with taxes!
Long live free trade!"*
—José Eustasio Rivera,
La vorágine

From Export Reverie to Export Real

By the 1920s, Spanish American literary texts began to offer a new way of envisioning export economies by way of a current known as regionalism. In the aftermath of the urban-based and intensely Europhilic literary movements of the late nineteenth and early twentieth centuries, particularly *modernismo,* regionalism marked a turn inward, to the peripheries of the already peripheral nation-state. Jungles, plains, and mountains are the settings par excellence of regionalism, a geographical shift frequently encoded as marking a turn away from the preciousness and artifice of Frenchified letters toward a more virile, if less sophisticated, form of cultural expression. The new protagonism of nature, in turn, has traditionally been seen as a turn toward a more authentic, if less modern, vision of Latin American societies at the turn of the nineteenth century. But as I argue in this chapter, regionalism's turn toward "nature," and "the land" marked anything but an escape from commercial culture: instead, the settings examined by regionalism were precisely those at the center of export-led modernization. Under a system organized around the extraction of natural resources, the rural hinterlands are always already marked as frontiers of accumulation and possible centers of production.

Focusing on a key text of regionalism, the Colombian author José Eustasio Rivera's *La vorágine* (*The Vortex*, 1935), a novel set in the early twentieth-century Amazonian rubber boom, this chapter explores an instance in which literature comes into direct contact with the social worlds created by export-led modernization.[1] These are worlds that earlier authors and texts had either idealized or ignored. Export reverie, a key modality of early liberal optimism, had imagined egalitarian polities and nations enriched beyond their wildest fantasies; the actual people who were to perform the labor required by full-scale export economies were rarely seen. *Modernismo*, by contrast, even in moments of crisis, focused almost exclusively on European objects and locales. Not coincidentally, it was in the 1920s, when the export model had already fomented numerous crises and was itself on the brink of collapse, that Rivera's regionalist text turned to examine the human consequences of liberal modernization. Like the novel examined in the previous chapter, José Asunción Silva's *De sobremesa*, Rivera's *La vorágine* focuses on an urbane poet from Bogotá; unlike Silva's novel, however, Rivera's takes the reader into the unmarked forests of rubber extraction to register the exploitation upon which this activity depended.

In turning to the exploitative and often murderous practices of extraction, *La vorágine* serves as a point of contact with what I call the export real, defined as that which the lettered creole subject didn't know he knew, but had been there all along. The ways in which this subject both sees and occludes what happens on the export frontier is the subject of what follows.

The Rubber Boom: Export Age (Ir)rationality

The Amazonian rubber boom, which reached its apex in the early 1900s, was long over by the time that the Colombian poet and lawyer José Eustasio Rivera wrote *La vorágine*. But the boom remained—and remains—an unparalleled episode of the rationalized irrationality of commodity booms. The extraction of rubber was so brutal that it stretched the putative rationality of capitalist accumulation to its outermost limits.

Before the 1890s, the Amazon rainforest had figured promi-nently in creole imaginaries as a place of indomitable wilderness that nonetheless hid vast stores of wealth.[2] Much of the region remained unmapped, and as numerous tracts of the early twen-tieth century attest, was inhabited only by Indian "savages" and "cannibals."[3] But this changed once demand for wild rubber grew to unfathomed heights with the invention of pneumatic tires at the turn of the century, first for bicycles and then for automobiles. White traders descended on the Amazon and its tributaries, prom-ising to "civilize" savages and create "progress" in the depths of the forest via the extraction of export commodities. These impera-tives had already been enshrined by generations of creole elites, but what happened during the ensuing boom quickly became the stuff of sheer fantasy. The trade soon created spectacular wealth for traders in the two cities built by rubber: Manaus, Brazil, and Iqui-tos, Peru. The extravagance of rubber barons became legendary: rich traders lit cigars with hundred-dollar bills, bathed their horses with champagne, and sent their laundry to Europe for cleaning. Previously remote frontiers of the nation-state became connected directly to Europe: boats loaded with rubber left Iquitos destined for Liverpool, and returned with champagne and other luxuries. Iquitos renamed itself the Chicago of the Amazon.[4] And then there was the most vivid and lasting monument to rubber-era excess: the opera house of Manaus. Today this structure, which was built by Parisian architects and hosted a famous performance by Caruso, stands as a ghostly reminder to the grandeur of the rubber era.[5] The presence of an opera house surrounded by the "wilds" of the jungle suggests a powerful and jarring juxtaposition of concepts of civilization and barbarism, nature and culture. Yet the strangeness of an opera house in Manaus, or the electric tram that ran through Iquitos, should not be measured in terms of the wildness of their

The civilized face of barbarism: the opera house at Manaus, Brazil, constructed between 1884 and 1892. Arquivo Fotográfico Ilustrativo dos Municípios Brasileiros.

jungle surroundings but rather in direct proportion to the violence on which these monuments to civilization were erected.[6]

The methods used to collect rubber became notorious for their brutality: debt peonage, outright slavery, and the massive dispossession and often murder of indigenous inhabitants in the region. Hence while rubber traveled to markets in the United States and Europe, where capitalist wage labor predominated (creating the paradigm of the Fordist worker in the United States), the extraction of this commodity generated contemporaneous forms of debt peonage and slavery in the Amazon basin. The violence became most closely identified with the rubber baron Julio César Arana, an entrepreneur from Lima whose Peruvian Amazon Company was incorporated in Great Britain and traded on the London stock exchange. In 1908 the North American engineer Walter Hardenberg released a report detailing the "devil's paradise" Arana had created along the Putumayo Rivera (a tributary of the Amazon). In 1910, the British consul Roger Casement, one of the men responsible for exposing the genocide in the rubber boom of King Leopold's Congo, wrote a similar denunciatory report detailing the torture and murder in the Putumayo river basin: thousands of Huitoto Indians had been forced into slavery, tortured, and murdered.[7] A scandal ensued in Britain, and the Peruvian Amazon

Company was officially disbanded. Arana and his overseers continued to operate in the area, using the same murderous methods
to extract rubber. By this time the South American trade in natural
rubber was already on the wane, not because of international outcry
caused by the killings in Putumayo, but rather because production
had been relocated to the British colony of Malaysia, where it could
be cultivated more efficiently on large plantations instead of amid
the brush of the rainforest.[8]

La vorágine: Epic of Nature / Novel of Rubber

La vorágine was written in the aftermath of the boom, as a reck-
oning with its effects. Rivera, trained as a lawyer and known in
his Bogotá milieu as a poet, wrote this novel on returning from a
Colombian expedition to mark the nation's borders with Venezuela. Even though the boom had ended over a decade earlier, the
border disputes provoked by the boom lived on. So too did stories,
legends, and rumors about the violence unleashed by the rubber
boom: overseers who controlled their corner of the jungle with
absolute impunity, and Indian workers beaten, tortured, and murdered at whim.[9]

    La vorágine's point of entry into these stories is by way of a poet
from Bogotá, Arturo Cova, a first-person narrator who serves as our
guide through the world created by the rubber trade. The action of
the novel begins as Cova flees Bogotá with his companion Alicia
under murky circumstances. To avoid detection by the law, Cova
cuts telegraph lines, and masks his and Alicia's true identities to
innkeepers and travelers they meet along the way. After days of
travel, the couple arrives to the plains region of Casanare, the setting of the first part of the novel. They stay with Griselda and Fidel
Franco, the owners of a small ranch. Cova, fancying himself a wom-
anizer, seduces Griselda. At the same time, he becomes fiercely
jealous of the attentions paid to his companion, Alicia, by Barrera,
a rubber trader who is in Casanare to recruit labor for his next expedition into the jungle. One day Alicia disappears from the ranch
with Griselda (who had planned to move to a rubber encampment

to sell food to the workers) and Barrera. Cova, accompanied by Griselda's husband Franco, goes after them.

While the first part of the novel focuses on Cova's stay in Casanare, the second and third parts trace his movements deeper and deeper into the jungle. In its recesses, he meets, loses contact, and reunites with other people circulating through its thick throng: these include the guide and interpreter (and also trickster) Pipa, the merchant Zoraida Ayram (also called *La turca* and *La madona*), and even a man Cova had known in Bogotá, who has in the meantime become a rubber trader. The multiplicity of characters populating the jungle is in turn refracted through a multiplicity of voices. While in the jungle, Cova's first-person narration begins to fuse with the voices and stories of other characters, in a practice Sylvia Molloy has insightfully named "narrative contagion" (1987). Most notably, Cova's narration melds with that of Clemente Silva, a man who has wandered the jungle for sixteen years with the bones of his dead son—a casualty of the brutal work of rubber tapping—strapped to his back; and also that of Helí Mesa, a tapper who has escaped enslavement by the trader Barrera.

Through a confusing mixture of Cova's first-person narrative and indirect free discourse, characters tell harrowing stories of the rubber economy, which revolve around forced advances of provisions to keep workers in debt (debt peonage) and outright slavery. Characters also tell of the perverse cruelty visited on the rubber workers, especially the indigenous inhabitants of the jungle. Helí Mesa, for example, tells a story of a baby infected with measles thrown overboard to crocodiles waiting below; the mother throws herself overboard to save the baby, and suffers the same fate. Newspaper reports from the port city of Iquitos, Peru, denounce the torture of Indians, which involves the sewing shut of eyes and lips, and pouring of hot wax into ears.

Through all this, Cova and his party continue their journey to find Barrera, Griselda, and Alicia. Finally they do. Cova attacks Barrera by plunging his head under water; the rubber trader is then finished off by a school of piranhas. Alicia, who had been pregnant, gives birth to a premature baby. While in the jungle, Cova reveals that he had been writing his story in a *libro de caja,* or accounting ledger, left behind by a rubber trader. While no one knows exactly what becomes of Cova and his party as the novel ends, his diary survives. This diary is presented in the novel's prologue by none other than José Eustasio Rivera, who in a letter to a Colombian official reveals himself as the editor of Cova's diary. The epilogue to *La vorágine,* in turn, contains a telegram sent from the Colombian consul in Manaus, Brazil, relating that no one has been able to find Cova: "¡Los devoró la selva!" ("The jungle devoured them!" 1990, 385).

La vorágine is one of the most famous texts of twentieth-century Latin American literature, passages of which are still memorized by schoolchildren in Colombia: "Antes que me hubiera apasionado por mujer alguna, jugúe mi corazón al azar y me lo ganó la Violencia" ("Before I experienced passion for any woman, I gambled my heart to chance, and it was won by Violence"; 1990, 79). These are the opening words of Arturo Cova's diary, in which woman, destiny, and violence with a capital "V" combine to form the epic register of the novel that has been privileged by many critics. The exclamation "The jungle devoured them!" has served, in turn, as shorthand for the novel's concern with the indomitable and crushing force of nature.

Borrowing from a larger repertoire of European colonial discourse, Rivera's novel identifies the jungle as vortex, *tobellino* (whirlpool), and "a mouth that devours men" (1990, 307). *La vorágine*'s treatment of the jungle has traditionally been evaluated in one of two ways: positively when seen as opening onto timeless, transcendental feats of "man" against "nature"; and negatively when seen as evidence of a mechanical, transparent, and/or documentary treatment of nature.

This second interpretation became predominant with authors of the Boom generation of the 1960s, who viewed regionalist fiction of the 1920s and 1930s "as the coarse, unfinished foundations" of the Latin American literary "structure" (Alonso 1990, 38). Along these lines, the Mexican novelist Carlos Fuentes cannot hide his impatience with regionalist narratives exemplified by *La vorágine.*

"The jungle swallowed them," Fuentes remarks, could be the summarizing statement for a whole century of Latin American novels: "the mountain swallowed them, the pampa swallowed them, the mine swallowed them, the river swallowed them. Closer to geography than to literature" (1969, 9). That regionalist literature amounts to little more than a geography lesson instead of "real" literature is already rendered suspect by the fact that Fuentes includes *mines* among his list of topographical markers. For a mine is not a naturally occurring geographical phenomenon, nor is the jungle once it is discovered by the caucho trade, or the plains once they are given over to cattle production. Instead, these are spaces that are transformed to different degrees by human action organized by a specific imperative: the production of commodities. This becomes especially important when we remember that "nature" never lies outside of the realm of capital—*especially* in Export Age Latin America, where this concept formed literal and figurative raw material of modernization in the region. In the Ricardian commodity lottery, nature was and remains the chief advantage designated to Latin American countries desirous of incorporation into global markets. The fact that novels of the 1920s and 1930s insist on people being devoured by rivers, mines, plains, and jungles (an image we have already seen with respect to the stock market in Martel's *La bolsa*) thus deserves our attention. Not, as Fuentes claims, because this shows a provincial naïveté or documentary lack of sophistication, but rather because these settings were at the very core of liberal projects of export-led modernization.[10]

Later novels of the 1930s and 1940s confirm this observation by naming novels after export commodities, or by organizing their plots around them. These include novels such as César Vallejo's *El tungsteno* (Tungsten, Peru, 1931) and Jorge Amado's *Cacau* (Cacao, Brazil, 1933), along with dozens of lesser known texts placed under rubrics such as "the novel of rubber" (of which *La vorágine* is the first), the "novel of nitrates," "the novel of oil," "the novel of timber," "the novel of coffee," etc. Hence if the mid-nineteenth century marked the proliferation of what we might call "the novel of the proper name" (*María, Cecilia Valdés, Martín Rivas*), the 1930s and 1940s witnessed the rise of "the commodity novel."[11] In broad strokes, the switch from the novel of the proper name to the commodity novel encapsulates the neocolonial predicament of Latin American countries, in which a single commodity appears to drive national history, independent of social agents. To paraphrase the Cuban anthropologist Fernando Ortiz in his 1940 essay on tobacco and sugar, single commodities had become the "main characters" of Latin American history (1978, 12). The proliferation of novels dedicated to single export products thus reveals a preoccupation with the place of the commodity in Latin American societies that cannot be dismissed on the grounds of literary naïveté or documentary realism. What I am concerned with in this discussion is how *La vorágine,* which might legitimately be considered one of the first commodity novels, allows us to ask different questions of early twentieth-century literature; namely, how global commodity relations can be seen and represented from the undergrowth of the capitalist world system.

This undergrowth arises not from "nature" or even from the persistence of "archaic" social forms; rather, as first postulated by critics such as Andre Gunder Frank (1967), what at first glance appears to be a non- or premodern social formation is in reality the product of the specific interactions with the capitalist world system. In contrast with classical Marxian accounts of imperialism, which stressed the progressive force of capital in overcoming "feudal" forms of exploitation (gradually replacing it with free wage labor) as it spread across the globe, later theorists of under- and uneven development have argued that capitalism does not necessarily produce bourgeois social structures. This is especially true in the periphery, where violent forms of coercion frequently coexist with free wage labor, and capitalist forms of exchange with noncapitalist ones.[12] Prabhat Patnaik notes, for example, that societies suddenly brought into the "vortex" of capitalism (his term) "are transformed by, and hegemonized by, metropolitan capitalism, but they themselves never get transformed into bourgeois societies." In this manner, he notes, "the capitalist mode is . . . both revolutionary and yet not revolutionary enough" (2006, 39).[13]

In concert with these interpretations, *La vorágine* responds to and represents a kind of capitalist development that was connected to bourgeois social relations at the same time as it relied on and profited from brutal violence. As noted, it is often the jungle itself—as a primitive space—that gets blamed for this violence. And yet the menace of nature is always linked to the action of human agents; beyond this, the overweening and oppressive force of nature is always linked to a world outside the jungle that can be grasped only by way of the ghostly stirrings of monetary exchange. As an example, we can turn to a statement made by Clemente Silva, the rubber tapper whose voice fuses with that of Cova's during long stretches of narrative:

> la selva trastorna al hombre, desarrollándole los instintos más inhumanos: la crueldad invade las almas como intrincado espino y la codicia quema como fiebre. El ansia de riquezas convalece al cuerpo ya desfallecido, y el olor del caucho produce la locura de los millones. (1990, 245)

> The jungle drives men crazy, breeding the most inhuman instincts: cruelty invades their souls like a tangled thorn, and greed burns like fever. The drive for riches takes over their already exhausted bodies, and the smell of rubber produces the insanity of the millions.

On the one hand, the greed identified by Clemente Silva is coded as atavistic, sparked directly by the animal and vegetable world of the jungle. On the other hand, it is the smell of rubber—a commodity produced for the global market—that conjures the "insanity of the millions."

Colonial Truth-Effects

Thus if there is a law of the jungle identified in *La vorágine*, it is not constituted solely by nature. Instead, the natural world can be grasped only in interaction with a particular human endeavor: the extraction of caucho. Similarly, if the jungle is frequently represented as a space of brute materiality in *La vorágine*—forged through images of the impenetrable foliage of the jungle, the mutilated and dead bodies of workers, and the thick stream of rubber, frequently likened to vital fluids like milk and semen—this materiality coexists with the seemingly groundless and invisible properties of money. The simultaneity of nature and money, and of material objects and airy discourse, is repeated on the level of the novel's form. For while *La vorágine* has frequently been misread as an overly documentary or "sociological" novel (a charge made particularly with regard to the denunciatory interventions made by Clemente Silva), its representational apparatus is not so straightforward. As literary critics Carlos Alonso (1990), Montserrat Ordóñez (1990), and Sylvia Molloy (1987), among others, have shown, the narrative apparatus of *La vorágine* is quite complex. On the one hand, the novel relentlessly incorporates stories and voices, to disorienting and frequently confusing effect. It is often difficult to know who is speaking at a given moment, and from which location. This shifting perspective is most notable when Cova's first-person narrative morphs into free indirect discourse, in which statements are marked neither by "I" or by quotation marks but instead float freely, as if unmoored from any single voice.

Adding to these difficulties is the fact that the narrative voice of Arturo Cova is itself characterized by unreliability and contradictoriness. In one scene in Casanare, for example, Cova enters into one of his many flights of fancy, imagining himself a "ricacho fastuoso" ("fabulously rich man") who has come to the region to bring "progress" in reality, he has come fleeing scandal. In another, he sees Alicia become sick, correctly infers that she is pregnant, and decides to keep the information from her. In short, even if Arturo Cova's narration is not purposefully deceptive, we cannot take his words at face value.

On a metalevel, the novel is not a work of documentary realism, but instead a self-conscious simulacrum of reality. In order to make this point, it is useful to note that Rivera's novel frequently cites previously published "documentary" works on the rubber trade, and in so doing dramatizes the extent to which the rubber boom itself created a context in which truth and lies, and reality and fiction became intertwined. As an initial example, we can turn to Rivera's citation of Eugenio Robouchon's *En el Putumayo y sus afluentes* (In the Putumayo and Its Affluents [1907]). Robouchon was a French photographer hired by the Casa Arana to take pictures of the rubber encampments for use as publicity. But after taking several pictures and writing an anthropological account of the Huitotos, Robouchon disappeared, never to be heard from again. The resulting work, *En el Putumayo,* appears after Robouchon's disappearance and is prefaced by a number of official letters to the Peruvian consul in Manaus and to the minister of foreign relations in Lima. The first letters document the arrival of the Frenchman and, finally, announce his disappearance. The last of these letters relates that only Robouchon's luggage and a few pages of writing were found: "The Mr. Arana brothers presume, with reason, that Mr. Robuchon has been a victim of the Indian cannibals who frequent those regions" (1907, xvii). Other documents of the era, however, suggest that Robouchon was really killed by Arana's henchmen after taking photographs of the torture and murder in the rubber camps. Robouchon's disappearance is alluded to in *La vorágine* by way of the character of Clemente Silva, who tells of *el francés* (the Frenchman) who disappeared into the jungle with his damning photographs. This historical referent is even more powerfully incorporated by way of the novel's framing device, which as we will recall is constructed as a letter from the author José Eustasio Rivera to the Colombian consul in Manaus. The novelist transforms himself into a fictional character—the curator of Arturo Cova's texts—just as he transforms his protagonist into a real character. Such an intermingling of truth and fiction has the effect of lending verisimilitude to the novel, a maneuver Rivera admits is part of his denunciatory aims. But this novelistic verisimilitude is anything but straightforward once we consider it has its roots in a *reality* that was itself only accessible through the hubris of consular letters and conflicting reports about "cannibals," on one hand, and the most barbaric forms of colonial violence, on the other. Thus the tendency to criticize *La vorágine* as a naïve form of realism misses a crucial point: that in the context of the rubber boom, reality was itself interwoven with elements of fiction and untruth.

Here it is useful to call on Michael Taussig's classic study of the Putumayo rubber boom and its aftermath, an unparalleled inquiry into the (il)logic of colonial cruelty. In this study he powerfully demonstrates the extent to which the business of rubber gathering depended on the perpetuation of colonial terror: first, the generation of whites' fears of the Indian as "wild man"; and second, the mobilization of these fears as justification for extraordinarily cruel discipline against Indian workers. The result was profoundly irrational, because rubber traders were killing the very labor from which they created wealth; with this, what Taussig names the "colonial mirror of production" (1986) took on a destructive logic all its own.

Citing literary criticism, Taussig holds that the only way to understand the violence generated by colonialism is through a mode of representation that "penetrate[s] the veil" of colonial violence, "while retaining its hallucinatory quality" (10).[14] The text in question is Conrad's *Heart of Darkness* (1899), a novel that for Taussig "combines a twofold movement of interpretation in a combined action of reduction *and* revelation" (1986, 10; emphasis in original). Though Conrad's novel of Leopold's Congo serves as a point of departure for Taussig, he makes only passing reference to *La vorágine,* giving it only enough time to dismiss it as a text that displaces the violence perpetuated against indigenous people on to a set of white characters. On some level, this is a valid critique. Rivera's novel is told exclusively from the perspective of whites: Arturo Cova is a poet from Bogotá; Helí Mesa and Clemente Silva, two subjects to whom the narrative is entrusted, are white slaves to the rubber traders, a significant detail given the fact that indigenous people bore the brunt of the violence during the rubber boom. Taking a cue from Taussig's hermeneutics of colonialism, *La vorágine*'s occlusion of reality is precisely the point, and its mystifications open onto insights about how the rubber trade and the violence it generates might be represented. Like Conrad's more famous novel, *La vorágine* simultaneously engages and folds into the hubris produced under (neo)colonial regimes of accumulation and extraction.[15]

To make this point, I now turn to two key tropes through which the novel reinforces its problematic relationship to reality and in so doing both occludes and catches sight of the "real" of export economies. Not coincidentally, these two tropes—counterfeiting and accounting—hail from the world of economic representation and as such permit a reading of *La vorágine* as a discourse on the deceptive systems of value through which the rubber trade reproduced itself. It is with these tropes, I argue, that *La vorágine* powerfully reflects on its own limits of representation.

Counterfeiting I: Money

First, let us consider counterfeiting. As noted, the novel begins with Cova and Alicia's flight from Bogotá. The reason for this flight is that Alicia had been promised in marriage to a rich landowner; Cova "steals" her and runs away, causing a scandal. But another intriguing possibility is alluded to on two separate occasions. On their way from Bogotá toward the llanos, Arturo and Alicia are stopped by Pipa, a character who will appear later in the novel as Arturo's guide in the jungle. In this first encounter, Pipa, claiming to be a representative of the mayor of Villavicencio, asks the pair to identify themselves lest they be the counterfeiters (*acuñadores de moneda*, literally "minters of coin") sought by the law. With this request, Arturo notes that Alicia lowers the veil on her hat, "to hide her pallor" (1990, 85). Does Alicia go pale simply because Cova is asked to identify himself, or because they might in fact be the minters of false coin? We are not given access to the thoughts of Alicia and so cannot know. We do know that just before the run-in with Pipa, an innkeeper in the previous town had assumed that they were indeed the counterfeiters and urged Alicia to show her "las monedas que fabricábamos" (the coins we fabricated/produced). It goes without saying that to literally *make* money is to counterfeit money. The innkeeper assures Alicia that there was nothing wrong with this activity, "dada la tirantez de la situación" (considering the severity of the situation; 1990, 83). Revealing complicity with the possible counterfeiters, the innkeeper suggests that falsification is a justifiable response to hard times. Here the innkeeper makes oblique reference to the grave economic instability in Colombia during the first decade of the twentieth century,

Exploitation

a time when severe hyperinflation was accompanied by a wave of counterfeiting.[16] Neither Cova nor Alicia responds directly to the innkeeper's charge. After recording her request to see the coins, Cova simply notes: "The next day we left before dawn" (83).

With these two references, something is clearly amiss. Cova never establishes firmly whether others have reason to suspect that he and Alicia are really counterfeiters, and we never see the coins the innkeeper encourages Alicia to show her. In the encounter with Pipa, Cova gets around the accusation with the lie that he is the *Intendente* (maximum official) of the region, traveling with his wife. Here, Cova deflects the possibility that he is a counterfeiter with the definite lie that he is the highest official of the land and that Alicia is his "legitimate" wife. Institutional and sexual legitimacy (marriage) are used as a cover for an accusation involving the illegitimate production of money. Even if Arturo Cova is not the counterfeiter, the accusation leads him to lie about who he really is. This lie, in turn, gives way to a further con. Pipa, with an obsequiousness that is always false in this novel, seemingly believes Arturo's story. He doesn't report them, but perhaps in exchange for his silence, he makes off in the middle of the night with Cova's horse. Pipa reappears later, after Cova has entered the jungle, to act as a guide and mediator with indigenous tribes they meet. He explains that he had really only borrowed the horse, with every intention of giving it back. He didn't, of course.

Counterfeiting is a crime of *representation*, one that substitutes the real thing for a fake and in the process causes us to question the boundary between the two. This is why monetary counterfeiting is so dangerous to a state: for what is so special about the state-issued currency if someone can make it on her own? In Rivera's hands, counterfeiting becomes a possible metaphor for the falsifications constantly occurring in *La vorágine*. There are several more instances of such fakery: the rubber trader Barrera, we learn, circulates falsely idyllic postcards of rubber encampments to recruit workers, and loaded dice win card games in Casanare.

The problem of counterfeit is that it circulates alongside real money; it is enough to know that counterfeit coins are somewhere lurking to cast suspicion on the rest of the money supply. How to tell a fake coin from a legitimate one? The same is true when we take the trope of counterfeiting to the linguistic economy of the novel. Jean Joseph Goux has explored money and language as parallel economies of representation, showing that when there is counterfeiting in the first, it is often signified as a crisis in the other (1994, 33).[17] The suggestion that Cova might be a counterfeiter in the realm of money thus opens the possibility that he also might be a counterfeiter in the realm of words. Whether or not Cova and Alicia are in reality counterfeiters is not the point; it is enough to know that counterfeiting is going on in our midst to give us pause. Even more unsettling is that our narrator does not give us the security to know whether or not he is circulating false money, but instead remains silent on the matter. Is he a counterfeiter or not? The point is to *not know*.

The suggestion of counterfeiting also gives us a different perspective from which to judge the much-criticized documentary thrust of the novel. The opening and ending of the novel deploy the documentary realism of official letters, signed by "José Eustasio Rivera," and the author himself admitted to wanting to create an effect of verisimilitude so as to create a greater sense of urgency vis-à-vis his subject matter. Read through the trope of counterfeiting, however, the will to verisimilitude loses some of its earnestness. Here we may consider Rivera's placement, in the first editions of the novel, of photographs identified as representations of "Arturo Cova" and "Clemente Silva," as though these were real people. The photo of Arturo Cova, supposedly taken by another fictional character, Zoraida Ayram, is really of José Eustasio Rivera (Pineda Camacho 2004, 485–86). While we might be apt to take this photograph as evidence that Cova is "really" a double of Rivera (an autobiographical reading that has on occasion been made), I think it is more interesting to view the photograph as an extension of the novel's own tropes of counterfeiting and falsification. Maybe the point is not that Cova is really Rivera or vice versa, but that we really don't know who *either* of them really is.

To what degree can we trust Cova the narrator or José Eustasio Rivera the novelist? This question is important because it leads us not only to question the deceptive practices at the heart of the rubber trade, but, on a different level, those perpetuated by the *letrado* himself with respect to this trade. The metaphor of counterfeiting within a literary text allows us to return to previous instances in which texts and/or narrators themselves behaved like money. In chapter 1, for example, I argued that José Martí's pamphlet *Guatemala* functioned as a promissory note, promising a glorious future by way of commodity production. In chapter 3, in the midst of severe financial crisis in Argentina, Julián Martel's novel *La bolsa* introduced a realist narrative principle that positioned itself as a kind of gold against the fictitious capital generated by the stock market. And in chapter 4, I showed how the protagonist of José Asunción Silva's *De sobremesa* allegorized the failure of the creole subject to secure value in the crisis-prone and ghost-filled realm of transnational exchange. *La vorágine,* in turn, posits a narrator who, both literally and figuratively, might be passing false coins.[18]

Counterfeiting II: Masculinity

The closest parallel to the counterfeit coin in the novel is Cova's own person, which is tied to another form of value circulating in the novel: masculinity. Again it is instructive to call on Jean Joseph Goux, who notes that crises in the realm of money are frequently expressed as a parallel crisis in the sexual economy: "For if the truth of language is contested along with the truth of gold, *the truth of the father* is also challenged" (1994, 32; emphasis in original). Like counterfeit coins, Cova's masculine identity is frequently *faked* and subjected to fierce irony on the part of Rivera.

At times, *La vorágine* seems to uphold an uncritical view of phallic power, as in the famous first sentence in which Cova positions himself between "Woman" and "Violence."[19] At other times, however, as other critics have shown, the novel reveals a great dose of irony toward Cova's masculine identity, which is by no

Real and simulacrum: photograph of the author José Eustasio Rivera published in the first edition of *La vorágine* (1924), in which he is identified as the protagonist of the novel. A translation of the original caption reads: "Arturo Cova in the barracks of Guaracú."

means sure-footed. While in Casanare, for example, Cova lavishly congratulates himself on having bedded both Alicia and Griselda; very shortly afterward, however, his macho mettle is tested when he learns that both women have gone to see Barrera. A character named Miguelito asks him: "¿Usté piensa matá al hombre?" (Are you gonna kill the man?) Cova's first reaction is "no, no." But when Miguelito suggests Barrera's affront, unaddressed, would make Cova look like a weakling, Cova asks: "Do you think I should kill him?" (1990, 136). In spite of the fact that Cova has been operating according to a hypermasculine code, he doesn't know that he is supposed to want to kill Barrera. Cova's uncertainty about how he should deal with the stealing of "his" woman (a patriarchal fantasy of proprietorship) shows that doubt lies at the very core of his performance of masculinity. This identity comes under question not so much because his honor has been offended, but because he is unsure as to what he should do to keep it intact.

After the scene with Miguelito, Cova drinks himself into oblivion and declares to Griselda and Alicia that he is going to kill Barrera. When Griselda tries to restrain him, he calls her a "procuress" (*alcahueta,* 138) and strikes her in the face, drawing blood. It is after this that Griselda and Alicia abandon Cova to join Barrera's expedition. Cova, obsessed with masculine "honor," is wholly unable to see his fault in driving them away and follows them into the jungle to find and kill Barrera.

At the end of the novel, he succeeds in doing so; but the novel has already indicated that the entire enterprise was based on an assertion of masculine power that was never assured, but instead shot through with holes. Here we might consider the very name "Cova," which alludes to a cave or a hollow space. This hollow, which needs to be compensated with drinking, womanizing, and killing, is a counterfeit insofar as it doesn't meet its ideal. At the same time, there is no self-assured gold standard behind the "faked" version of masculinity. But this is the point: it is the attempt to be "the real thing" that serves as the impetus for Cova's entire undertaking. We might go a step further and hold that this excessive, but at bottom empty signifier of masculinity motivates the entire rubber trade, which is run by men who rape and kill for no apparent reason except for shows of brute force. In this context, the real thing doesn't have to exist: the fake is lethal enough.

Counterfeiting III: Poetry

Earlier I noted that regionalist discourse is often posited as a virilized response to the urbanely artificial and hence "feminine" associations of *modernismo.* But as we have just seen, the poet of *La vorágine* boasts a hypermasculine identity at the core of which stands an empty shell. The novel enacts a similar response to poetry, not so much because it is considered feminized (and in need of virilization), but because in its context of enunciation—the jungles of rubber extraction—it too is rendered false.

If the suspicion of counterfeiting is poised to cause a crisis of representation in *La vorágine,* this crisis is most compellingly brought to bear on one of the key discourses circulating within the novel: poetry. What does it mean that the poet might also be a counterfeiter?

At the end of the previous chapter, I discussed how at the beginning of the twentieth century, José Enrique Rodó and others identified aesthetics as a true form of value, one that was immune to the fluctuations of the marketplace. Rodó's landmark text *Ariel* (1900) likened art to a gold coin inscribed with the word "hope." In Colombia, the writer Santiago Pérez Triana took a similar tack when he wrote in a little-known essay that poets are *acuñadores de la moneda del sentimiento* (minters of the coin of feeling). In an article dedicated to Henrich Heine and appearing in the journal *Repertorio Colombiano* in 1898, Pérez Triana writes that poets produce a kind of coin "that belongs to all of us, which once marked by their divine seal, circulates in the commerce of souls and ideas" (1898, 250).

The exact phrase *acuñadores de . . . moneda* (minters of coin) is repeated in *La vorágine,* but in a subversively adulterated form: in literalizing the metaphor—the poet as a possible *maker* of money—Rivera transforms this subject into a possible criminal, and *poetry* itself into a possible site of falsification and deceit. Pérez Triana's essay on poetry is not well known today, and I have not been able to ascertain whether Rivera read it or not. But two additional elements of his life make me think that Rivera might have found fertile grounds for parody: first, this intellectual wrote his own travel narrative detailing a trip from Bogotá through the jungle, entitled *De Bogotá al Atlántico* (1905). Second, this book was written after Pérez Triana was forced to flee Bogotá as a result of a scandal involving some murky business deals surrounding the construction of the Panama Canal, a context that transforms him into an intriguing site of possible inspiration for Rivera.[20] Even if Rivera is not citing this context, it is enough to note that the juxtaposition of counterfeiting and poetry in a novel about the rubber trade and its horrors serves to cast some doubt on the legitimacy of poetry in this context. Poetry, it should be noted, was the civilizing discourse par excellence in post-Independence Latin America: first as a fount of civic feeling, and later as a fount of refinement and disinterest. In Colombia, especially, poetry was together with grammar a chief mode of elite cultural expression: before the mid-twentieth century, there was scarcely a president of the nation who had not published a book of poems.[21] And Rivera, it is well known, before writing *La vorágine* had published a book of sonnets dedicated to the jungle, plains, and mountains of Colombia, entitled *Tierra de promisión* (1921).

In light of the novel's concern with deceit and counterfeiting, a concern that extends to poetry, we can reevaluate one of the most famous passages of the novel. It comes as the opening of Part 2, as Cova and his party move into the jungle. A voice we assume to be Cova's speaks in apostrophe:

> ¡Oh selva, esposa del silencio, madre de la soledad y de la neblina! ¿Qué hado maligno me dejó prisionero en tu cárcel verde? Los pabellones de tus ramajes, como inmensa bóveda, siempre están sobre mi cabeza, entre mi aspiración y el cielo claro, que sólo entreveo cuando tus copas estremecidas mueven su oleaje, a la hora de tus crepúsculos angustiosos. . . . ¿Aquellos celajes de oro y múrice con que se viste el ángel de los ponientes, por qué no tiemblan en su dombo?

> O jungle, wife of silence, mother of solitude and of fog! What evil sprite has made me a captive of your green prison? The pavillions of your roofs, like an immense vault, are always over my head, between my hopes and the clear skies, of which I only glimpse when your quivering treetops move their foliage, at the hour of your sorrowful twilights. . . . Those clouds of gold and purple with which the angel of the setting sun dresses, why do they not tremble in your abode? (1990, 189)

Critics have often accepted this lyrical outburst at face value, assuming that it is here that the "real" Rivera speaks as a poet of nature. Indeed, the collection of sonnets Rivera had published three years earlier also relies on the rarified terms and tropes associated with Spanish American *modernismo*.[22] But as Carlos Alonso has already pointed out, this resemblance has blinded many critics to the fact that the depiction of Cova the poet is "fraught with irony," as evidenced by his frequent self-aggrandizement, daydreaming, and failure to apprehend reality (1990, 148).[23] What I am most interested in here is how this ironic distance is effected in a particular way, in terms of poetry's *failure* to understand and apprehend the violence generated by the rubber trade.

The failure of poetry to represent the economy in which the novel as a whole inserts itself is powerfully illustrated in a scene appearing shortly after the lyrical apostrophe the jungle. By this time, Pipa—the man who stopped Cova and Alicia on their way to Casanare lest they be the counterfeiters sought by the law—has reappeared and offered his services as a guide. Pipa, we learn, has lived in and around the jungle for decades, and leads them to stay with a tribe of Guahiba Indians. Noting that the men will need provisions for their journey such as salt, mosquito nets, and gunpowder, Pipa leads them to a marsh to collect heron feathers to trade along the way. Cova, on seeing the habitat of the herons, moves immediately into lyrical mode: "¡Bendita sea la difícil landa que nos condujo a la región de los revuelos y la albura! El inundado bosque del garcero, millonario de garzas reales, parecía algodonal de nutridos copos" ("Blessed be the difficult journey that steered us to the region of flight and daylight! The replete forest of the royal heron marsh, enriched with millions of heron, looked like a field of well-nourished cotton balls") (203). The description goes on to depict the sky as made of "turquoise," the heron feathers as made of "whitening silk" (*seda albicante*), and their beaks as swordlike (203–4).

For any reader of the era, the tropes used here would have been immediately recognizable as borrowed from Spanish American *modernismo,* the late nineteenth- and early twentieth-century literary current considered in chapter 2. In that chapter, I showed how the artificial, precious, and luxury-inflected language helped to forge a discourse of import consumption through its flowing descriptions of luxuriously decorated interiors. Precious jewels, bronze statues, silk damasks, porcelain vases, and the like were the objects at the heart of this aesthetic.

But in Rivera's novel, something very different occurs: the jewel-toned descriptors usually reserved for human-made (and foreign) objects are applied to objects of American *nature,* and, moreover, inserted within an overt context of economic production and exchange. The narrative itself notes that the heron feathers—in high demand in Europe and the United States as decoration for women's hats—will arrive in faraway destinations, but that consumers will have no idea how they were produced: "the Indians penetrated the swamp bit by bit, crouching in the twilight with their sticks to ward off anacondas [*güíos*] and alligators. Thus they finish gathering feathers, the white handful that sometimes costs the lives of many before being taken to faraway cities to flatter the beauty of unknown women" (205).

With this revelation—that heron feathers sometimes cause the death of the Indians who collect them—the aesthetic pleasure culled from silky feathers and sword-like beaks abruptly comes to a close.[24] This is because, as Sylvia Molloy has pointed out regarding this same passage, the tropes of *modernismo* had become shopworn, and hence identifiable as "frivolous, pathetic, and commercialized" (1987, 755). We might go a step further and remark on the precise conditions under which the *modernista* fantasy of luxury and refinement evaporates; it happens once people—Indians, in fact—appear. In this way, *La vorágine* recognizes that the sparkling and artificial tropes of *modernismo* operate through a particular erasure, namely, that specific regimes of labor produce commodities before they can be transformed into objects of aesthetic value. While *modernismo*'s aesthetic privileges scenes of consumption, Cova's visit to the heron marsh in the jungle employs those same tropes, only to question their effect with the recognition of the erasure that sustains the fantasy of the commodity. The protective *étui* of poetry breaks down to reveal exploitation. In some sense, poetic discourse circulating in *La vorágine* bears a parallel with the ostentatious opera house in Manaus; both are empty signifiers of a "civilization" that does not recognize the exploitation on which it is built.

Accounting

Given the compromised status of narrative perspective by way of the metaphor of counterfeiting, a trope that refers to faulty practices of representation within a larger economic context, how might the novel grasp the real? It is crucial that these two concepts, counterfeit and real, are not opposed, but instead depend on one another; the counterfeit depends on verisimilitude, just as the real cannot express itself without recourse to deceptive apparatuses of representation. In this way, the novel's own apparatus resembles the caucho economy that Arturo Cova—mostly by way of other voices—encounters as he moves further and further into the jungle. Deceit is the mechanism of the caucho economy, and it is only by engaging deceit that shards of the truth might appear.

Poetry, as we have seen, is shown by the novel to be unable to represent adequately the social and economic relations taking place in the jungle. Which discourse, then, might provide a more trustworthy depiction? Here it is useful to remember that while Cova is a poet, and his narrative takes the form of a diary, the actual manuscript attributed to him is inscribed in a *libro de caja*, or book of accounts. This book, described as "useless and dusty" (1990, 345), had been left behind by a caucho trader and picked up by Cova to write his story months after his first foray into the jungle.

Accounting is a central mechanism of representation through which the violent system works. In the universe of caucho extraction, we learn at other points of the novel, such books were used to record the debts of rubber tappers, who received commodities as advance payment for labor. The information for how this accounting system functions comes not from Cova but from Clemente Silva, the white enslaved Colombian who narrates almost the entire second half of part 2. Silva was drawn into the jungle to search for his son, Lucianito, whose bones he carries as a "treasure" on his back, and who has been working for the past sixteen years to get out of debt with the rubber tappers. This is an impossible feat, however, because the system of labor employed in the jungle depends on the permanent maintenance of debt. Silva tells Cova and his party (now down to four people), about the onerous little books that keep these debts. The overseers (*capataces*)

> wait each night, notebook in hand, for the workers to bring in the extracted rubber and to enter its price in the account. They are never content with the work and the whip measures their discontent. They credit the worker who brings in 10 liters with only half of this and get rich by selling the surplus contraband to traders in another region, or they bury it to exchange it later for liquor and merchandise. (245)

The "sociological" or "documentary" quality of Clemente Silva's description of the methods of caucho extraction and exchange has been much maligned. But in the context of a social and narrative universe based on *deception,* Silva's straightforwardness takes on another cast. Again, it is only if we read this as a fragment it that seems contrived and/or naïve. Because in the larger context, the thing described—accounting ledgers—leads us to much more interesting questions about the system of representation through which the business of extracting caucho can be known.

If counterfeiting is the falsification of value, accounting is supposed to serve as an objective rendering of economic reality. But in this context, the numbers do not correspond with what a tapper actually produces; instead, these books alter reality in favor of the overseer. A crucial part of this alteration of reality by way of numbers is coercion, symbolized in the passage above by the whip. The secret of the *libreta* is outright stealing, a reality the numbers in their neutrality register but cannot themselves tell.

The trope of accounting remits to a longer history of capital accumulation. We might remember that Max Weber, for example, located the genesis of capitalism in the invention of double-entry bookkeeping, a development Mary Poovey has more recently traced to the creation of a modern epistemology in which numbers came to represent objective "facts." In *The History of the Modern Fact,* Poovey demonstrates how the emergence of modern forms of accounting in Renaissance Europe worked "to enhance the prestige of merchants as a group by proclaiming that the profits they earned were just" (1998, 32). Until this development, numbers had been associated with necromancy and the occult; accounting, however, would imbue numbers with an authority that would overtake narrative in the world of transactions.[25] But this new reliance on numbers had fiction built into its representational apparatus. This is because the key number in accounting—the zero—refers to no verifiable object in reality; rather, it is a convention imported so that the books might be balanced. The result was a system of accounting that is formally *precise,* but not accurate, for "only in relation to the other entries in the books could an individual entry be judged right or wrong" (56). This formal aspect of accounting as arithmetically precise became crucial to its truth-effects, essentially allowing merchants to banish from the books all elements of risk and uncertainty from its purview. On the eve of European imperial expansion, accounting created the illusion of stability in long-distance trade, even though instability and uncertainty "were the source of the profit that made commerce worth pursuing in the first place" (62).

What happens once we transpose Poovey's observations about accounting as a system of representation to the forests of commodity extraction? Here, too, the mechanism of accounting lends a sense of knowability to the whole enterprise in quantifying the amount of caucho extracted versus the cost of maintaining the labor that extracts it. But just as Poovey notes with regard to the accounting ledgers of early modern merchants, the system of accounting used in the jungle is a numerical and not a narrative system. As such, it might be numerically precise, but have absolutely no relation to reality. At the end of each day, the numbers shown in the overseers' books might balance out: there is no way of knowing by looking at them, however, how the values came to be assigned in the first place. Nor is there any way of knowing that in this context the ledger presupposes the simultaneous threat of the whip and the gun. Going back even further, the ledgers are unable to register the violence that had to take place before the rubber economy could be started at all. The violence has already taken place before the first number has even been entered.

Accounting is an internally precise system whose interaction with the larger social field reveals itself as false. And when we consider the scene of writing in this novel—Arturo Cova inscribing his story in a book of accounts—the novel offers itself as the site from which this falsity can be exposed. The whole novel tells the story that accounting ledgers—as numerical registers—*can't* tell and reintroduces narrative excess shorn from accounting in the pursuit of precision and elegance. The ledgers, on the other hand, take on a fictional quality precisely because of what their numbers hide: the brutal exploitation through which the rubber economy reproduces itself.

But as we have already seen, Arturo Cova's own system of accounting—the narrative diary—is itself unreliable, rooted in possibly counterfeit and most definitely skewed practices of representation. It is by reason of this partiality, however, that the novel gains access to the truth the ledger cannot grasp. The novel's very messiness and contradictoriness, that is, allow glimpses of the truth, much in the way that the affected poet sees glimpses of light between the moving treetops. In this manner, the novel gestures at, but does not claim to know "the truth," thus suggesting that it is in maintaining the hallucinatory quality that the real can be approached at all.

In *La vorágine*, Cova inscribes his personal account in an accounting ledger and in doing so attempts to flesh out an alternative narrative surrounding the exploitative practices occurring in the jungle. The novel, that is, tells what the accounting ledgers of the rubber companies cannot tell, and indeed actively hide. By the same token, the account provided by Cova is at every turn undermined by the skewed partiality and instability of his narrative voice, which, as noted earlier, bears some similarities to counterfeit money. Arturo Cova is also unable to provide a full "account" of the caucho economy; in part because of his perspective (that of a white lettered elite male), and in part because the economy itself is rooted in deceptive practices of representation. The novel is ultimately unable to register in a straightforward manner the exploitation at the core of the rubber economy. Even less is it able to account for how people become things, or how caucho gains its value within a larger system of production and exchange.

Fetish and Real: The Limits of Representation

I have been arguing that *La vorágine* simultaneously provides and bars access to the violence that sustained the rubber boom, resulting in what Taussig has discussed as a climate of "epistemic murk" (1986). This murk is certainly an effect of the sheer levels of brutality wrought by the rubber trade; at the same time, the state of unknowability in which violence flourishes is connected to the irreducible mysteries enshrouding the commodity form taken by rubber. On the level of the novel's form, Cova's narrative is constituted by an admixture of blindness and insight that coincides with the simultaneous visibility and invisibility of the social relations that allow the caucho economy to function as it does. On the one hand, the closer Cova moves into the space of production, the more its horrific practices are revealed and "accounts" rectified. On the other hand, this same journey becomes the occasion for new distortions. These distortions are frequently self-conscious on the part of the novel, as seen through the novel's tropes of counterfeiting and fakery. At the same time, the novel as a whole is unable to get very close to the "real" of exploitation. This is in part because, as Michael Taussig notes, the novel bars access to the indigenous people who bore the brunt of violence in the rubber trade: the narrative is entrusted to white characters, and the most important victims of slavery are also white. This choice is itself meaningful, if nothing else because it exposes an internal limit to what the subject imagined by *La vorágine* (and perhaps the one who wrote it) can perceive and understand. The novel can see that exploitation is the motor of the rubber trade, but it can't meet it head on; instead, the novel folds into its own narrative tricks and obfuscations.

And if Rivera's novel cannot *see* exploitation without the veil of deceptive practices of representation, neither can it *see* the larger system to which the rubber trade belongs. Everything that goes on in *La vorágine* is connected to the rubber trade, but the novel's focus on the jungle results in its paradoxical occlusion of the circuits outside of the space. In this manner, to travel to the jungle of the export boom is paradoxically to move closer to the site of commodity extraction at the same time as this movement makes the commodity itself lose any meaningful contact with outside reality. In other words, the closer the novel moves into the jungle, the closer it gets to the origins of the commodity as produced by human labor. By the same token, however, the deeper this perspective moves into the "real" of extraction, the less it is able to visualize the circuits outside of the jungle that are actually governing the production of the export commodity. The dense thicket of the jungle and text occludes any relation to this larger system, rendering individual actions, motivations, and relationships opaque and seemingly without referent.

At no point, for example, do we learn where the caucho extracted from the tree is being sent, or what it is used for. Rather, we are given grotesque images of trees and bodies comingling in the production of a dense white substance, likened at different moments to bodily fluids: milk, blood, and semen. Workers who cut the rubber tress, in turn, are transformed into things, property, petrified as trees. Caucho is the ghoulishly incomprehensible substance that performs this magic. And once smoked and ready for export, the milky white liquid is transformed into a malodorous black mass, referred to near the end of the novel as an *ídolo negro* (black idol; 1990, 348), a fetish object endowed with a power internal to itself. The etymology of the word "fetish" comes from the Portuguese *feitiço*, the term used by Europeans to denote the worship of totems and idols by the Africans they enslaved (the etymology of factory comes from a similarly colonial context, from the Portuguese word *feitoria*). When represented as a "black idol," the caucho fetish certainly carries connotations of primitivism, animism, and so-called black magic. And yet the fetishistic character of caucho hails more directly from modernity, as a commodity on the world market.

We will remember that Marx used the term "fetish" to discuss the magical and animistic qualities of all commodities in capitalist societies. For Marx, this magic resulted whenever commodities were removed from their "hidden abode of production" to appear to arrive to market on their own, independently of human agents (1976, 279). *La vorágine* is able to provide a particularly compelling rendering of commodity fetishism precisely because the text itself occludes and folds itself into its mystery. The novel also renders the specificities of the commodity fetish as it *appears* on the extractive periphery. First, as a generalized condition of export commodities, rubber is rendered even more mysterious and ghoulish because it appears to have no use-value at all. When rolled into enormous hulking masses and readied for export, caucho loses all of the utility it might have once had; and yet desire for the stuff drives an entire operation of exploitation. Endowed with an unsettling autonomy, the "black idol" becomes a diabolical signifier of sheer exchange-value.

Caucho is part of an integrated if uneven world system, and yet the enormous spatial and temporal divides within it render the export commodity mysterious *even in its abode of production*. In this case, it is only by reconnecting the time and space of rubber production in the jungle to that of its exchange and consumption elsewhere that the mystery of the commodity might be discovered. And yet as a reflection of the utter difficulty of reconnecting these fragmented spaces of the world market, the more *La vorágine* reveals the secrets of rubber production, the less it is able to visualize the circuits through which caucho travels to the B. F. Goodrich factories in Akron, Ohio, or somewhere else in North America. In this sense, *La vorágine* does not solve the riddle of the caucho fetish, but rather heightens its mystery. The novel—as an infinitely plastic genre—is able to explore these mysteries because the rubber economy is built on deceit and terror, but also because of the fictions and illusions generated by the commodity form itself. In this way, the novel offers itself to a reading in which it is not the jungle alone that functions as a devouring "vortex," but instead a global system of human interaction. This system, while producing concrete (horrific) effects on the ground, nonetheless remains invisible and opaque to those who operate within it.

Epilogue: A Letter to Henry Ford

In 1928, four years after publishing *La vorágine* to resounding success, and while he was preparing the English translation of the novel, Rivera wrote a letter to Henry Ford. Rivera knew that Ford was planning a major project to grow rubber for automobile tires on plantations in Brazil. The project was designed to reduce North American reliance on rubber from British plantations in Southeast Asia, the region of the world to which production had been transferred after 1910. The letter begins by congratulating Ford on his undertaking and goes on to offer his reflections on the recent history of the region. In the manner of *La vorágine*—a novel whose forthcoming English edition he recommends to the North American capitalist—Rivera recalls the horrors of the rubber boom of the early twentieth century. "I have had in my hands photographs of overseers who returned to their camps with baskets or *mapires* full of ears, breasts and testicles torn from unarmed Indians as punishment for not extracting the required amount of rubber for their bosses" (1991, 107–8). If Mr. Ford were to visit some parts of the rainforest, Rivera notes, he would find that all the people once living there had been exterminated. And in a gesture consonant with *La vorágine*'s investigations into the secrets of commodity fetishism, Rivera notes that no one in the metropolitan centers suspects the extreme violence that underwrites the history of rubber. Little do "the ostentatious banker, the elegant lady, and the satisfied worker" know just what had gone into the making of the tires on their automobiles. If rubber could talk, however, "it would exhale the most accusing wail, formed by the cries of flesh torn away by the whip, the moans of bodies devastated by hunger and swollen by *beriberi*, and the screams of the exploited and persecuted tribes" (1991, 108).

But the power of such images—analyzed in this chapter under the rubric of the "export real"—is undermined as Rivera lapses into the fantasy that with the help of Mr. Ford, things can now be different. Indians, understandably wary of whites, will flock to Ford as an "unexpected Messiah" once they understand that their work will be rewarded with wages and fair treatment. "The Amazon forest is a reserve of humanity and someone should, in its name, take the first step toward preparing and adapting it for future men [*las razas por venir*]." The rehetoric is familiar: the rainforest is a gigantic "reserve" awaiting human intervention. Though this intervention is explicitly named as that of private enterprise, it is justified in the name of humanity as a whole. Further, once nature is dominated, returns will be fantastic, exceeding even "the most optimistic calculation" (108).

Rivera wakes up from the nightmare of the novel (the export real) to walk right into the waking dream of export reverie. This well-worn legitimizing fantasy was rejected in *La vorágine* but reappears in Rivera's letter to the North American capitalist. Rivera disavows this knowledge of the real and hopes for the arrival of a more rational model of production (one associated with Fordism, no less). Things will now be different: the irrationality and cruelty unleashed by the previous commodity boom will result in lasting prosperity; Indians, still nameless and faceless in liberal discourse, will recognize the benefits of work; the jungle will respond to the rational intervention of engineers and technicians. There is, of course, no doubt that the conditions of workers under Fordism are preferable to those under slavery and debt peonage. But the Rivera of the letter expresses an illusory (if defensible) desire for a kind of capitalism that does not include violence.

The letter to Ford represents a step back into the waking dream of ideology, not because the periphery is destined to fail, as if by some congenital deficiency, in the order of capital. Rather, Rivera's position is illusory because it pretends not to know—against history and experience—how capital operates on a global scale. Capital, when given the chance, does not naturally produce well-fed workers and equitable social relations. Instead, capital must reproduce itself; the historical record shows that in order to do so, it frequently takes advantage of existing depredations and inequalities. More equitable relations do not come from an unexpected Messiah, no matter how magnanimous he might be, but from struggle. This struggle, of course, is more difficult to wage on the remote, lawless peripheries of production and exchange, where, if workers and resources become too much of a bother, capital can always go elsewhere. Shortly after writing his letter to Ford (which seems to have gone unanswered), Rivera died unexpectedly of pneumonia in New York City. Thus he did not live to see the results of Ford's creation of a model town in the Brazilian Amazon, named Fordlân-dia. There Ford undertook to recreate a felicitous copy of Ameri-can suburban life, complete with little houses, orderly streets and fire hydrants. Considering himself a philanthropist, Ford wanted to help modernize the backwaters of Brazil while efficiently produc-ing rubber for his automobiles in Detroit. The experiment, however, as Greg Grandin recounts in a recent book, was a disaster (2009). Conceived in the image of rationality, the planting methods used took rubber trees out of their natural environment, where they were attacked by parasites. The autocratic Fordist model of disci-pline—in which the polka and waltzes were imposed on workers— also failed miserably. After some years, Fordlândia became, like the opera house at Manaus, another ruin, this time with a North American suburban face.[26]

The continued relevance of *La vorágine* as a text that tries to understand exploitation is confirmed by the fact that these ruins continue to pile up. For the most part, yesterday's sites of colonial extraction remain the vortexes of today. These are places, to recall Patnaik's words, in which capitalism has been both revolutionary and not revolutionary enough, or, alternately, that are both too con-nected to global capital, and not connected enough to warrant pro-tection against ongoing waves of dispossession and violence. To go no further than Colombia, the plains and rivers traveled by Arturo Cova are the same as those traversed today by drug runners, para-militaries, leftist guerrillas, Colombian soldiers and U.S. marines fighting for control over cocaine production. Indeed, as the literary critic Juan Gustavo Cobo Borda (2004) notes, substitute "cocaine" for "rubber," and *La vorágine* lives on as part of "the recurring nightmare of history."

Conclusion

RETURN TO MACONDO

The Promise of Bananas

In 1908, the legendary Colombian Liberal and general Rafael Uribe Uribe delivered a speech to the Agricultural Society of Colombia. The subject of the conference: "El banano" (The banana). The hundred-page speech offers a wealth of information about the crop, with sections devoted to origins, uses and byproducts, growing conditions, labor needs, and varieties. Uribe Uribe knew something about agriculture. For when he wasn't fighting in civil wars against Conservatives (in 1876, 1886, 1895, and 1899), he was a coffee planter in Antioquia. And as a liberal visionary and man of "progress," he dedicated himself to outlining new sources of export wealth for the country. This search for new sources of national wealth became especially urgent in the aftermath of the War of One Thousand Days (1899–1902) fought between Liberals and Conservatives. Legendary for its destruction of human life and wreckage of an already precarious national economy, this war created a huge displaced population and massive hunger in its wake. Notably, for Uribe Uribe, the path toward national recovery would be the same as that proffered by earlier generations of liberal visionaries: export agriculture.

What is most striking to me about this speech is that it continues in a dogged defense of the export dream, even in the aftermath of war, ceaseless financial crises, and, after 1903, the loss of Colombia's most valuable asset, the isthmus of Panama. Though in the 1870s and 1880s coffee had been seen as a panacea to civil conflict, it had not lived up to its promise: Uribe Uribe himself played a significant role in starting the War of the Thousand Days—the greatest conflagration yet between Conservatives and Liberals. Moreover, coffee itself had proved a lucrative, though highly unstable source of national wealth. It is all the more unsettling, then, that Uribe Uribe writes as if awakening to the utopian possibilities of American agricultural abundance for the first time: "The possession of the banana is enough to justify the consoling proverb: *In América no one dies of hunger except he who desires it.* Might civilized Europe [*la Europa civilizada*] say the same?" (1908, 23; emphasis in original]. América, as proverbial land of natural plenty, is capable of feeding the "civilized" countries of Europe. Accompanied by improvements in education and transportation, "the banana and other tropical fruits will prove themselves to be elements of progress" (24).

The strains of export reverie, the mode of discourse studied in chapter 1, can be heard here, as Uribe Uribe announces a dream vision of the future rooted in export-driven agricultural production. Two dimensions of export reverie are worth recalling here: first, its conjuring of a prosperous future through the conversion of the gifts of nature into export commodities; and second, its overtly lyrical strains, through which economic expansion itself becomes a form of poetry. Not surprisingly, Uribe Uribe begins the speech with an epigraph from Andrés Bello's "Silva a la agricultura de zona tórrida" (Ode to tropical agriculture [1826]), an unavoidable reference point for nineteenth-century export reveries: "Y para tí el banano / Desmaya al peso de su dulce carga; / El banano, primero / De cuantos concedió bellos presentes / Providencia a las gentes del Ecuador feliz" (1908, 5; "And for you the banana plant/sags under dulcet weight. Banana, first/ of all the plants that Providence has offered/to happy tropic's folk with generous hand [Bello 1997, 30]). He goes on to cite the German naturalist Alexander von Humboldt, whose writings on the sublimity of American nature had inspired generations of creole writers as lauding the nutritional properties of the banana, and Bernardin Saint-Pierre, author of the Romantic novel *Paul et Virginie*, as naming the banana "king of all plants" (*rey de los vegetales,* 1908, 22).

But Uribe Uribe does not stop at gathering modern literary referents; instead, he shows that the banana belongs to the *mythic* origins of world civilization. I cite from the first paragraph of the speech: "This precious plant has been known to humankind since its origins. . . . A complete description of [the banana] is found in the *Vedas,* in the laws of Manu, and in other monuments of Sanskrit literature" (1908, 5). The banana, he notes, also makes its appearance in Semitic, Greek, and Arab texts. In medieval Europe, the banana was called *pomum paradisi,* because people thought it was the real fruit offered by the serpent to Eve in the Garden of Eden: according to this legend, "the banana was the true tree of the knowledge good and evil" (6). It is with these stories in mind that Uribe Uribe nominates the banana to the status of "mythical plant" (*vegetal mítico*), "or rather those [plants] for which nations have created some legend to explain how Providence graced them with their useful possession and enjoyment" (6).

It is only because Colombians have known the banana since childhood "that we do not fully realize . . . its worthiness of the honors of poetry" (35). The country might still have poets to sing to the banana: this aestheticizing labor is, of course, exactly what Uribe Uribe is performing, not in verse form but as reverie, through which aesthetics and political economy merge to produce a beautiful vision of the future. This lyrical opening sustains the technical discussion that constitutes the rest of the speech, on the multiple uses of the banana (beer, vinegar, flour, medicine, wood); its growth patterns and transport; and exploration of markets in Colombia and Costa Rica. Near the end, Uribe Uribe also outlines possible cooperation with a new partner: the North American firm United Fruit.

The United Fruit Company of Boston, of course, would go on to have an iniquitous history in South and Central America, its name becoming synonymous with a particularly egregious form of North American imperialism in the hemisphere. In addition to introducing the banana into wide consumption in the United States, United Fruit (today Chiquita) is credited with the creation of the "banana republic," a name for a type of polity almost entirely dominated by a foreign company. The company became especially reviled in the aftermath of a massacre of striking workers in Ciénaga, Colombia, in 1928, and after a C.I.A.-funded overthrow of the social democrat Jacobo Arbenz in Guatemala in 1954, after he attempted to carry out agrarian reform. The coup against Arbenz became a key reference point for future socialist revolutionaries, including Fidel Castro and Ernesto "Che" Guevara. Little could Uribe Uribe have known the magnitude of the storm that was gathering on the horizon as he sang so optimistically to the banana.

Macondo's Myths

The history of United Fruit in Latin America also inspired the novelist Gabriel García Márquez, who was born in the banana-producing town of Aracataca, Colombia, in 1927. His birth came just a year before a massacre of striking United Fruit workers by the Colombian army in nearby Ciénaga. This massacre, along with the arrival and departure of the banana company from the mythical town of Macondo, is famously depicted in his novel *Cien años de soledad* (*One Hundred Years of Solitude*, 1967), probably the most famous Latin American novel ever published. I will not attempt an in-depth analysis of this novel here, but I will remind the reader that it combines the history of the Buendía clan with the history of the town of Macondo. Macondo begins as a small, sleepy hamlet founded by the cousins Ursula and José Arcadio Buendía, who are cast out of their original home for committing the crime of incest. As Macondo grows, its peaceful life is interrupted by intermittent civil wars and by the arrival of foreigners, among them, Arab and gypsy peddlers and a vaguely Oriental figure named Melquíades, who writes down the prophecy of Macondo in a set of mysterious texts. No one in Macondo can understand these texts because they are written in Sanskrit. Macondo eventually becomes a bustling banana enclave, complete with a railway, electricity, and movie theaters, but also marked by violence and exploitation: the part of the novel dealing with the banana company culminates in a great massacre. After this, the banana company leaves, seemingly without warning, and Macondo is reduced to ruins. It is only after this ruin that the last of the Buendías is able to finally understand a prophecy that had been set down in Melquíades's texts. It says that the last of the line—Aureliano and his aunt Amaranta Ursula—will commit incest and give birth to a baby with a pig's tail, heralding the full-scale destruction of Macondo.

Critics have frequently discussed the mythic foundations of *Cien años de soledad* as a key component of the novel's poetics. But frequently, the mythic and circular time to which García Márquez and other "Boom" novels correspond is interpreted as hailing from premodern elements of social life in Latin America. On this reading, Macondo is a place where temporality can "still" be seen as mythic and circular rather than linear and progressive or, alternately, where mythmaking and magic have not been stamped out by the stultifying and rational logic of modern capitalism. From this perspective, García Márquez retains access to a past that is no longer available to people in technology-driven, ultra-specialized societies.

But if we reconsider *Cien años de soledad* in light of Uribe Uribe's speech "El banano," and indeed in light of the capital fictions assembled in this book, the mythic past to which the novel appeals takes on intriguing new meanings. To my knowledge, no one has discussed Uribe Uribe's speech "El banano" in relationship to García Márquez's novel. It is well known that Uribe Uribe inspired one of the most famous characters of *Cien años de soledad,* José Arcadio Buendía, who in the novel is a Liberal general who fights in a particularly destructive civil war. And so it is possible, and indeed probable, that García Márquez read or at least knew about "El banano," a foundational text of the banana industry in coastal Colombia.

This probability is made more meaningful if we consider *Cien años de soledad* as a mythologized rendering of Uribe Uribe's speech. Here we will remember that the very legends Uribe Uribe sets down in his speech reappear in García Márquez's novel as key elements of his story. As many critics have noted, the exodus of Ursula and José Arcadio from their birthplace echoes the biblical story of Adam and Eve, as does the incest plot that drives the novel forward (and backward). The Sanskrit texts, on the other hand, have been seen as a metaphor for history, or of language itself. These are valid interpretations, but I would like to entertain the possibility that the Sanskrit prophecy set down by Melquíades might hail from a more specific source. Two of the key mythical elements from *Cien años de soledad,* the story of Adam and Eve and ancient Sanskrit texts, are already present in Uribe Uribe's speech, distant referents invoked to predict the glorious future of the banana. In his role as liberal fortuneteller, Uribe Uribe looks back to an archaic past and forward to a wish-image of modernity. García Márquez, in his turn, transforms Uribe Uribe himself, along with his speech, into a foundation for his own myth of origins. For what is *Cien años de soledad* if not, to paraphrase Uribe Uribe, a legend about how Providence "graced" Macondo with the banana? From this perspective, the foundational Sanskrit texts that appear in the novel might overlap with Uribe Uribe's own mythical referents, referents that at the same time predict a glorious *future* under the sign of the banana. Is it not possible that Uribe Uribe's own text is incorporated as both myth and prophecy into *Cien años de soledad?* It just might be that the prophecy locked in Melquíades's old texts is none other than the future promised by Uribe Uribe, which, however, read from the present, seems only to foretell a catastrophe. In this sense, the true meaning of the export reverie, pointing simultaneously toward a mythical past and a glorious future, is unavailable at the time of writing. It becomes fully legible only once destiny has taken its course. But by then it is too late:

> Before reaching the final line, however, he had already understood that he would never leave that room, for it was foreseen that the city of mirrors (or mirages) would be wiped out by the wind and exiled from the memory of men at the precise moment when Aureliano Babilonia would finish deciphering the parchments, and that everything written on them was unrepeatable since time immemorial and forever more, because races condemned to one hundred years of solitude did not have a second opportunity on earth. (1991, 422)

It is entirely possible to read the demise of the Buendía clan and of Macondo in mythical terms, but this myth is of a more recent vintage than that generally assumed. Never simply a register of the "still" traditional/oral/superstitious societies of Latin America, it is rather an expression of a modernity that had already been envisioned by way of archaic foundations and futuristic dreams. For García Márquez, this futuristic dream is already a ruin, and the archaic ur-past is available as modern myth. The humble banana, never quite ordinary or self-evident as commodity, gives rise to a story of origins and a prophecy of a catastrophe. From amid these ruins, the order of capital itself becomes available as a foundational myth of Latin American societies.

Acknowledgments

It gives me great pleasure to acknowledge the debts I accrued in the process of writing this book. This book began as a dissertation under the direction of Mary Louise Pratt and Richard Rosa, the two teachers from whom I have learned the most. Mary continues to provide me with a model for rigorous and politically engaged scholarship. Richard's prodigious intellect is matched only by his generosity as a teacher and scholar, and this book never would have gotten off the ground without his guidance. Many other teachers and mentors in graduate school, especially Gordon Brotherston, Roland Greene, Lúcia Sá, Francine Masiello, Julio Ramos, and Ann Stoler gave intellectual sustenance while encouraging me to ask harder questions.

Many ideas developed in this book were shaped by long telephone conversations with my oldest friend and partner in crime, Marcial Godoy-Anativia. As an endlessly creative translator–roller skater–agitator–apostate, he has shaped my political and aesthetic sensibilities in many more ways than I can recogize. Thanks are also due to the beautiful and brilliant Karina Hodoyán for always giving me a home and for letting me become her *norteña* sister. With inimitable irreverence and clarity, Enrique Lima has taught me much about uneven development and literary form. Thanks also to graduate school buddies Raúl Coronado, Soledad Gelles, Marisol Negrón, Sara Rondinel, María Helena Rueda, and Kyla Wazana Tompkins. Across multiple time zones and states of mind, I have come to rely on my dear friends Alexander Regier and Laura Ceia to point me in the right direction.

The University of Illinois at Urbana–Champaign provided an ideal intellectual and institutional environment for the writing of this book. Members of my writing group (Ellen Moodie, Anna Stenport, and Yasemin Yildiz) offered insightful comments on several drafts of these chapters and unflagging encouragement to push on. Special thanks go to Yasemin for sharing with me the ups and downs of the writing process and for telling me when enough was enough. Martin Manalansan guided me through the unfamiliar territory of academic book publishing with wit and grace. Thanks to friends and colleagues at the University of Illinois who accompanied me as I wrote this book. These include Matti Bunzl, Nancy Blake, Eleonor Courtemanche, Luisa Elena, Delgado, Jed Esty, Dara Goldman, Lauren Goodlad, Behrooz Ghamari, Wail Hassan, Lilya Kaganovsky, Jean-Philippe Mathy, Manuel Rota, Michael Rothberg, Robert Rushing, and Eleonora Stoppino. I thank graduate students in Spanish and comparative literature for allowing me to test out my ideas in seminars and for breathing new life into readings in danger of becoming stale. I could not have asked for a better research assistant than Sally Perret in the preparation of this manuscript; thanks also to Arnaud Perret for help with illustrations.

I was fortunate to receive valuable input on different portions of this book from audiences at talks delivered at Columbia University, the University of California at Berkeley, and the University of Oregon. Thanks to Alessandro Fornazzari for co-organizing special panels at ACLA and LASA congresses. Jill Lane came to the rescue by reading and commenting on a draft of the manuscript at a crucial moment. I am grateful to the two anonymous reviewers at the University of Minnesota Press for helping me to clarify my main points and for saving me from some oversights and mistakes. The ones that remain are, of course, my own.

The completion of this book would not have been possible without generous institutional support. Travel grants from the Center for Latin American Studies at Stanford University and the Center for Latin American and Caribbean Studies at the University of Illinois financed research trips to libraries in Chile, Argentina, Peru, Bolivia, and Chile, where I began to gather many of the materials collected in this book. The Campus Research Board and the Department of Spanish, Italian, and Portuguese at the University of Illinois generously provided leaves from teaching, which allowed me to finish writing and editing. I recognize the assistance I received from librarians at Biblioteca Nacional in Buenos Aires and Biblioteca Luis Angel Arango in Bogotá. At the University of Illinois, Nelly González guided me to forgotten treasures in the university library. Thanks also to Alejandro Lajer for tracking down nineteenth-century newspapers in Argentina.

Thanks to Richard Morrison, my editor at the University of Minnesota Press, for believing in this project, and to his assistant, Erin Warholm-Wohlenhaus. Thanks also to John Eagleson for his copyediting skills.

The love and support of my parents, Michael and Pamela, and my brother, Kurt, predate this book by decades and hence comprise its most important point of origin.

Finally, my deepest love and gratitude go to my husband, best friend, and most trusted interlocutor, Marcelo Bucheli. More than anyone else, Marcelo has lived with and through this book, providing ideas and reassurance when I most needed them and inventing ever-new ways to make me laugh. Each day with him, and now Camila too, is truly a gift.

Notes

Dates of works are cited parenthetically, with original publication dates in brackets when relevant.

Introduction

1. The Bolivian "water wars" served as a symbolic referent for the James Bond movie *Quantum of Solace* (2008), much of it set in Bolivia, in which the final plot twist reveals that the evil multinational is not trying to secure oil reserves but water. This cinematic conspiracy fantasy, in which there lies a grain of truth, resonates with a claim attributed to Terry Eagleton, that "it would take a transformation of the political economy of the entire planet just to make sure everyone on it had access to clean drinking water" (qtd. in Žižek 2010, 199).

2. The memo is available at http://www.whirledbank.org/ourwords/summers.html.

3. In response to the Summers memo, Brazil's then-secretary of the environment, Jose Lutzenburger, wrote: "Your reasoning is perfectly logical but totally insane.... Your thoughts [provide] a concrete example of the unbelievable alienation, reductionist thinking, social ruthlessness and the arrogant ignorance of many conventional 'economists,' concerning the nature of the world we live in." This response cost Lutzenbuger his job (http://www.whirledbank.org/ourwords/summers.html).

4. Slavoj Žižek, in a series of recent interventions, has powerfully demonstrated the perverse logic by which we come to believe, in times of unprecedented financial crisis, that in order for people to be saved, capital must be saved: under this fiction, a global health pandemic like AIDS, Žižek writes, can wait, "but the call 'Save the banks!' is an unconditional imperative which demands and receives immediate action. The panic was here absolute, a transnational, nonpartisan unity was immediately established, all grudges between world leaders momentarily forgotten in order to avert *the* catastrophe. We may worry as much as we want about global realities, but it is Capital which is the Real of our lives" (2010, 334).

5. The nineteenth century did not mark the first time the present-day countries of Latin America were drawn into world markets as commodity producers. Aside from the well-known history of metal extraction initiated under Spanish colonialism, colonies such as Cuba and Saint-Domingue (later Haiti) belonged to an emerging world market as "sugar islands"; export commodity production increased gradually with the transition from mercantilism to capitalism, and from colonial rule to (mostly) independent

nation sovereignty in the early nineteenth century. It was during the last quarter of the nineteenth century, however, that market integration acquired unprecedented speed and intensity. See Halperín Donghi (1993, chapters 4 and 5) and Topik and Wells (1997, Introduction).

6. Eric Hobsbawm (1975, 1987) studies this period in Europe under the rubrics of the "Age of Capital" (1848–75), marked by the rise of industrial production, and the "Age of Empire" (1875–1914), when European states fought for control over the earth's resources.

7. Long before the rise of global capitalism, América had been considered a repository of wealth: from the sixteenth to the eighteenth centuries, American colonies filled the coffers of Europe with gold and silver, the very definition of wealth within the mercantilist system. With the rise of capitalism in the eighteenth and nineteenth centuries, however, the definition of wealth changed from one measured by specie to one defined by the store of useful commodities a given society could produce. Hence if América's worth had previously been judged by its stores of gold (an intrinsically valuable substance under mercantilism), the rise of the bourgeois order produced a system of value in which commodities, whose value was judged not internally but against one another, became the definition of wealth. Hence the value of gold, as commodity, itself became fungible and identifiable in myriad different forms. This is the logic behind Export Age variations on the old referent for value, such as "black gold" (oil), "white gold" (nitrates), "green gold" (bananas and henequen), etc.

8. Latin American history, it must be noted, is inscribed into the very origins of theories of underdevelopment and dependency. Andre Gunder Frank's classic study *Capitalism and Underdevelopment in Latin America* (1967) argued that the social structures of this region were not mired in "feudalism" (a term that implies a temporal disjuncture with properly capitalist metropolitan centers) but rather were a creation of modern capitalism. Capitalism, that is, and not its absence, was the source of the poverty of the periphery. Theorists loosely afilliated with the "dependency school" argued that the origins of Latin America's poverty lay in unequal trade relations between imperial centers and their peripheries (see, for example, Cardoso and Faletto's key work, *Dependency and Development in Latin America* ([1969] 1979). The world-systems analysis pioneered by Immanuel Wallerstein (1979), in turn, divided the entire globe into regions of "core," "periphery," and "semiperiphery," interacting within a single system of exchange. While the specific debates animating this diverse group of theories remains outside the scope of the present work, it remains indebted to the concept of a single capitalist system characterized by internal inequalities as a horizon for cultural analysis.

9. See Harvey, *The Limits to Capital* (2006a) particularly chapters 9 and 13; a more concise version of his theory of temporal and spatial fixes and accumulation by dispossession is found in Harvey, "Notes Towards a Theory of Uneven Geographical Development" (2006b).

10. I thank Richard Rosa for sharing his unpublished manuscript, "Finance and Literature in Spanish America." For a reading of the nineteenth-century Puerto Rican writer Eugenio de Hostos's understanding of emerging market society, see Rosa, *Los fantasmas de la razón: Una lectura material de Hostos* (2003).

11. On Britain's eighteenth-century "financial revolution," see J. G. A. Pocock (1975, 1985), Patrick Brantlinger (1996), and Laura Brown (2001); on the U.S. Gilded Age, see Walter Benn Michaels (1987) and Bill Brown (2003).

12. I am drawing here from Angel Rama's classic work *The Lettered City* ([1996] 1984), in which the Uruguayan critic identifies writing as a key mode of political power in Spanish America. Beginning with the edicts and legal documents of the Spanish colonial bureaucracy, through the deployment of scientific and literary discourses by the post-Independence state, Rama highlights the special prestige attached to the written word in Spanish American societies.

13. I am thinking of key studies from the 1990s by Francine Masiello (1992), Mary Louise Pratt (1992), and Doris Sommer (1991), among others, which mapped the dynamics of power involved in nineteenth-century writing, with particular attention to the interplay between gender, sexuality, and race as central points of conflict in emerging national cultures.

14. Classical political economy's reliance on fiction was long ago pointed out by Marx, who begins his "Introduction to the Critique of Political Economy" with an attack on Smith and Ricardo's depiction of economic man as an isolated hunter and fisher along the lines of Daniel Defoe's novel *Robinson Crusoe*. These isolated individuals, writes Marx, "are the fiction and only the aesthetic fiction of the small and great Robinsonades" (1998, 1). More recently, the economist Deirdre McCloskey (1985) has argued that the contemporary discipline of neoclassical economics relies on rhetorical (literary) maneuvers to establish its authority.

15. A number of studies have explored the formal similarities between money and fiction, and, on a larger scale, the relationship between monetary and literary economies. Marc Shell's *The Economy of Literature* (1978), Kurt Heinzelman's *The Economics of the Imagination* (1980), and Walter Benn Michaels's *The Gold Standard and the Logic of Naturalism* (1987) are early classics of this approach. Works such as these are often grouped under the rubric of the "new economic criticism," a loose categorization that refers to (post) structuralist, new historicist, and neo-Marxian analyses of economics and aesthetics. See Woodmansee and Osteen (1999).

16. One notable exception is Gootenberg (1993).

17. See, for example, studies by Molloy (1992, 1997) and Montero (1993) on gender and sexuality in *modernista* texts; Nouzeilles (2000) and Salessi (2000) on criminality and medicine in *fin de siglo* Argentina; and Aronna (1999) and Trigo (2000) on turn-of-the-century discourses on race and illness.

18. Of special interest to this study is a growing corpus of scholarly works on commercial practices such as collecting and national exhibitions. See González-Stephan and Andermann (2006), Fernández Bravo (2001), and López Mejías (2006). Another body of recent scholarship has examined the relationship between monetary and literary economies in the current neoliberal era. See, for example, Cárcamo Huechante (2007) and Fornazzari (2009).

19. See especially Schwarz's recently translated *A Master on the Periphery of Capitalism: Machado de Assis* (2001); and Rama's innovative but frequently overlooked *Las máscaras democráticas del modernismo* (The democratic masks of modernismo, 1985a). In my attempt to provide analyses of class, gender, and race as mutually supportive and reinforcing hierarchies, I recognize a special debt to the writings of Jean Franco, who perhaps more than any other Latin Americanist has been able to enrich Marxist modes of analysis with strong feminist critique. See especially *Plotting Women: Gender and Representation in Mexico* (1989), and *The Decline and Fall of the Lettered City: Latin America in the Cold War* (2002).

1. Production

1. A biweekly illustrated journal, *La América Ilustrada* (1871–75),was published by exiled Cuban liberals living in New York City and circulated throughout the hemisphere. This was just one of many Spanish-language publications dedicated to fomenting commerce between Latin American nations and centers of industrial development in Europe and the United States (see Greusz 2002, 187–92). In Latin American countries, the period after 1870 witnessed the creation of scores of illustrated liberal newspapers and magazines, with names like *El Progreso* (Progress) and *El Porvenir* (The Future).

2. All translations are my own unless otherwise noted. I also note that my use of the accented term "América" refers to the countries of Spanish- and Portuguese-speaking America.

3. Latin America was not alone in its specialization in these types of commodities for the global market. By the last quarter of the nineteenth century, European colonialism had succeeded in forcing the vast part of Asia and Africa into this role, securing resources in exchange for the supposed

benefits of European civilization. With the exception of Cuba and Puerto Rico, the nations of Latin America had won independence from Spain since the 1820s. But while formally independent, Latin American nations retained elements of colonial domination both externally and internally. As the Argentine historian Tulio Halperin Donghi has commented, independence from Spain marked the creation of a new set of neocolonial relations between Latin America and northern Europe, a "pact" that emerged with the first loans made to nascent governments in the 1820s and matured throughout the nineteenth century (1993).

4. The term "export reverie" is inspired by Mary Louise Pratt's "industrial reverie," a term she uses to describe the "modernizing, extractive vision" of early British travelers to independent Latin America (1992, 150). As a creole version of industrial reverie, export reverie continues to dream of a future in which blank, virgin American nature is incorporated into global commodity networks. Unlike the European industrial reveries studied by Pratt, however, creole export reveries tend to include a strong civic dimension together with their message of private economic enterprise, giving rise to a contradiction examined at length in the second half of this chapter.

5. Much recent literary and cultural criticism has studied representations of Latin American nature as emerging from within emerging scientific disciplines of geography and anthropology (González Echevarría 1998; Rodríguez 2004), or from within parallel discourses of sex and gender (Nouzeilles, ed. 2002). Many of these studies have expressed a Foucauldian-inspired concern with science as an ordering principle of modern epistemes. My contribution to this body of criticism, from a Marxian perspective, is to explore nineteenth-century articulations of nature as responses to the creation of a global capitalist division of labor, wherein Latin America's natural resources constituted its chief advantage.

6. The political projects grouped under the rubric of "liberalism" had many permutations in nineteenth-century Latin America, the specificities of which lie beyond the scope of this chapter. In focusing on the form of expression I call the export reverie, I will limit myself to a particular aspect of liberal projects: the belief, accepted by creole elites during the last quarter of the nineteenth century, that national modernity and well-being depended on individual nations' integration into global markets as exporters of raw materials and consumers of European manufactures. In studying the rhetorical articulations of this belief, I do not wish to flatten the extraordinarily variegated historical landscapes in which different articulations of liberalism flourished; to the contrary, my analysis aims to show the coherence of liberal tropes in a context of extremely uneven and tumultuous historical transformation. Readers with an interest in the intellectual history of liberalism in Spanish American contexts can consult Botana (1984), Castro Leiva (1992),

Gootenberg (1988 and 1993), Hale (1989), and Véliz (1994). A collection edited by Jacobsen and Love (1988), *Guiding the Invisible Hand,* contains essays on different countries' experiences with economic liberalism.

7. The classical theory of trade advantage was first articulated by Ricardo and then incorporated into the writings of subsequent theorists such as John Stuart Mill and Alfred Marshall. Ricardo was not himself widely read in nineteenth-century Latin America, but his theory of trade advantage percolated into discussions of political economy. As the historian Joseph Love notes, "an explicit articulation of the advantages of specialization in trade," derivable from Ricardo, was heard over the course of the nineteenth century in Latin America. "[Y]et the refrain was repeated much more frequently in the decades after 1880, corresponding to the beginning of a half-century of unprecedented production of agricultural and mineral goods, to be exchanged on the world market for manufactures" (1996, 395).

8. A more recent application of this neoclassical trade doctrine, and its hidden assumptions, might include tourism as a tropical country's main "advantage" in the world market. The Dominican Republic's advantage as tourist destination depends on a predetermined desire for warm weather and beaches on the part of northern tourists, coupled with the availability of cheap labor to clean hotels and provide other services. Here and in other cases, the cultural contingency of demand, as well as the inequality on which that demand is created, is erased and incorporated into the calculus of advantage.

9. See Coronil's discussion of nature as "the wealth of poor nations" in *The Magical State* (1997, 21–66).

10. In *A Century of Debt Crises in Latin America: From Independence to the Great Depression, 1820–1930,* the historian Carlos Marichal identifies several cycles of capital accumulation, followed by debt. The cycle beginning with Independence ended rapidly with the London stock market crisis of 1825. After this, the region remained in "hibernation" until around 1850, in the period elsewhere described by Eric Hobsbawm as initiating the "Age of Capital." See Marichal (1989), chapters 2 and 3.

11. The assumption that modes of production in different places implied *temporal* distance between them is one already written into early political economy. Adam Smith's *Lectures on Jurisprudence* posits stages countries must pass through on their way to becoming commercial nations: hunting, pasturage, farming, and commerce (1982, 200–222). This stagist approach is also incorporated into Sarmiento's *Facundo* (1845), in which he considers ranching as belonging to a "nomadic," "Oriental," and "barbaric" social order that should give way to commerce and "civilization." These stagist assumptions are more broadly incorporated into classical Marxist understandings of development, as in Marx's discussions of the Asiatic mode of

production as temporally and spatially removed from European capitalist societies. For a critique of this telos, see Chakrabarty (2008).

12. From the perspective of Sarmiento's dreams, we catch a glimpse of fantasy and imagination as integral components of bourgeois liberalism, something we are apt to overlook if we focus on Weberian readings of capitalism as an "iron cage" or condemnations of bourgeois utility and calculation waged from aesthetic quarters since the mid-nineteenth century. The Cuban Marxist historian Manuel Moreno Fraginals understood this when he wrote of the emergence of the Cuban bourgeois "soul" during the island's first major speculative boom near the end of the eighteenth century: "At the top of the curve there was a desperate investing and reinvesting fever, the grandiose awakening of the Cuban bourgeois soul, still with unlimited faith in its own strength and an irrepressible propensity to expand" (1976, 42–43).

13. See Mejías López (2006) for an analysis of incipient discourses of commercial display in three late nineteenth-century Spanish American magazines.

14. "¡Ya acaban las ruinas y comienzan los cimientos! Pierden las poblaciones su aspecto conventual, su tinte apático, su enfermizo matiz, y cobran, al ruido de las centrífugas, entre los pámpanos frondosos, entre los aromáticos cafetos, los colores de la juventud y las revelaciones de la vida. La libertad abrió esas puertas."

15. "Llaman Retalhuleu a un departamento que rebosa maderas, y suculento cacao, y el exquisito grano americano. Esto y caña produce Mazatenango, del mercantil Quezaltenango fiel tributario. En Quezaltenango abundan, sobre las fertilidades apuntadas, los ganados lanares. Inexplotado este ramo, es fuente segura de riqueza. Mucho tienen que hacer allí cardadores, exportadores, tejedores."

16. *Guatemala* is by no means the only instance in which Martí fuses aesthetic and commercial aims. As editor of the New York–based journal *La América* in the early 1880s, Martí wrote promotional essays for Latin American products ranging from coffee and bananas to quinine and cheese and penned advertisements for North American companies, including a tourist agency and brick company (1975h). Elsewhere I have argued that these texts—which have been mostly ignored by critics—should be taken seriously as representing an alternate direction taken by late nineteenth-century literary modernization in the region, helping to forge an incipient discourse of advertising (see Beckman 2008).

17. As the British intellectual historian J. G. A. Pocock has argued in *The Machiavellian Moment: Florentine Political Thought and the Atlantic Republican Tradition* (1975), the agrarian ideal rooted in classical political thought had been reinvented from the eighteenth century onward in the West as an antidote to the instability, fragmentation, and perceived feminization of

modern society in the wake of a wide-scale transition toward credit-based or "mobile" forms of wealth (see especially chapters 8 and 9). The dichotomy between the corrupt financial city and the salubrious countryside occurs over and again in Martí's oeuvre, especially in the writings he produced while living in New York City. The poem "Hierro," for example, represents the city as a feminized and corrosive space full of *copas de carne* (cups of flesh), and yearns for the virtue of the *campo inmenso* (immense countryside; 1975d, 16:142, line 29).

18. The pronouncement that agriculture should be Latin American countries' main source of wealth immediately calls to mind Physiocratic doctine of the seventeenth century. Founded by the court physician Quesnay, author of the *Tableau economique,* the Physiocrats provided an early challenge to mercantilists by maintaining that not money, but agricultural produce, was the basis for the nation's wealth. This doctrine was discredited, however, with the rise of eighteenth-century classical political economy, when wealth became defined as a country's store of useful commodities, agricultural or any other sort. Martí's observation that agriculture is Guatemala's main source of wealth, while perhaps owing something to the Physiocrats, was perhaps more directly influenced by aristocratic reformer Francisco Frías y Jacott, conde de Pozos Dulces, whose 1878 *Colección de escritos sobre la agricultura* proposes white ownership of small farms and crop variation as solutions to monocrop sugar plantations worked by slaves.

19. "¡Oh sí! El rico grano, que enardece la sangre, anima la pasión, aleja el sueño, inquietísimo salta en las venas, hace llama y aroma en el cerebro; el que afama a Urapan, mantiene a Colima y realza a Java; el *haschich* de América, que hace soñar y no embrutece; el vencedor del té; el caliente néctar, el perfumado cafeto, crece como la ilusión con los amores, como la marcha de la nube con el impulso de los vientos en los cerros y los planicies de la hospitalaria Guatemala."

20. *Guatemala* is not the only place in Martí's oeuvre that coffee is distinguished for its poetic properties: in a journalistic article from the same period, entitled "Los productos de Venezuela," Martí writes that "an ode boils in every cup" of the country's coffee (1975f, 7:242). And in one of his private notebooks, Martí went as far as to distinguish coffee as the ultimate inspiration: "Café, padre del verso. ¡Escencia viva!" ("Coffee, father of verse. Life essence!"; 1975b, 22:31).

21. These associations between coffee, pleasurable consumption, and poetic imagination cast a positive light on what Martí in other instances decries as corresponding to a corrosive ethic of luxury. From Martí's republican perspective, luxury is the maximum representation of excess and artifice as threats to the virtue and virility of citizens. In texts ranging from the "Prologue to the *Poema del Niágara*" (1882) to "Nuestra América" (1891),

luxury figures as a destabilizing and feminizing force, creating fantasy-ridden "damsels" (1975i, 7:223) and "seven-month men" (*sietemesinos*) instead of "real" or "natural" men (1975g, 6:16). In similar fashion, erotic desire frequently emerges in Martí's writings as a source of danger from which the virtuous male subject flees. And over and again in his oeuvre, Martí warns against overly imaginative and decorative forms of representation, insisting that writing correspond to the harmonious dictates of "nature." Together with "nature," "simplicity" and "sincerity" form core principles at the heart of Martí's literary aesthetic. Martí's incursion into erotic pleasure and flow occurs significantly around an export commodity, which is ultimately a source of productive national wealth.

22. For Marx the secret of the commodity resides in the particular way in which free labor finds its distorted mirror image in the commodities it produces, an observation that would seem to preclude a discussion of commodity fetishism in places where wage labor was not dominant. And yet, in volume 2 of *Capital,* Marx insists that on the world market, "the circuit of industrial capital, whether in the form of money capital or commodity capital, cuts across the commodity circulation of the most varied modes of social production" (1992, 2:189). He goes on to explain that whether the commodities are produced under conditions of slavery, serfdom, or non-capitalist hunting "is immaterial; they function in the market as commodities, and as commodities they enter both the circuit of industrial capital and the circulation of the surplus-value borne by it. Thus the circulation of process of industrial capital is characterized by the many-sided character of its origins and the existence of the market as a world market" (1992, 2:189–90). This comment would seem to suggest that any commodity, once set into global circuits of (industrial) capital, becomes a "social hieroglyphic" (1976, 1:167) worthy of examination.

23. The Cuban novel *Cecilia Valdés* (1882) by the abolitionist writer Cirilio Villaverde sets up a similar contrast between the brutality of the sugar plantation and the bucolic atmosphere of a coffee hacienda, which, while still worked by slaves, is coded as a less onerous system. In other countries, the association between coffee and democracy remains very much in force: countries such as Costa Rica and El Salvador continue to uphold the figure of the *colono,* or white settler, as an icon of self-sufficiency and entrepreneurship. In the region of Antioquia, Colombia, the romance of the smallholder is captured even more forcefully in the figure of Juan Valdez, the commercial ambassador of coffee par excellence.

24. This law, Greg Grandin notes, was modeled on the colonial *repartimiento* and drew from similar laws instituted in the 1830s (2000, 119).

25. Maria Josefina Saldaña-Portillo shows how during twentieth-century national liberation movements, indigenous people and women

remained at the outermost limits of revolutionary consciousness as subjects in need of education before they might become proper political subjects. See *The Revolutionary Imagination in the Americas and the Age of Development* (2003), especially chapter 3.

26. The period between 1930 and 1980, whose contours remain well outside the reach of this book, is often characterized as a reversal of the free-market, export-oriented reforms. Moreover, Martí's message of solidarity and cooperation among Latin American nations vis-à-vis imperial powers has provided a touchstone for a number of regionalist economic programs, most recently trade agreements such as ALBA (Alternativa Boliviariana para América Latina y el Caribe [Bolivarian Alternative for Latin America and the Caribbean]), proposed by Venezuelan president Hugo Chávez as an explicit alternative to the free trade treaties instated from the 1990s onward.

27. The rise of national industrial bourgeoisies in countries like Chile, Argentina, Mexico, Brazil, Colombia, and Venezuela in the twentieth century—and the rise of the modern Left to contest them—point to the reproduction of social inequality after the waning of the export-driven model and its replacement with economic protection and import-substitution industrialization.

2. Consumption

1. All translations are my own unless otherwise noted.

2. Martí and Casal are both considered forerunners of Spanish American *modernismo,* a continental literary current that sought to find an artistic language capable of representing the vast changes ushered in by modern life in the region at the end of the nineteenth century. My use of untranslated terms like *modernismo* and *modernista* seeks to distinguish the current from later and better-known articulations of Anglophone "modernism" (which in Spanish America is referred to as the *vanguardia* or "avant-garde"). The modifier "Spanish American," in turn, is meant to distinguish the current from Peninsular Spanish *modernismo* (a current that grew out of Spanish American *modernismo* after 1898) and from Brazilian *modernismo* (an avant-garde literary current of the 1920s). This confusion of terms already tells us something important regarding the transnational character of literary modernism(s): the need to mark the provenance and specificity of "Spanish American *modernismo*" speaks to its marginal, indeed peripheral position within world literary history. I will also note here that this chapter is concerned with what is generally studied as the "first wave" of Spanish American *modernismo,* running roughly between 1888 (the date of Rubén Darío's landmark work *Azul*) and 1900. This chapter examines three of the most important figures of this first wave—Darío, Casal, and Silva—as producers

of discourse on commodity consumption. For a broader discussion of this current in relation to Spanish American modernity, see Aching (1997), Kirkpatrick (1989), and Jrade (1998). Earlier studies by Jitrik (1970, 1978), Rama (1974, [1970] 1985) and Shulman (1969) continue to be useful guides to the central aesthetic propositions and influences of this current, which ranged from romanticism and the Parnasse to symbolism and decadence.

3. This shift is identified and traced in Julio Ramos's now classic study *Divergent Modernities* ([1989] 2001) in which José Martí is considered a key figure in the transition from a relatively undifferentiated sphere of civic writing (predominant until the 1870s), toward increasingly specialized and professional fields of writing. Ramos shows that what Angel Rama famously called "the lettered city" (in which state apparatuses provided writer's primary institutional and ideological framework) had by the 1870s begun to fragment and splinter into more specialized fields. On a material level, this fragmentation was pushed by the proliferation of print media such as newspapers, and with it the increasing professionalization of writing. This professionalization, Ramos argues, made possible the creation of a semiautonomous literary sphere, characterized simultaneously by the absorption of writing into the market, *and* the author's rejection of market logics through an incipient discourse of literary disinterest. This and other chapters examine different ways in which Latin American literary production interacted with market forces, not only through the differentiation of institutional spheres but through writers' specific engagements with different aspects of the economy, ranging from export production and import consumption to monetary speculation.

4. For useful discussions of *fin-de-siglo* literary production and questions of literary professionalization and autonomization, see Jitrik (1978), Rama ([1970] 1985b), Ramos ([1989] 2001), and Rotker (2000). A recent set of studies, such as those by Jrade (1998) and Aching (1997), in response to widespread perceptions about *modernismo*'s "apolitical" and "escapist" nature, have examined the deeply political investments of this current, especially with regard to contemporary issues like U.S. empire, social movements, and state politics.

5. In my focus on *modernismo* as a locus of discourses on consumption, I follow the lead of scholars who have already begun to ask after the significance of commodity consumption and display in late nineteenth-century Latin America, through exhibits at World Fairs, national museums, as well as through new practices of art collection and fashion. Taken together with scholarship on the gendered and sexual politics of *modernismo* (Kirkpatrick [1989], Molloy [1992], Montero [1993], among others), this chapter charts new ways of understanding emerging aesthetic discourses within a wider social and political frame. For this analysis, I have found it necessary

to return to a number of early, Marxist-inflected studies of *modernismo* as a basis for my critique of *modernista* commodity poetics, reevaluating contributions by critics such as José Blanco Aguinaga ([1980] 1997), Noé Jitrik (1978), Françoise Perus (1976), and Angel Rama (1974, 1985a [1970], 1985b, 1996).

6. Like the styles and images running through *Azul,* the term "bourgeois" was most likely adopted from French authors like Murget and Daudet. Additionally, the term "bourgeois king" has a historical referent in Louis Philippe, the last monarch of France, who earned this nickname from his close ties with industrialists and financiers, and for his abandonment of aristocratic pomp for bourgeois dress and manners. As such, the bourgeois king—in French history and in Darío's story—is a double-faced figure, rooted at once in the aristocratic past and in an emerging bourgeois present.

7. The critique of literary professionalization was itself intensely contradictory, Angel Rama reminds us, since Darío, rather than figuring as an enemy of this process in turn-of-the-century Latin America, was one of its greatest champions ([1970] 1985b, 52–53). Writing in the late 1960s and early 1970s, Rama is one of the first critics to view *modernismo* as not simply opposed to bourgeois society (essentially this current's vision of itself, which in turn became a central premise of Latin American literary studies in the early twentieth century), but as a contradictory outgrowth of this very society. In works like *Rubén Darío y el modernismo* ([1970] 1985b) and in *Las mascaras democráticas del modernismo* (1985a), Rama identifies this current as one defined by ambivalence and contradiction with respect to dependent, peripheral bourgeois societies. My approach remains heavily indebted to Rama's early work. The present work differs from Rama's approach, however, in that I am less concerned with the construction of a formalized literary sphere than I am with the manifold cultural expressions of capitalist modernity in Latin America.

8. Many critics have linked the proliferation of objects in Spanish American *modernista* texts to the tradition of the baroque. Gwen Kirkpatrick writes, for example, that *modernismo* borrows from a baroque sensibility in which objects are "not valuable for mimetic representation, but for their ability to be read as opposite signs, not straining to build bridges of relation between the objects of images themselves." Kirkpatrick further calls attention to the fetish quality of objects in *modernismo,* "emptied of their real (that is, tangible) information of representation, their physical density, and are presented in their signifying sense as signs" (1989, 9). At the same time, however, we should not lose sight of how such textual sublimations function not only to fetishize signs but actual commodities. In like manner, the relationship between baroque and *modernista* objects, while outside the

scope of this chapter, should be approached as a problem of form but also of material history.

9. Bill Brown has argued that Benjamin's appropriation of Marx's notion of commodity fetishism "misrepresents Marx because it seems to insist on understanding our desire for objects as more primary than understanding the structure through which they become commodities" (2003, 31). An aesthetic or psychological relation to objects, then, occludes the formal process by which objects become commodities in the first place. Brown might be right about Benjamin's reading of Marx; but if there is a misrepresentation, I think it is a productive one. For Benjamin shows that within the commodity system, the mystification of production *enables* the aesthetic properties in a special way, in a further mystification of social relations. That is, the structural relation of the fetish—present in all commodities under capitalism—works as a starting point for the commodity form as individual fantasy. The further an object might be removed from spheres of production and exchange, the more it might become an object of fantasy; paradoxically, the further this object travels from its site of production, in both literal and figurative terms, the more it may be shorn of its commodity character and invested with desire.

10. Along these lines, Colin Campbell argues that while most accounts of the rise of bourgeois societies in Europe and North America focus on a set of values Max Weber famously called "the Protestant ethic," this focus on bourgeois saving and austerity is unable to account for the "consumer revolution" of the eighteenth century. Campbell explains this discrepancy by arguing that the Protestant ethic coexisted and competed with a "Romantic ethic" (associated with pleasure, passion, and aesthetic sensation) that laid the foundations for modern consumerism (1987).

11. On the inventory in Balzac, Goncourt, and Flaubert, see Watson (1999).

12. Susan Buck Morss notes that early political economy's answer to the inequalities built into the new system of production was to reveal commodity consumption as a form of consumption for the drudgery and repetition inscribed into the new division of labor. This compensatory function of consumption depended, in turn, on the argument that European societies, no matter how unequal, enjoyed material comforts superior to other parts of the world. Buck Morss writes: "Despite distinctions between rich and poor, *all* members of 'civilization' can console themselves, because the *quantity* of *things they possess* marks them as superior to much of the world's population" (1995, 125, emphasis in original). In nineteenth-century Latin America, this compensatory logic expressed itself primarily as an elite justification for *international* division of labor; consumption of European manufactures and luxuries promised to compensate for the region's specialization

in the production of "raw" commodities for the global market. In another context, Anne McClintock has argued that the nineteenth century witnessed the rise of "commodity racism," a discourse through which consumer commodities themselves (soap especially) served as material indicators of the racial superiority of the English over colonized populations (1995, 32). Commodity racism is beneficial to the imperial power in two ways: first, it affirms white superiority as a justification for colonial rule; and, second, it effectively helps to create new markets for the manufactured goods the periphery is barred from producing. Empire does not only extract the natural resources of the colonial periphery; it turns around and sells them "civilized" goods.

13. A key text preceding Hume's "Of Refinement in the Arts" is Mandeville's poem *The Fable of the Bees* (1714), a satirical interpretation of proto-liberal arguments defending luxury consumption on the grounds that "private vice" created widespread "public benefits."

14. See Pike (1963, 16), and Villalobos (1987, 70–78).

15. On this point, see especially Schwarz's essay "Brazilian Culture: Nationalism by Elimination," in which he provides a thorough critique of the very notion of the "copy" as an objective mark of the intellectual and cultural inferiority of peripheral societies, seeing this concept instead as referring to the brutal inequalities of slave society in nineteenth-century Brazil. Hence for Schwarz the defect of the notion of the copy "presents as a national characteristic what is actually a malaise of the dominant class, bound up with the difficulty of morally reconciling the advantages of progress with those of slavery or its surrogates" (*Misplaced Ideas* 1992, 15).

16. On the feminization of consumer culture in fin-de-siécle Europe and its effects within masculine aesthetic discourse, see Emily Apter (1991), Rachel Bowlby (1985), and Rita Felski (1995).

17. In his reading of "El fénix," Oscar Montero has stressed the irony Casal employs with respect to the commodity spectacle of the department store. Montero suggests that this irony is the real position of the artist, who finds the commodity spectacle distasteful. But we should not take irony toward commodities at face value, especially when we turn to Casal's poetry (1993, 84–85).

3. Money I

1. The Desert Campaigns, led by General Julio Roca—who later became president of Argentina—took place at the same moment of westward expansion in the United States and similar projects of Indian removal in Chile. See David Viñas (1983).

2. Carlos Díaz Alejandro notes that in 1880, Argentina's population was 2,500,000. Over the next thirty years, the country would receive 3,200,000

immigrants, 80 percent of whom hailed from Italy and Spain. Around two-thirds of these immigrants settled permanently in Argentina (1980, 373).

3. While the Buenos Aires stock exchange was founded in 1854, it wasn't until the 1880s, with the huge influx of foreign loans, that it acquired material and symbolic significance as a mechanism for capital accumulation.

4. In the Revolution of 1890, the Unión Cívica political party ousted Juárez Celman in a coup, placing his vice president, Carlos Pellegrini, in power.

5. The first of such cycles of boom and bust was experienced in the immediate aftermath of Independence, when Argentina, together with other recently formed republics, became the recipient of British loans. This period of euphoria was brought to a sudden halt when overspeculation in Latin American bonds led to a stock market crash in England and new nations' subsequent default. After decades of financial "hibernation," cheap European credit became available again, only to culminate in the first global debt crisis in 1873, which placed Latin American countries again in default alongside the Ottoman Empire and Egypt. See Marichal (1989, chapters 2 and 3). In the context of the 1873 default, then-president Nicolás Avellaneda (in)famously remarked that the Argentine people would be content to suffer "hunger and thirst in order to save our compromised credit" (Avellaneda 1886, 103). This comment was frequently recalled in 2001, when Argentines were yet again called on to bear the brunt of financial crisis.

6. For a discussion of the Generation of 1880, see Foster (1990), Nouzeilles (1998), and Salessi (1995).

7. For discussions of the nineteenth-century Argentine stock market novels, see Jitrik (1970, 1980), Lewald (1983), Niemeyer (1998), and Wasserman (2001). The early twentieth century witnessed a continued fascination with the Baring Crisis in novels such as Osvaldo Saavedra, *Grandezas chicas* (1901), Roberto J. Payró, *Divertidas aventuras del nieto de Juan Moreira* (1910), and Emilio Gochon Cané, *El 90* (1928).

8. The up and down plotline of the stock market novel reaches well beyond this subgenre. As Franco Moretti (2000) has argued in his study of the European bildungsroman, the story of rise and fall is one of the central conventions of the nineteenth-century realist novel, which charts the "great expectations" and "lost illusions" of (male) bourgeois subjects.

9. Halina Suwala coins the term "novel of the stock exchange" to name a group of French novels, including Zola's *L'argent*, that were published after the 1882 collapse of the Unión Générale bank and investment company (qtd. in Wasserman [2001, 193, 210]).

10. See, for example, Morales (1997).

11. As Richard Rosa argues in his recent study "Finance and Literature in Spanish America" (book manuscript), credit-based forms of wealth have

exercised powerful effects on cultural discourse in Latin America since the founding of Independent nation-states in the 1820s. Examining works by figures ranging from Andrés Bello and Jorge Isaacs to Manuel Zeno Gandía and Jorge Luis Borges, Rosa argues that literature from the long nineteenth century refracts an oscillation between "mania" and "depression," categories that refer at once to psychosexual and monetary flows. Rosa notes, for example, that the plot of Jorge Isaacs's classic novel *María* (Colombia, 1867), which turns on the love story between Efraín and the epileptic Jewish convert María, can be read as corresponding to the financial upsets experienced by the seemingly idyllic hacienda in the rural Cauca Valley. The bodily twitchings of María coincide with the volatile movements of the family finances. In one instance, María experiences a fit just as Efraín's father learns of a huge loss he has incurred through mysterious speculative dealings. The closest historical and metaphorical referent for this dynamic of "mania" and "depression" is, Rosa reveals, the stock market (n.d., 34).

12. For an analysis of U.S. novels dealing with stock market speculation at the turn of the nineteenth century, including Norris's, see Alfred Zimmerman (2006).

13. A rich bibliography on Britain's eighteenth-century financial revolution examines anxieties surrounding emerging forms of credit-based wealth, including Laura Brown (2001), Patrick Brantlinger (1996), and J. G. A. Pocock (1975).

14. *The Thousand and One Nights* is a trope frequently used to signify the fantasy world embedded within the financial world and appears over and over in essays and novels about credit and finance in Latin America. Interestingly, Argentina's best-known writer, Jorge Luis Borges, incorporates frequent references to *The Thousand and One Nights* into his oeuvre, which might gain additional meaning as a trope for Argentina's financial history. Rosa has developed a related argument on Borges and finance (n.d. chapter 5).

15. For an integrated discussion of Marx's comments on credit and finance, scattered throughout his writings, see Harvey (2006a), especially chapters 9 and 10.

16. One critic writes that Miró seems to have fallen prey to "the very sickness he railed against"; see Bonet (1940, 50).

17. A similar switch in identity and voice was repeated two years later by the Brazilian novelist Alfredo Escargnole de Taunay. After losing money in the crisis of 1890, he wrote *O encilhamento* under the pseudonym of Heitor Malheiros, published in Rio de Janeiro's *Gazeta de Noticias* in 1893. For a discussion of Taunay's novel in relation to Zola's *L'argent* and Norris's *The Pit*, see Wasserman (2001).

18. On this point, see Julio Ramos ([1989] 2001). Ramos's main argument is the specificity of late nineteenth-century Latin American literary production hails in large part from an incomplete distinction between aesthetic, political, and economic fields.

19. As Josefina Ludmer writes in her study of intertwined fictions of state and crime in modern Argentina, "'the story' of 'the Jews' (a place of margin, alterity, and exclusion) is a story of the Latin American modernity that appears at the end of the nineteenth century," cohering on its identification of destabilizing elements within the nation. Referring to an "anthology" of these stories, ranging from López's *La grand aldea* and Martel's *La bolsa* to Borges's "Emma Zunz" and Arlt's *Los siete locos,* Ludmer continues that within the Argentine literary imaginary "[t]he Jews' are always the *representatives of money,* and the narrative that includes them is an economic narrative: banks, stock exchanges, and gold. 'The Jews' are the sign of the money sign: a sort of representation squared. Or better yet, 'the Jews' are the representatives of money, which is itself *an apparatus of representation"* (2004, 155; emphasis in original).

20. The racist markings of Jews as agents of finance capital (itself fashioned from medieval tropes) will be familiar to readers of nineteenth-century European or North American novels. In fact, as Evelyn Fishburn has noted, Martel's physical description of the Baron Von Mackser was lifted almost verbatim from Drumont's 1885 anti-Semitic tract *La France juive* (Fishburn 1981, 99). Also, *La bolsa* borrows liberally from Zola's portrayal of the Jewish banker Gundermann in *L'argent,* himself molded after the figure of the Parisian banker Jacob Rothschild. For a reading of Martel's anti-Semitism as a response to conflated anxieties surrounding cosmopolitanism and money, see Graff-Zivin (2008, 80–82).

21. The Rothschild and Baring families had already been counterposed in Byron's *Don Juan* (1822): "Who holds the balance of the world? Who reign / O'er congress, whether royalist or liberal? . . . / Jew Rothschild, and his fellow-Christian, Baring" (Canto XII, verse 5, qtd. in Russell 1986, 107). In South America, a tacit agreement had long divided investment in the continent between the houses of Baring, dominant in Argentina, and Rothschild, dominant in Brazil and Chile; see Ferns (1977).

22. To further illustrate the process of reconcentration of capitals that inevitably follows on the heels of financial disaster—including the one we are living today—David Harvey cites the cynical wisdom of the robber baron Andrew Mellon: "'In a crisis, assets return to their rightful owners' (i.e., him)" (2006a, 11). This upward redistribution can occur within a nation, or in case of Argentina in 1890 (as well as in later debt crises) from peripheral capitalists to imperial ones. The outcome, in both cases, is the same: the ensuing devaluation of assets carries out its most brutal effects on workers

and the poor, effects that are worsened in proportion to the society's weakness within the global system.

23. Along these lines, Marx's controversial essay "On the Jewish Question" argued that the qualities that European Christians identified as particularly "Jewish" aberrations ("huckstering," worship of money) were the very qualities that marked the relentless drive of capital (1978). Slavoj Žižek furthers the analysis begun by Marx by asking, "[I]s the anti-Semitic capitalist's hatred of the Jew not the hatred of the excess that pertains to capitalism itself, i.e., of the excess produced by its inherent antagonistic nature? Is capitalism's hatred of the Jew not the hatred of its own innermost, essential feature?" (1993, 206). In this manner, anti-Semitism functions as a supreme act of ideological displacement. With specific regard to Marx's complex and contradictory position regarding Judaism, it is necessary to mention that while cognizant of the ideological utility of racial and religious divisions within capitalist society, he (himself a converted Jew) sometimes sought uncritical resource to stereotype to align Jews with moneylending and usury. Discussing circulation, for example, Marx writes that the sum of values in circulation cannot be augmented by a change in distribution, "any more than a Jew can increase the quantity of the precious metals in a country by selling a farthing from the time of Queen Anne for a guinea" (1976, 265–66). I would in no way suggest, however, that the use of such metaphors would place Marx in the same category as those anti-Semitic writers (among them, Martel), who seek to *explain* the internal contradictions of capitalism by way of racial scapegoating.

24. In identifying finance capital as simultaneously "poison" and "cure" for peripheral nations, I am drawing from Pheng Cheah's essay "Crises of Money." Though Cheah focuses on the East Asian financial crisis of 1997 (and maintains the novelty of financial forms of power), his observations extend beyond this contemporary moment: "Financial flows are autoimmune processes. On the one hand, inflows of money strengthen the well-being of the economy and are therefore a source of power and security that can be drawn on in self-defense against any external threats. On the other hand, since this integrates the nation into a circuit of capital market processes in which other actors who have even more money can attack and weaken the nation through currency speculation, what is medicine is also poison" (2008, 213).

25. The previous wave of violence that made the economic boom of the 1880s possible comes closest to surfacing in another stock market novel, *Quilito*. In its opening scene, the protagonist pinches and kicks a female indigenous maid named Pampa (bought in the *mercado de indios*), who serves as an allegorical referent for the brutality of the

Desert Campaign. Pampa further serves as a feminized referent for the land that speculators abused or ignored under the regime of runaway speculation. For a discussion of this scene, see Viñas (1983, 287–89). The solution to this abuse is not posed as the liberation of indigenous people, but rather as the reinvigoration of the dream of white agrarian settlement. This desire is expressed through an Irish character, Míster Robert (a figure uniting northern European and Catholic creole masculine identity), who in the throes of crisis resolves to leave the stock exchange to "go and dig up the earth" with his own two hands ([1891] 1985, 237). *Quilito* invokes the land—and the productive economy it represents—as an antidote to illusory speculative wealth. Recalling the vocabulary employed in the "export reveries" studied in chapter 1, agriculture is figured once more as an honorable, stable, and morally fortifying activity. What Mr. Robert's desire does not recognize, however, is that it was the productive promise of "the land" that allowed speculation to get under way in the first place.

26. A notable exception is Ian Baucom's *Specters of the Atlantic,* which argues that transnational financial speculation in eighteenth-century Britain has one of its origins in bets placed on whether slaves would survive the Middle Passage. These bets took the form of a macabre life insurance policy, put in place to assure property. As a chilling reminder of how early finance capital incorporated racial violence into its self-representation, Baucom relates that the façade of the Liverpool stock exchange was originally decorated with bas-reliefs of African heads (2005, 52).

27. Ludmer notes more generally that in turn-of-the-century Argentine literature, "the Jews" were frequently accompanied by "other 'enemies' or 'guilty parties,'" such as adulterous women (2004, 156). See also Theweleit's *Male Fantasies* (1987), in which post–World War I Germany was represented as threatened by "engulfment" by femininity and Jewishness.

28. On the centrality of gender as a shifting signifier within nation-building projects in nineteenth-century Argentina, see Masiello (1992). On the linkage between femininity and criminality in the 1880s particularly through prostitution, see Guy (1991).

29. Taunay's *O encilhamento* goes even further than Martel by introducing a causal relation between feminine luxury and financial speculation. In this novel, women compete with one another in the conspicuous display of wealth, "ardently inciting their husbands to luxury, to chance . . . and to all manners of squandering money" ([1893] 1923, 136).

30. Argentina's recovery after the Baring Crisis was quite slow: it was not until the 1910s that the country gained access to credit once more. The resulting bubble in the 1920s was even bigger than the one of the 1880s, and culminated in the global crash of 1929.

4. Money II

1. See, for example, Jorge Holguín, "La bestia negra" (1892). The most vocal defender of paper money was the renowned conservative intellectual, grammarian, and then-vice-president Miguel Antonio Caro, whose justifications for the *curso forzoso* are collected in a volume dedicated to economic matters (1943). The complex issue of paper money, it should be noted, blurred what we might expect to be divisions between Conservatives and Liberals, the two main political factions in nineteenth-century Colombia. If on one hand Conservatives like Caro were stalwart defenders of church and "tradition," they also freely experimented with the devilish innovation of paper money.

2. Cacao and coffee beans were often depicted on nineteenth-century banknotes as representatives of money, because their shape resembles that of coins, and because of the function of cacao as an instrument of exchange in pre-Columbian Meso-America. At the same time, the shape of the chocolate bar and the bank note might share the rectangular form of the gold ingot. I thank Jesús Rodríguez Velasco for this last insight.

3. Benjamin's words come from a section of *One Way Street* (1928) titled "a tour of German inflation." In Weimar Germany, as is well known, hyperinflation reaching 29,500 percent helped to pave the way for Hitler's rise to power. For an analysis of responses to the sense of irreality that resulted from this hyperinflationary moment, see Widdig (2001).

4. According to one of the many legends the figure of Silva continues to evoke, Silva had asked his doctor days earlier to outline the exact place of his heart, assuring that the bullet would arrive swiftly to its destination. Today, graffiti images of Silva's silhouette, made recognizable by top hat and red heart, appear on the walls of Bogotá's colonial neighborhood, La Candelaria.

5. In addition to owing money to his grandmother, Silva owed money to family members and friends who cosigned his loans (see Vallejo 1995; and Silva 1996a). And while elite Bogotá society has long been considered provincial (as much for its geographical isolation as for its Catholic conservatism), Silva's debts show that his milieu was held together by an eminently modern form of social glue: credit. The genteel members of Bogotá society who attended literary *tertulias,* gathered in salons to hear piano recitals, and met up with each other on consular business in Paris or London were drawn together by their status as lettered elites, but also perhaps for another reason: they owed each other money.

6. Part of this letter is reproduced in *Cartas,* 87–97. The rumored length of the letter is complemented by its tone of utter desperation: "News of my bankruptcy spread across the city. . . . Only one promissory note was presented to the court, that of Señor Pratt, for which you were a guarantor. Why? Because Señor Pratt very courteously collected from you and you answered

him in a manner that offended him. Nonetheless, I covered that debt. How, with what funds? Not with those of the shop, which belonged to my creditors, but by pawning my mother's jewels and enduring exceptional sacrifice, which I do not wish tell you about because it would cause you pity" (1996a, 93). With the debtor's attempt to reestablish his good name through a language of honor and sacrifice, the letter itself becomes a credit mechanism, albeit a weak one unable to generate much-needed cash. The debtor's letter is one of the still-unexamined genres of the Export Age; numerous private letters surely exist. At least two were published as pamphlets. These include the Colombian novelist and entrepreneur Jorge Isaacs's *A mis amigos y a los comerciantes de Cali* (To my friends and to the merchants of Cali, 1871), written in the aftermath of his (first) bankruptcy; and the Brazilian financier Visconde de Mauá's *Exposição . . . aos Credores de Mauá e C e ao Público* (Statement to the creditors of Mauá and Compan and to the public, 1878). Like Silva's letter, both of these pamphlets mark the debtor's last-ditch effort at reestablishing credit within his economic and social milieu.

7. Silva's polemics against the paper money regime of the *Regeneración* were published in the Bogotá newspaper *La Nación* under the titles "La confusión de hechos" (Confusion of facts, June 28,1887) and "Confusiones varias" (Various confusions, July 12,1887). In these two texts Silva takes on the voice of a liberal political economist, maintaining that "to prohibit currency exchange is like prohibiting the rain" (1887a), and defending "private credit" as a linchpin of "civilization" (1887b).

8. Here I am thinking of early Marxist literary critics such as Angel Rama, whose approach I find limited insofar as he continues to view Silva's business activities as significant only insofar as they create a contradiction between "the ecomomic demands of the milieu, and artistic vocation" ([1970] 1985b, 64). While it is probably true that Silva would have written more poems and novels had he been able to earn his living as a writer, I am more interested in how failure itself becomes meaningful to an analysis of the contradictions of peripheral capitalism and their precise modes of expression in literary texts.

9. Brigard Silva notes that Silva "left ten pesos in paper money in his wallet: it was all that remained of his patrimony" (1946, 300).

10. Many critics place the emergence of decadence in turn-of-the-century Europe in the aftermath of Darwin's theory of evolution and natural selection. Decadence offered itself as a counter-narrative to bourgeois notions of progress, positing that societies did not always improve but often declined; instead of evolving, they could devolve. See Hustvedt (1998).

11. *De sobremesa* is widely considered the first Spanish American decadent novel. On the cusp of the twentieth century, a corpus of decadent novels began to emerge, including Manuel Díaz Rodríguez (Venezuela), *Idolos*

rotos (Broken idols, 1901) and *Sangre patricia* (Patrician blood, 1902); Amado Nervo (Mexico), *El bachiller* (The student, 1896); Carlos Reyles (Uruguay) *Primitivo* (1896) and *El extraño* (The stranger, 1897); and Abraham Valdelomar (Peru), *La ciudad de los tísicos* (The city of consumptives, 1911) and *La ciudad muerta* (The city of the dead, 1911). For a discussion of this corpus, see González (2007) and Olivares (1984). Literary decadence, of course, was but one way in which creole elites expressed their growing sense of malaise with regard to the future of Latin American nations. The end of the nineteenth century witnessed the rise of racial positivism, which allowed economic failures to be explained in terms of racial inferiority. Hence the liberal visionary D. F. Sarmiento, who decades earlier had expressed great optimism regarding the future of Latin American nations, wrote *Conflicto y armonía de las razas en América* (1883) as an attempt to explain the failure of liberal dreams to realize themselves. Race had always been present in Sarmiento's thought (inscribed into the very notion of civilization and barbarism), but the later work marks a turn toward a formalized discourse of racial science. At the beginning of the twentieth century, works like the Bolivian writer Alcides Arguedas's *Pueblo enfermo* (1909), and the Chilean author Francisco Encina's *Nuestra inferioridad económica* (1912) attempted to explain national economic failures in terms of race. On the rise of racial positivism in Latin America, see Leys Stepan (1991). For an analysis of intellectuals' discourses surrounding "sickness" in turn-of-the-century Latin America and Spain, see Aronna (1999) and Trigo (2000).

12. Fernando Vallejo highlights this difference in characteristically sardonic manner: "*De sobremesa* is the novel of one madman written by another. . . . José A. Silva is José Fernández with the simple difference that the latter is rich, immensely rich, and the former poor, immensely poor. Poor and in debt. In debt and without credit" (1995, 258).

13. All English translations of *De sobremesa* are from Kelly Washbourne's translation, *After-Dinner Conversation: The Diary of a Decadent*, unless otherwise noted.

14. *A rebours* was also an important site of inspiration for Spanish American contemporaries of Silva's such as the Cuban poet Julián del Casal, who corresponded with Huysmans, and the Nicaraguan poet Rubén Darío, who signed some of his journalistic chronicles with the pen name "Des Esseintes."

15. The cultural expression that best expresses nineteenth-century elites' patterns of luxury consumption is, of course, *modernismo*, as studied in chapter 2. *De sobremesa*'s suggestion that peripheral elites consumed luxury at the cost of accumulation later became a linchpin in twentieth-century Marxist readings of (neo)colonialism and underdevelopment. In his 1928

Siete Ensayos de interpretación de la realidad peruana, Carlos Mariátegui calls the Peruvian landower an "unproductive consumer" (1970, 64). Similarly, in *The Wretched of the Earth* (1961), Frantz Fanon writes that the local bourgeoisie is unable to fulfill its "historical mission" (2005, 116) as a class, living off the money paid to them by multinational corporations instead of producing.

16. See Fernández Retamar's 1971 essay *Calibán*.

17. See Ramos (2001), in particular.

18. González Echevarría notes a contradiction between the airiness of Ariel and the solidity of the coin: "The inescapable association between language and money constitutes a considerably contradictory figure; instead of flowing from words, we have the heavy, repeatable, though divisible, materiality of coins. The coin, in contrast with the undifferentiated air, is sculpted, fixed, written" (2009). I would locate the contradiction arising from Rodó's association between language and money elsewhere, in Rodó's disavowal of money as a scale of value, even as he employs a gold coin to metaphorize it.

19. At different moments, José Enrique Rodó and Pedro Henríquez Ureña have also appeared on national currency in Uruguay and the Dominican Republic, respectively. Today, authors such as Juana de Ibarbourou (Uruguay), Gabriela Mistral (Chile), and Jorge Isaacs (Colombia) can be found on banknotes. One author noticeably absent from currency is Jorge Luis Borges, perhaps because placing this literary master of duplicity and deception would be asking for trouble. Then again, perhaps not; the Brazilian writer Machado de Assis—himself a master of blurring boundaries between truth and fiction—graced the one-thousand-cruzado note, a currency that lasted for only two years (1986–89) before hyperinflation took the bills out of circulation.

20. Here it is germane to mention that the genesis of the five-thousand-peso note bearing Silva's image was made possible by the money mischief that continues to wrack the Colombian economy. In 1994, in the city of Valledupar, bank robbers carried out the biggest heist in the nation's history. The Banco de la República was robbed of $24,075 million pesos, much of it in bills of small denominations. The bank quickly invalidated the stolen notes, but this did not resolve the problem. People across the country had to check the serial numbers on their notes on a daily basis, lest they be stuck with what came to be called "vallenatos," a humorous reference to the famous musical style of Valledupar. The Banco de la República finally phased out the old notes, and introduced newly designed one-thousand, five-thousand, and ten-thousand peso notes. This is how Silva landed on the five-thousand-peso note, as once again monetary disaster paved the way for literary intervention. I thank Oscar Iván Useche for bringing this story to my attention.

5. Exploitation

Original epigraph text: ¿Por dónde escapar, a dónde acudir? Mujeres y chicuelos, desorbitados por un refugio, daban con la pandilla que los abaleaba antes de llegar. "¡Viva el coronel Funes! ¡Abajo los impuestos! ¡Viva el comercio libre!" I have had access to *The Vortex*, Earl K. James's 1935 translation of the text.

1. The trio of novels most often associated with regionalism is formed by *La vorágine*, with Ricardo Güiraldes's *Don segundo sombra* (Argentina, 1926), about an illegitimate farmhand and his gaucho friend), and Rómulo Gallegos's *Doña Bárbara* (Venezuela, 1929), about a wicked female hacienda owner. While the first novel takes place in the jungle, the latter two take place on the plains. As Carlos Alonso has shown in his important rereading of regionalism, these three novels employ very different styles and symbolic resolutions and deserve to be studied separately (see Alonso 1990).

2. The space of the jungle was already mythic in Euro-American colonial discourse before the rubber boom. The Spanish legend of El Dorado (The Golden One) held that an indigenous chief lived deep in the jungle, where he bathed himself in gold dust. In the seventeenth century, Dutch bankers financed expeditions to the region to find El Dorado, once again demonstrating the importance of fantasy in the genesis of modern capitalism. The mythical status of the Amazon rainforest is even more fundamentally captured in the name itself, which refers to the one-breasted women warriors of European myth.

3. In Colombia, the future president Rafael Reyes was one of the first to provide such a map, filled with ciphers of caucho and cacao plants interspersed with skulls to denote the presence of "cannibals." Reyes, who was a quinine trader, claims that his brother was killed by cannibals on the same exploratory voyage; the other succumbed to yellow fever (Reyes [1907] 1979).

4. As part of a promotional campaign for rubber, a Brazilian pamphlet entitled *Brazil: The Land of Rubber* (1912), approvingly cites a document written by a European, who says that Manaus, even though surrounded by "wild Indians . . . is as modern as New York or Chicago" (116).

5. The opera house at Manaus cost millions of dollars and took fifteen years to build by the time it was finished in 1896. The story inspired the German film director Werner Herzog to make his film *Fitzcarraldo*, about an Irish adventurer in Iquitos who becomes a rubber trader to build an opera house to rival the one in Manaus. On *Fitzcarraldo* as a "high tech" reinvention of Amerindian primitivism versus European "civilization," see Franco (1999).

6. I thank Marcial Godoy for this insight.

7. I am drawing here from Michael Taussig's discussion of the Hardenberg and Casement reports (1986, 17–36).

8. The rubber plant is indigenous to equatorial South America, and its transplant to other parts of the world came only after British officials managed to smuggle tens of thousands of seeds to Kew Gardens in London in 1876. The plant subsequently traveled to British Malaysia, where plantation production quickly displaced South American wild rubber on the market; see Loadman (2005, 87–107). The market for natural rubber itself waned in the 1930s with the rise of synthetic substitutes.

9. Rivera's biographer Eduardo Neale Silva notes that the writer was most struck by the stories he kept hearing about the cruelty and savagery of a man named Funes—the colonel referred to in the epigraph to this chapter—an associate of Arana's who had spread terror throughout the environs (1960, 242–44).

10. This point has also been made recently by Jennifer French, who writes that discourses on nature in post-independence Latin America do not signal an "'escape' from the realities of industrial capitalism" but instead a representation of "the continent's predominant economic forms and, as a result, its gradual incorporation into the international capitalist system" (2005, 13).

11. While an analysis of these "commodity novels" is beyond of the scope of this chapter, I would like to note that the 1930s and 1940s witnessed a veritable explosion of regionalist and social realist novels centered on rural commodity production. These include the "novel of oil," such as Uribe Piedrahíta's *Mancha de aceite* (Oil stain, Colombia, 1935), Arturo Pietri Uslar's *Mene* (Venezuela, 1936) and Adolfo Costa du Rels's *Tierras hechizadas* (Enchanted lands, 1940, Bolivia). Before his untimely death in 1929, José Eustasio Rivera was planning a novel about oil. This corpus also includes the "novel of nitrates," such as Andrés Sabella's *Norte grande: Novela del salitre* (The big north: Novel of nitrates," Chile, 1945); "the novel of coffee," such as Jose Antonio Osorio Lizarazo's *La cosecha* (The harvest, Colombia, 1935); "the novel of timber," such as Marta Brunet's *Humo hacia el sur* (Smoke to the south, Chile, 1946); and of course "novels of rubber" published in the aftermath of *La vorágine,* such as Uribe Piedrahitas's *Toá: narraciones de caucherías* (Toá: Stories from the caucho camps, 1942), and Diómedes Pereya's *Caucho* (1938, Bolivia).

12. Rosa Luxemburg was among the first Marxist theorists to recognize that so-called primitive accumulation was not simply a first stage of capitalism Europe, overcome with time, but rather a tactic continued under colonial policy. In the colonies, she writes, "[f]orce is the only solution open to capital: the accumulation of capital, seen as a historical process, employs force as a permanent weapon, not only at its genesis, but further on down to the present day" (1951, 351).

13. I thank Enrique Lima for calling this passage to my attention.

14. Taussig is citing Fredrick Karl, *Joseph Conrad*.

15. *La vorágine*, as Jennifer French has recently argued, should be read alongside *Heart of Darkness* for engaging commensurable imperial contexts and problematics (2005). Though I will not attempt such a reading here, it is relevant to remark on how these novels speak from radically different points of enunciation within the imperial world-system they try to represent. We will recall that Conrad's novel begins and ends aboard a cruising yawl on the Thames River, as Marlow begins to tell his colleagues of his trip to Africa and encounter with the trader Kurtz (ivory is substituted for rubber in the novel). The colonial African "heart" of the novel is thus contained within a European narrative frame. *La vorágine*, in contrast, is a novel that unfolds without any access to the imperial centers that shaped the rubber boom, or even to the urban spaces of the periphery. Instead, it unfolds entirely within ever more peripheral reaches of the South American nation-state. This locus of enunciation gives *La vorágine* the sense of being confined to the margins of the larger imperial system to which the rubber trade belongs, without recourse to the metropole. Here the fact that the novel begins and ends with official communications becomes important, since these documents do not serve to anchor the narration to a more stable context (as literally occurs aboard the *Nelly* in *Heart of Darkness*), but instead sets it adrift into the unmarked forests of peripheral nation-states. This lack of a narrative anchor is in turn reflected in what one critic has referred to as the "broken" voice of the first-person narrator (Ordóñez 1990).

16. Counterfeiting was a huge problem in early twentieth-century Colombia, especially during and after the Thousand Days' War (1899–1903), a conflict between Liberals and against Conservatives that led to the worst hyperinflationary crisis in the country's history and left the national economy in ruins. See Bergquist (1986) or Deas (1982). Today, Colombia is the world capital of counterfeiting: not of *pesos*, for these are worth little outside of Colombia, but of U.S. dollars (Stone). The main counterfeiting operations, incidentally, have been discovered not in Bogotá but under the cover of the rainforest.

17. Goux elaborates this argument in his reading of André Gide's 1925 *The Counterfeiters* (1994). In Spanish American literature, counterfeiting becomes an important rhetorical and plot device in the Argentine author Roberto Arlt's 1929 *Los siete locos* (The seven madmen) about a motley band of Buenos Aires con-men. That the novelistic economy of *La vorágine* is altered by the suggestion of counterfeiting shows again that this novel should be removed from strictures of "nature," and allowed to circulate as a novel about modern and sophisticated practices and regimes of representation.

18. David Viñas uses a different economic metaphor, inflation, to describe the narrative principle of excess in *La vorágine*. Speaking of Cova's participation in a dice game in Casanare, Viñas argues that on a

metaphorical level, Cova lets money flow even though he doesn't have any, which amounts to "an inflationary process [*proceso inflacionario*] in the discourse of the protagonist" (1974, 20).

19. In *La vorágine*, Cova feels called upon to prove his masculine mettle over and over again, drinking, bedding different women, and confronting the dangers of the jungle. The Uruguayan writer Horacio Quiroga provides additional evidence of this hypermasculine performance as a key trope of 1920s *regionalismo*. Quiroga, who began his career as a Europeanized dandy along the lines established by *modernismo*, underwent a vast transformation after visiting and then moving to the frontier region of Misiones, Argentina, where he became a self-described "agricultural pioneer" and author of short stories about the jungle. On Quiroga's experiences in Misiones, see Delgado and Brignole (1939).

20. Beyond Rivera, Pérez Triana was a model for none other than Joseph Conrad, who reveals in letters to Cunningham Greene that the Colombian writer served as inspiration for the character José Avellanos in his novel *Nostromo* (1904), as discussed by Deas (1993). In *Nostromo*, Avellanos functions as a pitch-perfect parody of the nineteenth-century *letrado*: urbane and fiercely patriotic, he is the author of a work on the post-Independence politics of his country, titled *Fifty Years of Misrule*. When attending tea at the home of Mr. and Mrs. Gould (owners of the mine around which the novel centers), he declaims poetry whenever given the chance. Intriguingly, the Spanish American man of letters serves in this case as a point of contact between Rivera and Conrad's literary visions. When Conrad—the writer of European colonialism—is called upon to invent a Spanish American character, he chooses a poetry-declaiming *letrado*, a choice that becomes even more significant in light of Rivera's choice of a poet as his narrative point of contact with the rubber trade. While this choice is frequently explained by the fact that Rivera was himself a poet, I believe it points to the ubiquity of poetry as mode of expression par excellence of Latin American elites, and hence to its availability as parody.

21. On the special relationship between poetry and Colombian politics in the nineteenth century, see Deas (1993) and Rodríguez García (2010).

22. For an analysis of the relationship between this collection of sonnets and the poetic discourse in *La vorágine,* see Alonso (1990) and French (2005). *La vorágine*'s salvo to the jungle resembles the poetic language used in *Tierra de promisión* and reveals an uncanny similarity with Pérez Triana's *De Bogotá al Atlántico* (translated as *Down the Orinoco in a Canoe*): "The light scarcely filtered through the dense mass of leaves, so that we felt as if we stood constantly behind some cathedral stained-glass window. The air was full of the peculiar fragrance of tropical flowers and plants; the orchids swung high above our heads like lamps from the vaults of a temple" (1902, 51). Even more compellingly, Pérez Triana enters into a moment of reverie

in which an apparition speaks to him: "Listen to me, O pilgrim, lost in these vast solitudes; listen to the voice of the wandering streams!" (1902, 101). In a reverse of the apostrophe used in *La vorágine*, Pérez Triana allows the jungle to speak to him.

23. A particularly amusing moment of this ironization comes in the scene when Cova is introduced to Barrera for the first time in Casanare. Barrera gushes admiration for the national poet: "Alabada sea la diestra que ha esculpido tan bellas estrofas. Regalo de mi espíritu fueron en el Brasil, y me producían suspirante nostalgia." ("Praise be to the hand that has sculpted such beautiful stanzas. In Brazil they were a gift to my spirit, producing a sighing nostalgia," 1990, 114). The humorous effect is produced by Rivera's imitation of the lofty strains of poetry as patriotic discourse. As we learn who Barrera is and what he does, however, the effect of such discourse rings more sinister: this is a man, after all, who lures people into the jungle on the basis of false promise, enslaves them, and sells them. He loves poetry, however, and is on the surface a civilized man. In this manner, Barrera is similar to the legendary rubber trader Julio César Arana, who named one of his riverboats *El Liberal*, and cut an impressive figure in European suits when he traveled to his trial in London.

24. This break in pleasure generated by *modernista* language recalls the moment, analyzed in chapter 2, when the Cuban poet/journalist Julián del Casal steps outside the Havana department store El Fénix to encounter the disorder and heat of the street. Casal preserves his fantasy by saying that he prefers *poetry* to the spectacle of the department store; in *La vorágine*, however, poetry can no longer be used as a shield from its conditions of enunciation.

25. Poovey's history of accounting has a fascinating gendered component. Poovey notes that early accounting systems have three parts: the inventory, the diary (a narrative of all transactions), and the ledger (composed solely of numbers). Whereas women and youth were often entrusted to the first two types of books, only males had access to the ledgers. Hence *narrative* is feminized; the precision of arithmetic masculinized. Poovey's history of accounting hence has wider relevance for the gendering of literary forms that occurs throughout the eighteenth and nineteenth centuries, when the novel is associated with rhetorical excess and hence femininity (1998). In terms of *La vorágine*, the juxtaposition of the "precise" (but inaccurate) ledgers against the messy reality of the caucho trade parallels Cova's ambiguous sexual identity/hysteria; that is, incursion into the murk beyond the ledgers might imply a symbolic identification with the feminine.

26. See Greg Grandin's *Fordlândia* (2009) for an in-depth analysis of this failed experiment.

Bibliography

Aching, Gerard. 1997. *The Politics of Spanish American Modernismo: By Exquisite Design.* Cambridge: Cambridge University Press.

Alberdi, Juan B. [1872] 1898. "La literatura es una industria." In *Escritos póstumos.* Vol. 8, 246. Buenos Aires.

Alonso, Carlos. 1990. *The Spanish American Regional Novel: Modernity and Autochthony.* Cambridge: Cambridge University Press.

———. 1998. *The Burden of Modernity: The Rhetoric of Cultural Discourse in Spanish America.* New York: Oxford University Press.

Álvarez Curbelo, Silvia. 2001. *Un país del porvenir: El afán de la modernidad en Puerto Rico (siglo XIX).* San Juan: Ediciones Callejón.

Apter, Emily. 1991. *Feminization of the Fetish: Psychoanalysis and Narrative Obsession in Turn-of-the-Century France.* Ithaca, N.Y.: Cornell University Press.

Armas, Emilio de. 1981. *Casal.* La Habana: Editorial Letras Cubanas.

Aronna, Michael. 1999. *"Pueblos Enfermos": The Discourse of Illness in the Turn-of-the-Century Spanish and Latin American Essay.* Chapel Hill: University of North Carolina Department of Romance Languages.

Arosema, Justo. 1873. "El Porvenir de Colombia." *La América Ilustrada.* March 20.

Arrellano, Jorge Eduardo. 1993. *Azul . . . de Rubén Dario. Nuevas Perspectivas.* Washington, D.C.: Organization of American States.

Avellaneda, Nicolás. 1886. *Nicolás Avellaneda: In memoriam.* Buenos Aires.

Balestra, Juan. 1935. *El noventa: Una evolución política argentina.* Buenos Aires: Librería y Editorial "La Facultad," J. Roldán y cía.

Baucom, Ian. 2005. *Specters of the Atlantic. Finance Capital, Slavery, and the Philosophy of History.* Durham, N.C.: Duke University Press.

Bauer, Arnold J, and Benjamin Orlove. 1997. "Chile in the Belle Epoque: Primitive Producers, Civilized Consumers." In *The Allure of the Foreign: Imported Goods in Postcolonial Latin America.* Ed. Benjamin Orlove, 113–49. Ann Arbor: University of Michigan Press.

Beckman, Ericka. 2008. "Man on the Market: José Martí and the Poetics of Commerce." *Revista Hispánica Moderna* 61, no. 1: 19–35.

Bello, Andés. 1997. "Ode to Tropical Agriculture." *Selected Writings of Andrés Bello.* Trans. Frances M. López-Morillas, 29–37. New York: Oxford University Press.

Benedetti, Mario. 1966. *Genio y figura de José Enrique Rodó.* Buenos Aires: Editorial Universitaria de Buenos Aires.

231

Benjamin, Walter. 1978. *Reflections: Essays, Aphorisms, Autobiographical Writings*. Trans. Edmund Jephcott. New York: Schocken Books.

Benson, Todd. 2005. "An Oasis of Indulgence amidst Brazil's Poverty." *New York Times*, July 16. http://www.nytimes.com/2005/07/16/business/worldbusiness/16daslu.html (accessed Nov. 5, 2010).

Bergquist, Charles W. 1986. *Coffee and Conflict in Colombia, 1886–1910*. Durham, N.C.: Duke University Press.

Blanco Aguinaga, Carlos. 1997. "La ideología de la clase dominante en la obra de Rubén Darío." In *From Romanticism to* Modernismo *in Latin America*, ed. David William Foster and Daniel Altamiranda, 316–51. New York and London: Garland Publishing.

Blanco Fombona, Rufino. 1994. "José Asunción Silva." In *Leyendo a Silva*. Vol. 1. Ed. Juan Gustavo Cobo Borda and Luis Fernando García Núñez, 67–86. Bogotá: Instituto Caro y Cuervo.

Bonet, Carmelo Melitón. 1940. *Voces argentinas*. Buenos Aires: Librería del Colegio.

Botana, Natalio. 1984. *La tradición republicana: Alberdi, Sarmiento y las ideas políticas de su tiempo*. Buenos Aires: Editorial Sudamericana.

Bowlby, Rachel. 1985. *Just Looking: Consumer Culture in Dreiser, Gissing, and Zola*. New York: Methuen.

Brantlinger, Patrick. 1996. *Fictions of State: Culture and Credit in Britain, 1694–1994*. Ithaca, N.Y.: Cornell University Press.

Brazil, the Land of Rubber at the Third International Rubber and Allied Trades Exhibition. 1912. [New York].

Brigard Silva, Camilo. 1946. "El infortunio comercial de Silva." *Revista de América* 17:281–300.

Brown, Bill. 2003. *A Sense of Things: The Object Matter of American Literature*. Chicago: University of Chicago Press.

Brown, Laura. 2001. *Fables of Modernity: Literature and Culture in the English Eighteenth Century*. Ithaca, N.Y.: Cornell University Press.

Buck Morss, Susan. 1995. "Envisioning Capital: Political Economy on Display." In *Visual Display: Culture beyond Appearances*. Ed. Lynne Cooke and Peter Wollen, 111–41. Seattle, Wash.: Bay Press.

Bulmer-Thomas, Victor. 2003. *The Economic History of Latin America since Independence*. Cambridge: Cambridge University Press.

Burns, E. Bradford. 1983. *The Poverty of Progress*. Berkeley: University of California Press.

Cambranes, J. C. 1985. *Coffee and Peasants in Guatemala: The Origins of the Modern Plantation Economy in Guatemala, 1853–1897*. Stockholm: Institute of Latin American Studies.

Campbell, Colin. 1987. *The Romantic Ethic and the Spirit of Modern Consumerism*. Oxford: B. Blackwell.

Cárcamo Huechante, Luis. 2007. *Tramas del mercado: Imaginación económica, cultural pública y literatura en el Chile de fines del siglo veinte.* Santiago: Cuarto Propio.

Cardoso, Fernando Henrique, and Enzo Falletto. *Dependency and Development in Latin America.* [1969] 1979. Berkeley: University of California Press.

Caro, Miguel Antonio. 1943. *Escritos sobre cuestiones económicas.* Bogotá: Imprenta del Banco de la República.

Casal, Julián del. 2001. *Poesía completa y prosa selecta.* Ed. Alvaro Salvador. Madrid: Editorial Verbum.

Castro Leiva, Luis. 1992. "The Dictatorship of Virtue or the Opulence of Commerce." *Jahrbuch für Geschichte von Staat, Wirtschaft und Gesellschaft Lateinamerikas* 29: 194–240.

Chakrabarty, Dipesh. 2008. *Provincializing Europe: Postcolonial Thought and Historical Difference.* Princeton, N.J: Princeton University Press.

Cheah, Pheng. 2008. "Crises of Money." *Positions* 16, no. 1: 189–219.

Clark, Odis H., Jr. 1971. *Paper Money of Guatemala.* San Antonio, Tex. Almanzar.

Cobo Borda, Juan Gustavo. 2004. "November 254, 1924. En el corazón de la selva." In *Semana.* May 30. http://www.semana.com/especiales/noviembre-25-1924bren-corazon-selva/79076-3.aspx (accessed September 3, 2011)

——, ed. 1988. *José Asunción Silva. Bogotano universal.* Bogotá: Villegas Editores.

Coronil, Fernando. 1997. *The Magical State: Nature, Money, and Modernity in Venezuela.* Chicago: University of Chicago Press.

Darío, Rubén. [1888] 1965. *Azul . . . ; El salmo de la pluma; Cantos de vida y esperanza. Otros poemas.* México: Porrúa.

——. 1983. *Prosas políticas.* Managua: Ministerio de Cultura, Nicaragua Libre.

——. 1988. *Historia de mis libros.* Managua, Nicaragua: Editorial Nueva Nicaragua.

——. 2006. *Selected Writings.* London: Penguin.

Deas, Malcolm. 1982. "The Fiscal Problems of Nineteenth-Century Colombia." *Journal of Latin American Studies* 14, no. 2: 287–328.

——. 1993. *Del poder y la gramática. Y otros ensayos sobre historia, política y literatura colombianas.* Santafé de Bogotá, Colombia: Tercer Mundo Editores.

Delgado, José M., and Alberto J. Brignole. 1939. *Vida y obra de Horacio Quiroga.* Montevideo: Claudio García y Cía. Editores.

Derrida, Jacques. 1991. "Plato's Pharmacy." In *A Derrida Reader: Between the Blinds.* Ed. Peggy Kamuf, 112–42. New York: Columbia University Press.

——. *Given Time: I.* 1992. *Counterfeit Money.* Trans. Peggy Kamuf. Chicago: University of Chicago Press.

Díaz Alejandro, Carlos F. 1980. "La economía argentina durante el período 1880–1913." In *La Argentina del ochenta al centenario.* Ed. Gustavo Ferrari and Ezequiel Gallo, 369–75. Buenos Aires: Editorial Sudamericana.

Esteves, Luis. 1882. *Apuntes para la Historia Económica del Perú.* Lima.

Estrade, Paul. 2000. *José Martí: Los fundamentos de la democracia en América Latina.* Aranjuez and Madrid: Ediciones Doce Calles/Casa de Velázquez.

Fabian, Johannes. 2002. *Time and the Other: How Anthropology Makes Its Object.* New York: Columbia University Press.

Fanon, Frantz. [1961] 2004. *The Wretched of the Earth.* New York: Grove Press.

Felski, Rita. 1995. *The Gender of Modernity.* Cambridge, Mass.: Harvard University Press.

Fernández Bravo, Álvaro. 2001. "Ambivalent Argentina: Nationalism, Exoticism and Latin Americanism at the 1889 Paris Universal Exposition." *Nepantla: Views from South* 2, no. 1: 115–39.

Fernández Retamar, Roberto. 1971. *Calibán: Apuntes sobre la cultura en Nuestra América.* México: Editorial Diógenes.

Ferns, H. S. 1977. *Britain and Argentina in the Nineteenth Century.* New York: ArnoPress.

Ferreira, Francisco. 1890. *La crisis.* Buenos Aires: Imprenta Europea.

Fishburn, Evelyn. 1981. *The Portrayal of Immigration in Nineteenth Century Argentine Fiction (1845–1902).* Berlin: Colloquium-Verlag.

Fornazarri, Alejandro. 2009. "A Stock Market Theory of Culture: A View from the Latin American Neoliberal Transition." *Social Identities: Journal for the Study of Race, Nation, and Culture* 15, no. 3: 373–81.

Foster, David William. 1990. *The Argentine Generation of 1880: Ideology and Cultural Texts.* Columbia: University of Missouri Press.

Franco, Jean. 1989. *Plotting Women: Gender and Representation in Mexico.* New York: Columbia University Press.

——. 1999. "High-Tech Primitivism: The Representation of Tribal Societies in Feature Films." In *Critical Passions: Selected Essays.* Ed. Mary Louise Pratt and Kathleen M. Newman, 181–95. Durham, N.C.: Duke University Press.

——. 2002. *The Decline and Fall of the Lettered City: Latin America in the Cold War.* Cambridge, Mass.: Harvard University Press.

Frank, André Gunder. 1967. *Capitalism and Underdevelopment in Latin America: Historical Studies of Chile and Brazil.* New York: Monthly Review Press.

French, Jennifer. 2005. *Nature, Neo-colonialism, and the Spanish American Regional Writers.* Hanover, N.H.: Dartmouth College Press.

Fuentes, Carlos. 1969. *La nueva novela hispanoamericana*. México: J. Mortiz.

Galbraith, John Kenneth. 1990. *A Short History of Financial Euphoria*. New York: Penguin.

Gallagher, Catherine. 2006. *The Body Economic: Life, Death, and Sensation in Political Economy and the Victorian Novel*. Princeton, N.J.: Princeton University Press.

García Márquez, Gabriel. [1967] 1991. *One Hundred Years of Solitude*. Trans. Gregory Rabassa. New York: Harper Perennial.

———. 1975. *El otoño del patriarca*. Esplugas de Llobregat: Plaza & Janés.

Gilman, Sander. 1991. *The Jew's Body*. London and New York: Routledge.

González, Aníbal. 1993. *Journalism and the Development of Spanish American Narrative*. Cambridge: Cambridge University Press.

———. 1994. "Retratos y autorretratos: El marco de acción del intelectual en *De sobremesa*." In *Leyendo a Silva*. Vol. 2. Ed. Juan Gustavo Cobo Borda and Luis Fernando García Núñez, 269–306. Bogotá: Instituto Caro y Cuervo.

———. 1997. " 'Estómago y cerebro': *De sobremesa*, el *Simposio* de Platón y la indigestión cultural." *Revista Iberoamericana* 63: 233–48.

———. 2007. *A Companion to Spanish American Modernismo*. Woodbridge, U.K.: Tamesis.

González Echevarría, Roberto. 2009. "El extraño caso de la estatua parlante: *Ariel* y la retórica magisterial del ensayo latinoamericano." *Cervantes Virtual*. Alicante: Biblioteca Virtual Miguel de Cervantes. http://www. cervantesvirtual.com/FichaObra.html?Ref=34622 (accessed June 4, 2011).

———. 1998. *Myth and Archive: A Theory of Latin American Narrative*. Durham, N.C.: Duke University Press.

González-Stephan, Beatriz. 2003. "Showcases of Consumption: Historical Panoramas and Universal Expositions." In *Beyond Imagined Communities: Reading and Writing in Nineteenth-Century Latin America*. Ed. Sara Castro-Klarén and John Charles Chasteen, 225–38. Washington, D.C.: Woodrow Wilson Press.

González-Stephan, Beatriz, and Jens Andermann, eds. 2006. *Galerías del progreso: Museos, exposiciones y cultura visual en América Latina*. Rosario: Beatriz Viterbo Editora.

Gootenberg, Paul. 1988. "Peru's Beleaguered Liberals." In *Guiding the Invisible Hand: Economic Liberalism and the State in Latin American History*. Ed. Joseph L. Love and Nils Jacobsen, 63–97. New York: Praeger.

———. 1993. *Imagining Development: Economic Ideas in Peru's "Fictitious Prosperity" of Guano, 1840–1880*. Berkeley: University of California Press.

Goux, Jean-Joseph. 1994. *The Coiners of Language*. Trans. Jennifer Curtiss Gage. Norman: University of Oklahoma Press.

Graff Zivin, Erin. 2008. *The Wandering Signifier. Rhetoric of Jewishness in the Latin American Imaginary*. Durham, N.C.: Duke University Press.

Grandin, Greg. 2000. *The Blood of Guatemala: A History of Race and Nation*. Durham, N.C.: Duke University Press.

———. 2009. *Fordlândia: The Rise and Fall of Henry Ford's Forgotten Jungle City*. New York: Metropolitan Books.

Gruesz, Kirsten Silva. 2002. *Ambassadors of Culture: The Transamerican Origins of Latino Writing*. Princeton, N.J.: Princeton University Press.

Guy, Donna. 1991. *Sex and Danger in Buenos Aires*. Lincoln: University of Nebraska Press.

Hale, Charles. 1989. *The Transformation of Liberalism in Late Nineteenth-Century Mexico*. Princeton, N.J.: Princeton University Press.

Halperín Donghi, Tulio. 1993. *The Contemporary History of Latin America*. Trans. John Charles Chasteen. Durham, N.C.: Duke University Press.

Harvey, David. 2006a. *The Limits to Capital*. London: Verso.

———. 2006b. "Notes toward a Theory of Uneven Geographical Development." In *Spaces of Global Capitalism*, 69–116. London: Verso.

———. 2006c. *Spaces of Global Capitalism: Toward a Theory of Uneven Geographical Development*. London: Verso.

———. 2010. *The Enigma of Capital*. New York: Oxford University Press.

Heinzelman, Kurt. 1980. *The Economics of the Imagination*. Amherst: University of Massachusetts Press.

Henríquez Ureña, Pedro. 1991. *Del ensayo crítico a la historia literaria*. Ed. J. Lasarte Valcárcel. Alicante: Generalitad Valenciana/Instituto de Cultura Juan Gil-Albert.

Hernández Gamarra, Antonio. 2006. *La moneda en Colombia*. Bogotá: Villegas.

Hobsbawm, Eric. 1975. *The Age of Capital*. London: Weidenfeld and Nicolson.

———. 1987. *The Age of Empire*. London: Weidenfeld and Nicolson.

Holguín, Jorge. 1892. *La bestia negra*. Bogotá: Imprenta de la Nación.

Hume, David. [1777] 1898. "Of Refinement in the Arts." In *Essays Moral, Political, and Literary*. Vol. 1: 299–308. London: Longmans, Green.

Hustvedt, Asti. 1998. "The Art of Death: French Fiction at the Fin de Siècle." In *The Decadent Reader: Fiction, Fantasy, and Perversion from Fin-de-Siècle France*. Ed. Ari Hustvedt, 10–29. New York: Zone Books.

Huysmans, Joris-Karl. [1884] 1998. *A rebours [Against Nature]*. Trans. Margaret Mauldon. Oxford: Oxford University Press.

Irigaray, Luce. 1985. "Women on the Market." In *The Sex Which Is Not One. 1977*. Trans. Catherine Porter. Ithaca, N.Y.: Cornell University Press.

Isaacs, Jorge. 1875. *A mis amigos y a los comerciantes del Cauca*. Cali.

Jacobsen, Nils, and Joseph L. Love, eds. 1988. *Guiding the Invisible Hand: Economic Liberalism and the State in Latin American History*. New York: Praeger.

Jitrik, Noé. 1970. *La Revolución del Noventa*. Buenos Aires: Centro Editor de América Latina.

———. 1978. *Las contradicciones del modernismo*. México: Colegio de México.

———. 1980. "El ciclo de la bolsa." In *Historia de la literatura argentina*, 159–66. Buenos Aires: Centro Editor de América Latina.

Jrade, Cathy Login. 1998. *Modernismo, Modernity, and the Development of Spanish American Literature*. Austin: University of Texas Press.

Kirkpatrick, Gwen. 1989. *The Dissonant Legacy of Modernismo: Lugones, Herrera y Reissig, and the Voices of Modern Spanish American Poetry*. Berkeley: University of California Press.

La bolsa de comercio de Buenos Aires en su centenario, 1854. 1954. Buenos Aires: Ministerio de Cultura y Educación de la Nación.

"La República Dominicana." 1872. *La América Ilustrada*. September 30, 275.

"Las Riquezas de Bolivia." 1872. *La América Ilustrada*. February 15, 34.

Lewald, Ernest. 1983. "La Bolsa como símbolo y crónica en la literatura argentina." *Chasqui* 12, no. 2–3: 19–26.

Leys Stepan, Nancy. 1991. *The Hour of Eugenics: Race, Gender, and Nation in Latin America*. Ithaca, N.Y.: Cornell University Press.

Loadman, John. 2005. *Tears of the Tree: The Story of Rubber—a Modern Marvel*. Oxford: Oxford University Press.

López Mejía, Alejandro. 2006. "'Conocer y ser conocido': Identidad cultural, mercado y discursos globales en tres revistas latinoamericanas de entre siglos." *Revista Iberoamericana* 72, no. 214: 139–53.

Love, Joseph. 1996. "Economic Ideas and Ideologies in Latin America since 1930." In *Ideas and Ideologies in Twentieth-Century Latin America*. Ed. Leslie Bethell, 207–74. Cambridge: Cambridge University Press.

Ludmer, Josefina. 2004. *The Corpus Delicti*. Trans. Glen S. Close. Pittsburgh: University of Pittsburgh Press.

Luxemburg, Rosa. 2003. *The Accumulation of Capital*. London: Routledge Classics.

Machado de Assis, Joaquim Maria. 1996. *A semana. Cronicas (1892–1893)*. Ed. John Gledson. São Paulo: Editora HUCITEC.

Mariátegui, Carlos. [1928] 1979. *Siete ensayos de interpretación de la realidad peruana*. Caracas: Biblioteca Ayacucho.

Marichal, Carlos. 1989. *A Century of Debt Crises in Latin America: From Independence to the Great Depression, 1820–1930*. Princeton, N.J.: Princeton University Press.

Martel, Julián [José María Miró]. 1891. *La bolsa. Estudio social*. Buenos Aires: Editorial Huemul.

Martí, José. 1975a. "Arboles de Quina." In *Obras Completas*. Vol. 7, 189–90. La Habana: Editorial de Ciencias Sociales.

———. 1975b. "Fragmento 40." *Obras Completas*. Vol. 22, 31–32. La Habana: Editorial de Ciencias Sociales.

———. [1878] 1975c. *Guatemala*. In *Obras Completas*. Vol. 7, 115–69. La Habana: Editorial de Ciencias Sociales.

———. 1975d. "Hierro." In *Obras Completas*. Vol. 16, 141–44. La Habana: Editorial de Ciencias Sociales.

———. 1975e. "La América Grande." In *Obras Completas*. Vol. 8, 297. La Habana: Editorial de Ciencias Sociales.

———. 1975f. "Los productos de Venezuela." In *Obras Completas*. Vol. 7, 242. La Habana: Editorial de Ciencias Sociales.

———. 1975g. "Nuestra América." In *Obras completas*. Vol. 6, 15–23. La Habana: Editorial de Ciencias Sociales.

———. 1975h. *Obras completas*. Vol. 28. La Habana: Editorial de Ciencias Sociales.

———. 1975i. "Prólogo al *Poema del Niágara*." In *Obras completas*. Vol. 7, 223–238. La Habana: Editorial de Ciencias Sociales.

———. [1891] 2001. "Our America." Trans. John D. Blanco, 295–303. In Julio Ramos, *Divergent Modernities: Culture and Politics in Nineteenth-Century Latin America*. Durham, N.C.: Duke University Press.

Marx, Karl. 1976. *Capital: Volume I, A Critique of Political Economy*. Vol. 1. Trans. Ben Fowkes. New York: Vintage Books.

———. 1978. "On the Jewish Question." In *The Marx-Engels Reader*. Ed. Robert C. Tucker. New York: Norton, 26–52.

———. 1991. *Capital: Volume III*. London: Penguin Classics.

———. 1992. *Capital: Volume II*. London: Penguin Classics.

———. 1993. *Grundrisse*. London: Penguin Books.

———. 1998. "Introduction to the Critique of Political Economy." Printed in *The German Ideology*. New York: Prometheus Books.

Marx, Karl, and Friedrich Engels. 1978. *Manifesto of the Communist Party*. In *The Marx-Engels Reader*. Ed. Robert. C. Tucker, 469–500. New York: Norton.

Masiello, Francine. 1992. *Between Civilization and Barbarism: Women, Nation, and Literary Culture in Modern Argentina*. Lincoln: University of Nebraska Press.

Mauá, Visconde de. 1878. *Exposição do Visconde de Mauá aos Credores de Mauá e C e ao Público*. Rio de Janeiro.

McClintock, Anne. 1995. *Imperial Leather: Race, Gender, and Sexuality in the Colonial Contest*. New York: Routledge.

McCloskey, Deirdre. 1985. *The Rhetoric of Economics*. Madison: University of Wisconsin Press.

Meisel Roca, Adolfo, and Alejandro López Mejía. 1990. "Papel moneda, tasas de interés y revaluación durante la Regeneración." In *El Banco de la República: Antecedentes, evolución y estructura*, 67–102. Bogotá: Banco de la República.

Meléndez, Concha. [1938] 1988. "José Asunción Silva, poeta de la sombra, (1865–1896)." In *José Asunción Silva, bogotano universal*. Ed. Juan Gustavo Cobo Borda, 203–18. Bogotá: Villegas.

Michaels, Walter Benn. 1987. *The Gold Standard and the Logic of Naturalism*. Berkeley: University of California Press.

Molloy, Sylvia. 1987. "Contagio narrativo y gesticulación retórica en *La vorágine*." *Revista Iberoamericana* 53, no. 141: 745–66.

———. 1992. "Too Wilde for Comfort: Desire and Ideology in Fin-de-Siècle Spanish America." *Social Text* 10, no. 2–3: 187–201.

———. 1997. "Voice Snatching: *De sobremesa*, Hysteria, and the Impersonation of Marie Bashkirtseff." *Latin American Literary Review* 25, no. 50: 11–29.

Montero, Oscar. 1993. *Erotismo y representación en Julián del Casal*. Amsterdam: Rodopi.

———. 1997. "Escritura y perversión en *De sobremesa*." *Revista Iberoamericana* 63: 249–61.

Morales, Carlos Javier. 1997. *Julian Martel y la novela naturalista argentina*. Logroño: Universidad de La Rioja, Servicio de Publicaciones.

Moreno Fraginals, Manuel. 1976. *The Sugarmill: The Socioeconomic Complex of Sugar in Cuba, 1760–1860*. New York: Monthly Review Press.

Moretti, Franco. 2000. *The Way of the World: The Bildungsroman in European Culture*. London: Verso.

Morton, Timothy. 2000. *The Poetics of Spice: Romantic Consumerism and the Exotic*. Cambridge: Cambridge University Press.

Neale Silva, Eduardo. 1960. *Horizonte humano: Vida de José Eustasio Rivera*. Mexico City: Fondo de Cultura Económica.

Neiemeyer, Kathleen. 1998. "Este pueblo que se desarrolla de golpe." *Revista de Crítica Literaria Latinoamericana* 47: 123–45.

Nouzeilles, Gabriela. 1998. *Ficciones somáticas: Naturalismo, nacionalismo y políticas médicas del cuerpo*. Rosario, Argentina: Viterbo.

Nouzeilles, Gabriela, ed. 2002. *La naturaleza en disputa: Retóricas del cuerpo y el paisaje en América Latina*. Buenos Aires: Paidós.

Ocampo, José Antonio. 1984. *Colombia y la economía mundial (1830–1910)*. Mexico City: Siglo Veintiuno Editores.

Ocantos, Carlos María. [1891] 1985. *Quilito*. Madrid: Hyspamérica.

Olivares. 1984. *La novela decadente en Venezuela*. Caracas: Editorial Armitano.

Ordóñez, Montserrat. 1990. "Introducción." In José Eustasio Rivera, *La vorágine*, 11–58. Madrid: Cátedra.

Ortiz, Fernando. [1940] 1978. *Contrapunteo cubano del tabaco y el azúcar.* Caracas: Biblioteca Ayacucho.

Pardo, Manuel. [1860] 1988. *Estudio sobre la provincia de Jauja.* In *Manuel Pardo y el primer estudio económico sobre la región central.* Ed. Manuel J. Baquerizo. Huancayo: Universidad Nacional del Centro del Perú.

Patnaik, Prabhat. 2006. "The Concept of Mode of Production and Theory of Imperialism." In *The Great Divergence: Hegemony, Uneven Development, and Global Inequality.* Ed. K. S. Jomo, 25–43. New Delhi: Oxford University Press.

Perelman, Michael. 1987. *Marx's Crises Theory: Scarcity, Labor, and Finance.* New York: Praeger.

Pérez Triana, Santiago. 1898. "Monumento a Henrich Heine." In *Repertorio colombiano* 18, no. 4 (August): 245–56.

———. 1902. *Down the Orinoco in a Canoe.* New York: Thomas Y. Crowell and Co.

"Peru: Leading the Way." N.d. http://www.forbes.com/peru/famesa.html (accessed November 10, 2010).

Perus, Françoise. 1976. *Literatura y sociedad en América Latina: El modernismo.* La Habana: Casa de las Américas.

Pike, Fredrick B. 1963. "Aspects of Class Relations in Chile, 1850–1960." *Hispanic American Historical Review* 43, no. 1 (February): 14–33.

Pineda Camacho, Roberto. 2004. "Novelistas y etnógrafos en el infierno de la Casa Arana." *Boletín de Historia y Antigüedades* 91, no. 826: 485–522.

Pocock, J. G. A. 1975. *The Machiavellian Moment: Florentine Political Thought and the Atlantic Republican Tradition.* Princeton, N.J.: Princeton University Press.

———. 1985. *Virtue, Commerce, and History.* Cambridge: Cambridge University Press.

Polanyi, Karl. [1944] 2001. *The Great Transformation: The Political and Economic Origins of Our Time.* Boston: Beacon Press.

Poovey, Mary. 1998. *A History of the Modern Fact: Problems of Knowledge in the Sciences of Wealth and Society.* Chicago: University of Chicago Press.

Pratt, Mary Louise. 1992. *Imperial Eyes: Travel Writing and Transculturation.* London: Routledge.

Quantum of Solace. 2008. Directed by Marc Forster. Sony Pictures.

Rama, Angel. 1974. "La dialéctica de la modernidad en José Martí." *Estudios martianos: Memoria del seminario José Martí.* Ed. Manuel Pedro González et al. San Juan: Editorial Universitaria, Universidad de Puerto Rico.

———. 1985a. *Las máscaras democráticas del modernismo.* Montevideo: Fundación Angel Rama.

———. [1970] 1985b. *Rubén Darío y el modernismo.* Caracas: Alfadil Ediciones.

———. 1996. *The Lettered City*. Ed. and trans. John Chasteen. Durham, N. C.: Duke University Press.

Ramos, Julio. [1989] 2001. *Divergent Modernities: Culture and Politics in Nineteenth-Century Latin America*. Trans. John D. Blanco. Durham, N.C.: Duke University Press.

Raventos, José María. *1880–1980: Un siglo de publicidad gráfica en Colombia*. Bogotá: Puma Editores, 1984.

Reyes, Rafael. [1907] 1979. *A través de la América del sur: Exploraciones de los Hermanos Reyes*. Bogotá: Flota Mercante Grancolombiana.

Richmond, Douglas W. 1989. *Carlos Pellegrini and the Crisis of the Argentine Elites, 1880–1916*. New York: Praeger.

Rivera, José Eustasio. [1924] 1990. *La vorágine*. Madrid: Cátedra.

———. 1935. *The Vortex*. Trans. Earl K. James. New York: G. P. Putnam.

———. 1991. "Carta a Henry Ford." In *José Rivera, Intelectual: Textos y documentos 1912–1928*. Ed. Hilda Soledad Pachón-Farías, 105–9. Bogotá, Colombia: Empresa Editorial Universidad Nacional de Colombia.

Rodó, José Enrique. [1900] 1991. *Ariel*. Madrid: Ediciones de Cultura Hispánica.

Rodríguez, Ileana. 2004. *Transatlantic Topographies: Islands, Highlands, Jungles*. Minneapolis: University of Minnesota Press.

Rodríguez-García, José María. 2010. *The City of Translation: Poetry and Ideology in Nineteenth-Century Colombia*. New York: Palgrave Macmillan, 2010.

Rojas, Cristina. 2002. *Civilization and Violence: Regimes of Representation in Nineteenth-Century Colombia*. Minneapolis: University of Minnesota Press.

Rojas, Ricardo. 1925. *La literatura argentina. Los modernos II*. Buenos Aires: Librería "LaFacultad."

Rosa, Richard. 2003. *Los fantasmas de la razón: Una lectura material de Hostos*. San Juan and Santo Domingo: Isla Negra Editores.

———. 2007. "Crédito, propiedad y narración en la novela tropical de Zeno Gandía." *Estudios: Revista de investigaciones Literarias y Culturales* 15, no. 21: 95–122.

———. n.d. "Finance and Literature in Spanish America." Manuscript.

Rotker, Susana. 2000. *The American Chronicles of José Martí: Journalism and Modernity in Spanish America*. Trans. Jennifer French and Katherine Semler. Hanover, N.H.: University Press of New England.

Roubouchon, Eugenio. 1907. *En el Putumayo y sus afluentes*. Lima: Imprenta de la Industria.

Russell, Norman. 1986. *The Novelist and Mammon: Literary Responses to the World of Commerce in the Nineteenth Century*. Oxford: Clarendon Press.

Saldaña-Portillo, María Josefina. 2003. *The Revolutionary Imagination in the Americas and the Age of Development*. Durham, N.C.: Duke University Press.

Salessi, Jorge. 1995. *Médicos maleantes y maricas: Higiene, criminología y homosexualidad en la construcción de la nación argentina (Buenos Aires, 1871–1914)*. Rosario, Argentina: Viterbo Editora.

San Román, Gustavo. 2009. "Money, Culture, and Enterprise in José Enrique Rodó." *Modern Language Review* 104: 83–105.

Santos Molano, Enrique. [1990] 1997. *El corazón del poeta: Los sucesos reveladores de la vida y la verdad inesperada de la muerte de José Asunción Silva*. Bogotá: Presidencia de la República.

Sarmiento, Domingo Faustino. [1841] 1887. "Un viaje a Valparaíso." In *Obras de D. F. Sarmiento. . . .* Vol. 1, 115–42. Santiago: Imprenta Gutemberg.

———. [1850] 1968. *Argirópolis*. Buenos Aires: Editorial Universitaria de Buenos Aires.

———. [1845] 1976. *Facundo*. Caracas: Ayacucho Editores.

Schwarz, Roberto. 1992. *Misplaced Ideas: Essays on Brazilian Culture*. London and New York: Verso.

———. 2001. *A Master on the Periphery of Capitalism: Machado de Assis*. Trans. John Gledson. Durham, N.C.: Duke University Press.

Shell, Marc. 1978. *The Economy of Literature*. Baltimore: Johns Hopkins University Press.

———. 1993. *Money, Language, and Thought: Literary and Philosophical Economies from the Medieval to the Modern Era*. Berkeley: University of California; Baltimore: Johns Hopkins University Press.

———. 1995. *Art and Money*. Chicago: University of Chicago Press.

Shulman, Ivan. 1969. *Martí, Darío y el modernismo*. Madrid: Biblioteca Romántica Hispánica.

Silva, José Asunción. 1887a. "La confusión de hechos." Bogotá: *La Nación*. June 28, 4.

———. 1887b. "Confusiones varias" Bogotá: *La Nación*. June 12, 4.

———. 1996a. *Cartas: 1881–1896*. Ed. Fernando Vallejo. Bogotá: Ediciones Casa Silva.

———. [1896] 1996b. *De sobremesa*. In *Obra Completa*. Ed. Héctor H. Orjuela. Madrid: Colección Archivos.

———. 2005. *De sobremesa [After-Dinner Conversation: The Diary of a Decadent]*. Trans. Kelly Washbourne. Austin: University of Texas Press.

Smith, Adam. 1982. *Lectures on Jurisprudence*. Indianapolis: Liberty Fund.

Smith, Neil. 1984. *Uneven Development: Nature, Capital and the Production of Space*. Oxford: Basil Blackwell.

Smith, Paul. 1997. *Millennial Dreams: Contemporary Culture and Capital, in the North*. London: Verso.

Sombart, Werner. [1911] 1951. *The Jews and Modern Capitalism.* Trans. M. Epstein. Glencoe, Ill.: Free Press.

Sommer, Doris. 1991. *Foundational Fictions: The National Romances of Latin America.* Berkeley: University of California Press.

Sommi, Luis. 1957. *La revolución del 90.* Buenos Aires: Ediciones Pueblos de América.

Spivak, Gayatri. 2005. *Death of a Discipline.* New York: Columbia University Press.

Stone, Alexander. 2001. "Illegal Tender: Counterfeit Dollars and Colombian Crime." *The Future of War* 23, no. 2. http://hir.harvard.edu/ index.php? page= article&id=893 (accessed June 11, 2011).

Summers, Lawrence. 1991. "Memo." http://www.whirledbank.org/ourwords/ summers.html (accessed June 11, 2011).

Taunay, Alfredo d'Escragnolle [Conde de Taunay]. [1893] 1923. *O encilhamento: cenas contemporâneas da Bôlsa do Rio de Janeiro em 1890, 1891 e 1892.* São Paulo: Edições Melhoramentos.

Taussig, Michael. 1986. *Shamanism, Colonialism, and the Wild Man: A Study in Terror and Healing.* Chicago: University of Chicago Press.

Theweleit, Klaus. 1987. *Male Fantasies.* Vols. 1 and 2. Trans. Stephen Conway. Minneapolis: University of Minnesota Press.

Thompson, James. 1996. *Models of Value: Eighteenth-Century Political Economy and the Novel.* Durham, N.C.: Duke University Press.

Topik, Steven C., and Allen Wells, eds. 1998. *The Second Conquest of Latin America: Coffee, Henequen, and Oil during the Export Boom, 1850–1930.* Austin: University of Texas Press, 1998.

Trigo, Benigno. 2000. *Subjects of Crisis: Race and Gender as Disease in Latin America.* Middletown, Conn.: Wesleyan University Press.

Uribe Uribe, Rafael. 1908. *El banano. Conferencia dictada por el Doctor Rafael Uribe Uribe ante la Sociedad de Agricultores de Colombia.* San José, Costa Rica: Imprenta de Avelino Alsina.

Vallejo, Fernando. 1995. *Chapolas negras.* Bogotá: Editorial Santillana.

Véliz, Claudio. 1994. *The New World of the Gothic Fox: Culture and Economy in English and Spanish America.* Berkeley: University of California Press.

Villafañe, Segundo I. [1891] 1960. *Horas de fiebre.* Buenos Aires: Universidad de Buenos Aires, Facultad de Filosofía y Letras.

Villalobos, Sergio. 1987. *Origen y ascenso de la burguesía chilena.* Santiago: Editorial Universitaria.

Viñas, David. 1971. *Literatura argentina y realidad política. Apogeo de la oligarquía.* Buenos Aires: Ediciones Siglo Veinte.

———. 1974. "*La vorágine:* Crisis, populismo y mirada." *Hispamérica: Revista de Literatura 3*, no. 8: 3–21.

———. 1983. *Indios, ejército y frontera.* Mexico City: Siglo Veintiuno Editores.

Wallerstein, Immanuel. 1979. *The Capitalist World-Economy*. Cambridge: Cambridge University Press.

Wasserman, Renata. 2001. "Financial Fictions: Emile Zola's *L'Argent*, Frank Norris' *The Pit*, and Alfredo de Taunay's *O Encilhamento*." *Comparative Literature Studies* 38, no. 3: 193–214.

Watson, Janell. 1999. *Literature and Material Culture from Balzac to Proust: The Collection and Consumption of Curiosities*. Cambridge: Cambridge University Press.

Widdig, Bernd. 2001. *Culture and Inflation in Weimar Germany*. Berkeley: University of California Press.

Williams, Raymond. 1973. *The City and the Country*. Oxford: Oxford University Press.

Woodmansee, Martha, and Mark Osteen, eds. 1999. *The New Economic Criticism: Studies at the Intersection of Literature and Economics*. London: Routledge, 1999.

Zeigler, Philip. 1988. *The Sixth Great Power: Barings, 1762–1929*. London: Collins.

Zimmerman, David A. 2006. *Panic! Markets, Crises ,and Crowds in American Fiction*. Chapel Hill: University of North Carolina Press.

Žižek, Slavoj. 1993. *Tarrying with the Negative: Kant, Hegel, and the Critique of Ideology*. Durham, N.C.: Duke University Press.

——. 2010. *Living in the End Times*. London and New York: Verso.

Zumeta, César. [1899]1961. *El continente enfermo*. Caracas: Colección "Rescate."

Index

245

Ericka Beckman is associate professor of Spanish and comparative literature at the University of Illinois at Urbana-Champaign.